PHOENIX RISING
the making of a desert metropolis

Philip VanderMeer, author • Mary VanderMeer, photo editor

Published by

Heritage Media Corp.
Heritage Building
1954 Kellogg Avenue, Carlsbad, California 92008
www.heritagemedia.com
ISBN: 1-886483-69-8
Library of Congress Control Number: 2002107935

Philip VanderMeer *Author*
Mary VanderMeer *Photo Editor*
Charles E. Parks *CEO/Publisher*
Lori M. Parks *Editorial Director*
Stephen Hung *Executive Vice President*
Randall Peterson *CFO*

Design	**Editorial**
Gina Mancini *Art Director*	Betsy Baxter Blondin *Editor-in-Chief*
Robert Galmarini	Betsy Lelja *Softcover Managing Editor*
Chris Hamilton	Mary Campbell
Marianne Mackey	John Woodward
Charlie Silvia	**Staff Writers:**
	Gregory Lucas
	Julie Gengo
Administration	
Kelly Corcoran *Human Resources Manager*	**Production**
Lisa Barone	Deborah Sherwood *IT/Production Manager*
Melissa Coffey	Dave Hermstad
Juan Diaz	Arturo Ramirez
Cyndie Miller	
Stephanie Stogiera	**Client Services**
Vicki Verne	Aina Grant

Profile Writers
Poppy Behrens
Lana Gates

Printed by Heritage Media Corp. in the United States of America

table of contents

acknowledgments

■ In many ways my ideas for this book grew out of 15 years of teaching community history and historical methods to graduate and undergraduate students at Arizona State University. Working with students to locate resources, design projects and analyze historical materials stimulated my interest and informed my thinking about the history of Phoenix and the Valley. Working with graduate students who pursued such investigations further, often in dissertations and theses, provided additional impetus. I wish particularly to thank the following students: Fred Amis, Teresa Baker, Jerry Briscoe, David Dean, Jane Lawrence, Robin LaVoie, Heidi Osselaer and Mark Scott.

In his characteristically gentle manner, my colleague Peter Iverson strongly encouraged me to undertake this project, understanding that I really did want to do this, and he provided valuable critiques of draft chapters. My department chair, Noel Stowe, rearranged my teaching schedule to allow me more time for writing. For help in accessing their collections I am indebted to the staffs of the Arizona Historical Society Library and Archives, Central Division, in Tempe (particularly Dawn Nave and Dave Tackenberg); the Luhrs Reading Room of Arizona State University (particularly Chris Marin and Rob Spindler); the Arizona Historical Foundation at Arizona State University; and the Phoenix Public Library (especially Linda Risseeuw). Becky Burke of the Government Documents Division of the ASU Library located reports that had disappeared and the Planning Department of the City of Phoenix supplied useful

Easter Lily Cactus, Desert Botanical Garden
Photo by César Mazier

information about annexation; and Dick George provided helpful materials about the Phoenix Zoo. I wish to thank George Kishiyama for talking with me about himself and his family, and I am especially grateful to Terry Goddard for speaking so generously and candidly about his memories and perspective of the city's development.

By far my greatest debt in completing this book is to my wife, Mary. I agreed to undertake this type of project, combining text and photos, only after she agreed to be photo editor. This allowed us to fulfill a longtime goal of collaborating on some project, and it used her expertise in editing, organizing and photo layout. She could not have realized, however, that as a result of our collaboration, she would also hear unceasingly about my ideas and progress on this project, read all of my drafts, and encounter my unnecessary suggestions about what kinds of photographs were desirable and where to place them. For her unflagging support, enormous patience and good humor, and her invaluable expertise I am more than grateful.

Phil VanderMeer

■ When my husband suggested this collaboration, I had no idea how involved the process of finding relevant historical photos could be. I owe special thanks to Bob Rink, photographer for the City of Phoenix, who is responsible for taking many of the photos we used and who helped me find historical photos of people, places and events long before his tenure with the city. Sheila Brushes, archivist for the Arizona Historical Foundation, helped me dig through the Goldwater Family Collection to find the previously unpublished photos of Barry Goldwater, and LaRee Bates, archivist for the Heard Museum, contributed Goldwater's photo of the Grand Canyon. Dawn Nave, Dave Tackenberg and Lee Pierce helped me look through boxes upon boxes of Phoenix History Project, HomeBuilders Collection and numerous smaller collections at the Arizona Historical Society. Elizabeth Bentley, Rob Spindler and other staff at the University Archives helped me collect both easy-to-find and obscure photos as well as Reg Manning's cartoons and examples of Daniel Noble's art. Nancy Van Leeuwen scoured the *Arizona Republic* archives to find negatives that no longer exist of the 1963 protest marches and illustrations of the proposed raised Papago Freeway.

John Olson, communication specialist for America West Arena and the Arizona Diamondbacks, brought me up to speed (well, he tried) about sports facts and provided great photos of the Suns, Mercury, Diamondbacks and Jerry Colangelo. Dick George, photographer and historian for the Phoenix Zoo, shared information as well as his photos of Ruby, Robert Maytag and the Zoo's farm. Oscar Munoz, archivist for the Frank Lloyd Wright Archives, not only supplied a number of wonderful Wright photos and drawings, he also patiently answered my trivia questions about Wright and Taliesin. Gary Martinelli supplied historical photos of Sky Harbor Terminals 2 and 3 from the airport's archives. Nelda Cromwell and Kristin Jarchow helped find photos of Frank Snell; Jessica Roe and Cezar Mazier shared numerous slides of the Desert Botanical Gardens; Officer Mike Nikolin, curator of the Phoenix Police Museum, reproduced the photo of the PPD's Studebacher Lark patrol cars. Public relations and library staff from Glendale, Mesa, Scottsdale, Tempe and ASU welcomed my questions and shared photos as did staff from the Pioneer Living History Museum, the Herberger Theater Center, the Phoenix Art Museum and the Heard Museum. Tot Long lent us personal photos of John F. Long; Ruth and David Manning gratiously allowed us to use Reg's cartoons.

I owe a debt of thanks to my co-workers at Banner Health System, especially my boss, Vice President of Communications Dan Green, for his patience and support, and to my colleague Al Luna for his help and good humor. And I am particularly thankful to Phil, for giving me this opportunity to share his work and love of history.

Mary VanderMeer

Saguaro cactus in bloom, Desert Botanical Garden *Photo by César Mazier*

People have come to Arizona and the Valley for many

reasons. The warm, dry climate has always attracted many

health seekers, the famous and the not-so-famous. Others

sought economic opportunities, first in agriculture and later

in industries. Beginning in the 1940s the Phoenix Chamber

of Commerce recruited businesses to move to the Valley.

Many of them, such as AiResearch or Goodyear, profited

from federal defense spending, first in World War II and

(Opposite page)
Mrs. Gertrude Divine
Webster's influence,
financial support and
passion "not to destroy but
glorify" the Valley's unique
desert landscape helped
found the Desert Botanical
Garden in 1939.
Desert Botanical Garden

then in the Cold War, and a growing number like Motorola and Sperry were part of the "new economy" of electronics and computers. Still other migrants came first as visitors or tourists, marveling at the Sonoran Desert and nearby mountains, enjoying the mild winter climate, and experiencing a variety of outdoor living styles from resort to ranch. The recruitment of tourists started with the pacesetting *Arizona Highways*, and became a staple of the Valley's economy. Visitors often returned not only as vacationers, but also as workers in the expanding economy, or as "snowbirds"— winter residents, or retirees in a growing number of residential communities for retirees such as Sun City, Sun Lakes or Leisure World.

From its frontier beginning Phoenix was praised by dreamers, promoted by "boosters" and sold by hucksters. People were assured that the possibilities were limitless, and the future was whatever one wished to make of it. But the Valley also had particular characteristics that made it amenable to dreaming — which suggested a malleable environment. Abundant sun, level land and water — after the advent of "climate controls" like evaporative coolers and air conditioning — allowed migrants to remake the land with structures and landscaping into whatever they wished: a typical American suburb, a desert oasis, a tropical paradise, a ranch, or even a midwestern lakeside community (one joker claimed that inside a Valley planner's head was a map of Minnesota).

Growth has been the dominant focus of Phoenix, "like cars to Detroit." Phoenix grew rapidly in the first three decades after statehood, but small cities can achieve high growth rate easily, and in 1940 the Phoenix population was still only 65,414. During the next 60 years, however, both Phoenix and the remainder of its

metropolitan area not only grew at an impressive rate but also gained huge numbers of people: Phoenix itself added more people than any city except Los Angeles and Houston. This growth was not literally unprecedented in U.S. history — Chicago in the late 19th century, Detroit in the 1910s and Los Angeles 1920-40 had grown even more phenomenally — but it was still enormous. Phoenix was one of the perennial cases in national discussions of growth — Phoenicians spoke with pride about its transformation and rising status, and longtime residents saw the fulfillment of their dreams.

So it seems all the more surprising that Phoenix should have ended the 20th century in a struggle over growth. Public policy debates over limiting growth have been common in the United States during the last 25 years, and western states and cities (notably Portland and Boulder) have imposed controls. What makes it surprising — if not a bit shocking — to have such a debate in Phoenix is that Phoenix pursued growth so aggressively, so successfully and for so long. To understand the contentious, even traumatic, nature of recent struggles, one must see them as the product of a particular environment and a history starting in the 1940s. During an era when virtually every place in the country wanted to grow, why did Phoenix succeed so well? What was the initial vision and who were involved in bringing it about? By the 1960s Phoenix had national visibility as the leading city of the Southwest, but it also began to confront urban problems of transportation, providing urban amenities and the needs of less fortunate within the population. By the 1980s the city was confronting even more serious urban problems, and because of its size and the huge number of inmigrants, its decisions more clearly reflected and affected

*Greater Phoenix
Convention & Visitors
Bureau, Photo by
Jessen Associates, Inc.*

national urban policy. The creation of this desert metropolis has involved not only jobs and elections, but also touches on the growing diversity of built environments — the variety of architecture and landscapes, the focus on lifestyle, and the development of urban amenities. While patterns can often be more easily and clearly seen from a distance — certainly an historical distance — it seems clear that in the year 2000 Phoenix was experiencing a transition from an era that began in the 1940s with war clouds on the horizon.

Throughout his life, Barry Goldwater spent his free time capturing the beauty of Arizona's landscape and the character of her people on film.
The Goldwater Family Collection, The Arizona Historical Foundation, Arizona State University

Making A New Vision Real
1940-1960

Phoenix began on dry land and grew with water and air. Set in a broad valley, well-watered by rivers but with near cloudless skies that gave only seven inches of rain per year, Phoenix started as an agricultural center, providing food to army posts. Its growth relied on canals to distribute water from the Salt River, an enterprise vastly expanded in 1911 by the federally financed construction of nearby Roosevelt Dam.

chapter one

City	Population	Rank in top 100 U.S. cities	City	Population	Rank in top 100 U.S. cities
Los Angeles	1,504,277	5	Oklahoma City	204,424	42
San Francisco	634,536	12	Tulsa	142,157	62
Seattle	368,302	22	Denver	322,412	24
Portland	305,394	27	Salt Lake City	149,934	57
San Diego	203,341	43	Spokane	122,001	68
Tacoma	109,408	82	El Paso	96,810	98
Dallas	294,734	31	Phoenix	65,414	na
Fort Worth	177,662	46	Tucson	35,752	na
San Antonio	253,854	36	Albuquerque	35,449	na

Western Cities in 1940

With this economic base, its role as a regional marketing and distribution center, its connection with mining (the other major economy of the area), and its nascent tourist industry, Phoenix resembled many other western places. By 1940 Phoenix was a growing but modest-sized western city, larger than its nearest competitors, Tucson and Albuquerque, but dwarfed by its California neighbors and substantially smaller than interior Western cities or cities in the Southwest.

Like all American cities, Phoenix sought growth, and like most cities not far from their frontier past, it had its boosters and dreamers. In 1940 their vision of the future comprised only a larger version of its present. Phoenicians touted their agriculture and to a much lesser degree, the surrounding mining and timber prospects. They boasted about the dry desert air, the dramatic scenery and the warm winter climate (and suggested that hot summers were a time to relax). Tourism brought the city an estimated $50 to 75 million a year and, as one writer joked, showed visitors that "we live in houses, can read and write English, and are not violent." Phoenicians praised their city as ideal for families: a place of affordable homes, pleasant parks and good schools. After noting the current economic resources and suggesting future economic growth, one author predicted, "This does not mean that the Phoenix of 1993 will be a large industrial city, nor would that be desirable."

But the city's future would not be a simple extension of the past. Soon

Downtown Phoenix in 1940
Arizona State Archives

large national and international forces would intervene, dramatically changing possibilities. A group of economic and political leaders would capitalize on these possibilities with a new vision of the future — and make their vision a reality.

World War II brought the military, conflict, and new ideas to Phoenix

War is a tremendously powerful force in human history, changing the lives of contemporaries in ever-widening ripples of consequences. Phoenix grew up with the army and gunfire in the 19th century, supplying army posts that protected miners and settlers. World War I had significantly reshaped the Valley's agriculture and economy when the Goodyear Company encouraged cotton growing for making airplane wings and tires. But World War II had more dramatic and long-lasting effects. Historian Gerald Nash claims that it "accomplished a reshaping of the [West's] economic life that would have taken more than 40 years in peacetime." Phoenix shared in that transformation but less dramatically or permanently than, for example, California or Texas.

War first touched Phoenix in 1939. When fighting began in Europe, the federal government increased its spending on aviation, providing money for construction at Phoenix's Sky Harbor Airport and funding a program to train civilian pilots. Carl "Pappy" Knier started training 30 fliers at Sky Harbor. Southwest Airways took over the operation and in 1941 contracted to train pilots at two new fields: Thunderbird Field north of Glendale provided primary training to Army pilots, and Falcon Field in northeast Mesa trained British cadets. Less than two years later, the federal government was operating four bases: a naval testing facility in Litchfield Park; Thunderbird II north of Scottsdale; and two very large bases — Luke Field, west of Glendale, furnished advanced training, and Williams Field, south of Mesa, provided basic or intermediate training. Concentrating these bases in the Valley made very good sense for aviation: there were mild winds, level ground and vast areas without population, and the skies held few clouds and little rain. Another essential reason to choose this area was its inland location that provided safety from possible attacks along the coasts. But Phoenicians also had worked hard to attract these

facilities, through lobbying by a municipal commission and the Chamber of Commerce, by purchasing the land for Luke Field, and especially benefiting from the considerable influence of Carl Hayden, then one of the most senior Democrats in the Senate and a relatively loyal supporter of the administration.

The Valley also benefitted from the federal government's support for war-related manufacturing. Following the war-time principle of geographic dispersal and continuing the New Deal's earlier goal of encouraging economic development in the West and South, the Defense Plant Corporation funded the construction of three plants in the Valley: in Litchfield Park (1941) where Goodyear Aircraft built airplane parts and balloons, near Sky Harbor Airport (1942) where AiResearch made equipment for high altitude flying, and west of Phoenix (1943) where Alcoa operated an aluminum extrusion plant (also located because of efforts by Senator Hayden). At their peak these plants employed nearly 15,000 workers, creating a huge influx of population and a tremendous housing shortage in the Valley. Phoenicians were encouraged to take in boarders, and the government funded the construction of housing projects near the AiResearch and Alcoa plants.

Phoenix also felt the impact of the Army Desert Training Center bases that General Patton had established in southeastern California and western Arizona, including two (Camps Horn and Hyder) relatively close to Phoenix. With troop trains constantly coming through the Valley and caravans of vehicles coming from the camps, Phoenix was flooded by young men looking to spend money and find entertainment. Rowdiness became a problem in Phoenix, as in all nearby towns. One night soldiers took over Yuma, and another time 300 troops rioted in Las Vegas. Race complicated these conditions, and armed confrontations involving black troops occurred in Phoenix and Indio, California. The most serious problems were gambling and prostitution. Phoenix, like many communities, had previously "controlled" these vices with limited arrests and bribery, but the huge influx of soldiers made vice a much greater issue. An epidemic of venereal disease created a health problem for the military and a political crisis for Phoenix.

Our Own 'Secret Weapon'
By Reg Manning
Arizona Republic Staff Artist

Pilots train in A-6s over Luke Air Force Base, 1942. *Arizona Historical Society-Central Arizona Division*

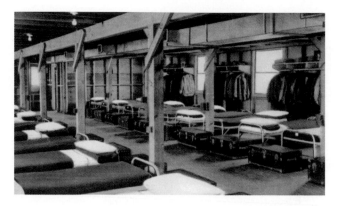

(Far right)
St. Monica's (later Phoenix Memorial Hospital) was funded and built, at least in part, as a response to the venereal disease outbreak in 1942.
Arizona Historical Society-Central Arizona Division

Williams Air Force Base barracks during World War II.
Arizona Historical Society-Central Arizona Division

On November 31, 1942, Col. Ross Hoyt, the military control officer for the region, employed a tactic that had worked in Las Vegas and Fort Worth. He declared Phoenix temporarily off-limits to military personnel and threatened to make the order permanent. This action provoked great concern in Phoenix because, Mayor Newell Stewart admitted, "the army's pay rolls constitute one of the community's largest sources of revenue." City officials sought to resolve the crisis by increasing arrests and establishing venereal clinics. The military faulted these as half-hearted efforts but admitted that prostitutes comprised only part of the problem — noting that "most of the disease cases we now encounter are nonprofessional." The solution the military envisioned went beyond controlling brothels and eliminating bribery of police to much broader restrictions on activities of minors and adult women.

As the crisis continued, the proposed violations of civil liberties became more draconian. State Adjutant General A. M. Tuthill suggested running guilty women out of the state. Phoenix City Manager Richard Smith recommended stopping incoming trains to check for prostitutes. And Governor Sidney Osborn threatened to declare martial law.

The issue reached a dramatic conclusion on December 15, 1942, but it defined a political conflict that lasted for another seven years. On December 12, Col. Hoyt had warned Frank Snell, chairman of the local USO and former head of the Phoenix Chamber of Commerce, that he might make the off-limits order permanent. Snell quickly conferred with the chamber's board of directors, which then forced the city commissioners to meet with them at the Adams Hotel. The meeting, which Snell later jokingly referred at to as the "Card

Phoenix Bell Hop & Chamber Maid Games, 1948
Arizona Historical Society-Central Arizona Division

(Far left)
The Arizona Biltmore, 1930
Arizona Historical Society-Central Arizona Division

By the mid-1950s, winter visitors were packing trailer parks and travel courts.
Arizona Historical Society-Central Arizona Division

Room Putsch," was no laughing matter at the time. Working into the early morning hours of December 15, chamber members defined the problem as political management and forced the commissioners to take immediate and drastic action. They fired the city clerk and city manager, and the new manager fired the police chief. These changes satisfied Col. Hoyt, and on December 17 he lifted the off-limits order.

But three weeks later, after the crisis was over and the military threat had disappeared, the council revoked the deal and rehired the original officials. This angered chamber of commerce leaders, persuading them of the need for larger political changes. City elections thereafter reverberated with charges of inefficiency, croneyism and corruption.

A Troubled Peace and Reasons to Grow

When the war ended in 1945, Phoenix quickly felt the consequences. The army bases closed first, followed by the smaller air fields, and then even Luke Field shut down in late 1946. War-related production stopped, and the federal government took possession of all three of the Phoenix war-materials production facilities. Manufacturing, which had played only a minor role in Phoenix's economy before the war, had boomed even more dramatically than the national economy in 1942-43. Now it dipped below national levels and seemed headed toward the prewar condition, bearing out a common prediction "that Phoenix would go back to being pretty much what it had been before the war." War-time expansion and changes, it appeared, might only have been a deviation, not a basic shift in course.

Instead, it was the postwar slump that proved temporary. Mild winter temperatures, the dry desert air and dramatic scenery enticed veterans like lawyer and later congressman John Rhodes, who had gone through military training in Phoenix, to resettle. Military benefits helped veterans buy homes, start businesses, or return to school. (By the late 1940s enrollment at Phoenix College and Arizona State College in Tempe tripled

from prewar levels and tripled again by 1960.) In 1956, Daniel Noble of Motorola claimed, only half facetiously, that "if the engineers and the scientists of the country knew about the perfection of Phoenix's winter weather and understood the joys of Western living without snow, or ice, or smog, there would be such a rush of applicants for positions that corporations of the country would have to set up shop in Phoenix to stay in business."

Moving to the Arizona desert had long been a life-saving prescription for people suffering from respiratory ailments and arthritis. Dwight Heard, one of the Valley's wealthiest and most influential citizens, had come in the 1890s because of respiratory problems and stayed. Del Webb arrived in 1928, a carpenter recovering from typhoid fever; John Goettl, a metal worker, came in the 1930s because of lung problems; and in 1943 John C. Hall, rejected by the military for health problems, moved to the Valley to work in the AiResearch plant. Surveys in the early 1950s found that three-fourths of the workers who moved to Phoenix did so because of health.

During the 1930s Phoenix began catering to wealthy winter visitors with swank resorts like the Arizona Biltmore, owned by Philip Wrigley, and the Camelback Inn, built in part by Cleveland businessman John C. Lincoln (who came for his wife's health). After the war the traffic of wealthy winter visitors increased, as did the number of resorts. Phoenix appreciated these visitors for what they spent, but a different goal grew increasingly important. As Valley National Bank Chairman Carl Bimson noted, demonstrating the Valley's natural and business climates to people with wealth and connections often attracted important new residents and investors. A winter visitor like Merle Cheney might stay and help develop north Scottsdale.

Arizona attracted more than the very wealthy. By the early 1950s, tourism provided a major part of the state's economy. Trailer parks and travel courts filled to capacity, and tourism revenues contributed roughly $180 million annually to the state's coffers — triple the prewar levels and more than the state's

continued on page 23

frank lloyd wright

■Frank Lloyd Wright, America's most brilliant architect, first came to the Valley in early 1928. At a low point in his professional career, he arrived to help a former student, Albert McArthur, build the Arizona Biltmore, but within a few months Dr. Alexander J. Chandler had commissioned him to design a luxury resort — San Marcos in the Desert — for Chandler's town, located some 25 miles southeast of Phoenix. Wright drafted a basic design before leaving for home in Wisconsin that summer, then returned in January of 1929 to complete the designs.

During this second visit, he built and lived in a camp that he called "Ocatilla" and loved the openness of the desert. Ocatilla burned shortly after he returned to Wisconsin that summer, and the Great Crash of 1929 killed the San Marcos project, but Wright remained fascinated with the desert's light, topography and natural materials. In the winter of 1934 he returned to the Valley, camping with some of his architecture students in what would much later become north Scottsdale. In 1937 he bought substantial acreage there and with associates and students began building Taliesin West, his winter school and retreat for the last 22 years of his life.

Wright was brilliant, imperious and eccentric, and in both Wisconsin and Arizona he remained cavalier about paying his bills. During one of his winter sojourns in the Valley, Wright went to see Walter Bimson, head of Valley National Bank, complaining that his car had been repossessed. Knowing that this world-famous architect must have earned enough to afford a car, Bimson asked what Wright did with the commission checks he received. "I don't know," Wright responded. "I just stick them in my pocket." Then he dug in his pockets and came up with checks totaling about $30,000. A composed but amazed Bimson assured Wright that he would get the car back, and he set up a savings account for Wright with the remaining funds.

Wright achieved much of his early architectural success designing private residences, and he designed seven homes in the Valley as well as Taliesin West and First Christian Church. But as he grew older he became increasingly interested in designing public buildings. In 1957 he volunteered a design, "Oasis, Pro Bono Publico," for a proposed new Arizona State Capitol. He envisioned a vast copper-plated, hexagonal dome that covered buildings and gardens set in Papago Park. Critics objected that moving the government eight miles would be too expensive, and the legislature rejected it in favor of a more traditional and less expensive addition on the current capitol grounds. For Wright, the primary issues were quality of life and beauty. Speaking at Glendale's American Institute for Foreign Trade in 1958, Wright scathingly described 20th century cities as "overgrown feudal villages crammed with gadgetry and blocked by cars — useful only as headquarters of banking, newspapers, and prostitution."

(Above)
Frank Lloyd Wright in the Taliesin West drafting room, 1946
Frank Lloyd Wright Archives, Scottsdale, Arizona

(Right)
Wright's 1957 design for a new Arizona State Capitol building in Papago Park — "Oasis, Pro Bono Publico"
©2001 The Frank Lloyd Wright Foundation, Scottsdale, Arizona

Wright was in his late 80s when the legislature rejected his capitol design, and some prominent Arizonans grew concerned that the Valley had no major public example of his architecture. So when Arizona State University sought to build a performing arts center, Walter Bimson and Lewis Ruskin lobbied state legislators to pay Wright for a design, and this time they agreed. Wright completed the design for Grady Gammage Auditorium in 1959, and construction began in 1960 and finished in 1964. It was Wright's last design and a striking example of his later work — built for the public's ease and pleasure, it is still renowned for its superb acoustics and beauty. ■

manufacturing revenue. By the 1970s, annual tourism revenues exceeded the state's agriculture revenues, and by 1978 tourists were spending $1.6 billion in and around Phoenix alone.

Growth was in the air!

Even Phoenix's summer heat, which had traditionally deterred people from living in the desert, began to yield. In the early 1930s several manufacturers had developed a simple and effective evaporative cooler — a grilled metal box holding a pad (or other substance) over which water was dripped, and a fan blowing the moistened air into the room. Window-sized evaporative or "swamp" coolers sold very rapidly. By 1941 window or central units were typical in Phoenix homes, and thereafter on military bases. By 1950 local firms owned by the Goettl brothers and by Oscar Palmer led the country in manufacturing evaporative coolers, and Phoenix was considered the "cooler capital" of the nation.

Coolers worked well if the weather was hot and dry but not during the two months of Phoenix's hotter, wetter "monsoon" season. For this, at least, Phoenicians needed refrigerated air. Refrigeration or "air-conditioning" systems were much more complex and expensive for home or small business owners. In the 1930s only a few office buildings, hotels, and theaters made the investment. But technology improved after the war as did the supply of metal, and by the late 1940s, Phoenix led the nation in the number of homes cooled by window air-conditioning. Demand for central air-conditioning for homes grew more slowly, but the market boomed after 1957 when the FHA agreed to finance new homes with central air-conditioning. By 1960 a fourth of all Phoenix homes enjoyed central air, and the city also served as a center for manufacturing these units.

Although Phoenix had adequate rail and road connections, it suffered the disadvantage of being far from the nation's economic hubs, except those in southern California. In 1945, however, the nation began entering the air age, and Phoenix became a primary beneficiary. Air transportation not only dramatically shortened travel time, it also encouraged fewer stops and centralized locations. Phoenix's weather and terrain promoted passenger, commercial, and private travel to and through Phoenix, just as it had earlier attracted (and would again win) military air traffic. Tourism flourished because of easy air

access, and passenger traffic more than tripled in each of the next two decades.

By the mid-1950s Sky Harbor Airport was the 10th busiest in the nation; in 1961 it ranked sixth. American Airlines had begun servicing Phoenix in 1930, joined in the 1940s by TWA. Before 1950 both airlines flew nonstop flights to larger cities in California and Texas, to Chicago, and shortly thereafter to New York, while two smaller carriers — Frontier and Bonanza — flew to communities within the state and to nearby cities like El Paso and Las Vegas. By the end of the decade, Western and Continental airlines added travel options.

Combined with easy trucking to and from California, aviation proved crucial for business expansion, especially for manufacturing high-value, lightweight goods. City leaders understood the importance of aviation and actively supported it. They had courted TWA to foster competition and expand passenger service, encouraged smaller carriers, and campaigned

for the passage of bonds in 1946, 1948, and 1957 to expand runways, provide equipment and increase infrastructure. They also understood that financing airport expansion required obtaining federal funds, and they lobbied eagerly and effectively.

The Cold War Heats up the Phoenix Economy

Air service, air-conditioning, and the desert environs provided the basic conditions that encouraged development in the Valley and attracted people to the area. But U.S. foreign policy most fundamentally affected the area's economy and growth. The actual shape and content of the developing Phoenix economy (as in much of the inland West) stemmed directly from the Cold War.

The end of World War II necessarily meant lower spending for military personnel, weapons, and war-related manufacturing — a transition with less impact in areas like California, where military-related activity had already reached a critical mass, and more in places like Phoenix, where it had not. While World War II laid important groundwork, America's subsequent international role and the size of its military changed the Valley's future most profoundly. As President Harry Truman pressed Congress in the spring of 1947 to increase military assistance to Greece and Turkey, Phoenix was fighting its own war, threatening to use police to prevent the federal government from removing any buildings from Luke Field. As the Cold War expanded, with the Marshall Plan (1948), the Berlin Airlift (1949), and continued development of nuclear weapons, America's military budget rose. Finally, the outbreak of the "hot" war in Korea in June 1950 brought America's role and military

spending back to their World War II levels, where they would remain. This new commitment provided a significant, direct and continuing impact on Phoenix.

Phoenix Charts a New Course

Like many growing young cities, Phoenix had been guided during its early years by an elite primarily composed of established residents with money, but that group accepted newcomers and talented but less wealthy men. During the 1930s and 1940s, when the city was still relatively compact in size and modest in population, this elite of wealthy, influential men met often and informally: "You couldn't go two blocks without meeting 10 people that you knew well," said one. Together they ran associations, social clubs, and met informally for dinner, particularly during the summer. But as Frank Snell later recalled, the discussions around their table in the Luhrs Hotel's Arizona Room went beyond weather or golf: "This table was more important than you think, because we really did talk about important things and many were carried out." The city's three service clubs included many more members, but each drew somewhat different types of members. According to a common saying: "The Rotary Club owned the town, the Kiwanians ran it, and the Lions enjoyed it."

The Chamber of Commerce was the city's largest business group, having grown steadily to about 500 members by 1944. This association fostered friendships and communication between members and helped construct a consensus about developing the community. Into the 1940s the chamber supported balanced development with agriculture as the leading economic force, but in 1944 the new chamber president, F. W. Albury, advocated a postwar program with different goals. Under his direction, the Chamber appointed a Post-War Development Committee with subcommittees on aviation and tourism.

In the spring of 1945, chamber president Herbert R. Askins (who would later serve as Assistant Secretary of the Navy) moved the organization in a radically new direction. New bylaws defined the chamber's purpose as economic development and allowed it to purchase and hold property for that end. More than a dozen committees advised the chamber about manufacturing, conventions, public relations and state trade. The chamber hired a full-time staff and recruited Lewis E. Haas from San Francisco to be director. An energetic membership drive and the chamber's clear focus increased total membership to

In the late 1930s downtown Phoenix ranked 13th in the nation for retail sales.
The Herb and Dorothy McLaughlin Collection, Arizona Collection, Arizona State University Libraries

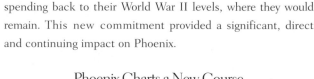

Throughout the 1950s the "Valley of the Sun" Chamber of Commerce office welcomed visitors with "Wild West" hospitality.

Arizona Historical Society-Central Arizona Division

nearly 2,000 by the end of the decade and made it a driving force in the Valley's future.

A handful of leaders with a combination of family ties, wealth, vision, and energy linked these organizations. From the beginning, downtown merchants had fostered the city's growth. Charles Korrick had come to Phoenix in 1900, and with his brother Abe built the city's largest department store. Public spirited and aware that local connections could help his business, Charles actively participated in community programs and the Arizona Club. In 1896 Baron Goldwater opened the Phoenix branch of the family store (based in Prescott), which his sons Bob and Barry continued to manage throughout the 1930s and 40s. Both brothers were active in community service, but while Bob focused on Phoenix and the store, Barry became more interested in the state and, increasingly after 1950, politics.

Other business leaders had long connections with some aspect of building and construction. The O'Malley Lumber Company began in 1908, and during the next several decades the family expanded into various building supply companies, development and investment firms. Ted O'Malley, a second-generation Phoenician, worked in these enterprises, participated in the chamber, belonged to many charitable and social groups, and worked especially with hospitals and health care.

Media owners significantly influenced community life. During the 1940s Wes Knorpp, the influential business manager of the city's two newspapers, the *Arizona Republic* and *Phoenix Gazette*, participated visibly in community organizations such as Kiwanis, the chamber, and the Community Chest. And in 1942, he had helped force the "Card Room Putsch" that ousted ineffectual city leadership. But in 1946, when *Indianapolis Star* publisher Eugene Pulliam purchased both the *Republic* and the

Gazette, the papers' influence became more overt, with major consequences for the Valley.

The son of a Methodist minister, Pulliam had acquired a string of Midwestern newspapers by the mid-1940s, and he took a few years to move his newspapers' base of operations to Phoenix. Although he believed in local service and contributed money to local causes, his personal involvement took place behind the scenes with other community leaders. Even more important, he pushed his papers into the forefront of public debates, especially on local matters, and pursued a political and economic agenda with a style reminiscent of press barons of an earlier era. Both the *Republic* and the *Gazette* featured front page editorials and banner headlines, blistering stories and sarcastic critiques, bombast and hyperbole that sometimes seemed no more than a vehicle for Pulliam's personal views — of labor unions, the federal government, the Democratic party, and taxation as the road to socialism. People complained about preferential coverage (or lack of coverage) of some issues or about slanted stories (denounced as "Pulliamism"). But no one denied that the *Republic* and *Gazette* provided significant coverage of community issues, or that they significantly affected the outcome of public debates.

Walter Bimson was born in Colorado, struggled to acquire an education, and became a banker in Chicago after World War I. His work involved providing agriculture loans, which brought him to the Valley during the 1920s. He moved to Phoenix as the new head of Valley National Bank in January of 1933 during the depths of the Depression and on the brink of a terrible banking crisis. His suggestions helped save the Arizona banking system, his loan policies provided money for home-ownership and economic growth, and by 1945 his bank made two-thirds of all loans in the Valley. Then the largest bank in the Rocky Mountain states area, VNB expanded further under Bimson's direction, acquiring control of other banks (including Frank Brophy's Bank of Arizona by 1955) and becoming the dominant bank of the Valley and state. Bimson's strategy of building branch offices and focusing on consumer and small business loans helped VNB prosper, and it also stimulated the Valley's economic development. He believed that the reverse also held true — that promoting Arizona's growth would benefit VNB. This philosophy shaped two VNB programs not directly connected with bank business: in 1944 the bank began producing the *Arizona Statistical Review*, an annual summary of Arizona data; in 1946 VNB published *Arizona Progress*, a pamphlet describing Arizona's growth, which it distributed to banks around the country. This philosophy and his position as the chair of Arizona's leading bank put Bimson at the forefront of important economic and social institutions in the Valley and made him a key player in efforts to recruit new businesses. Because he cared greatly about culture, he gave vital support to the arts and helped develop important cultural institutions in the Valley.

Frank Snell was the central figure among Phoenix leaders. "He was probably the most powerful man that ever existed in Arizona," recalled Tom Chauncey, another prominent city leader, at the time of Snell's death. "But I'll tell you, he was humble with it." Born in Kansas City, Missouri, in 1899, Snell graduated from law school in 1924 and accepted the invitation of an uncle in Miami, Arizona, to try his luck in Arizona copper country. In 1927 he married a local school teacher, Elizabeth Berlin, and moved to Phoenix. During the next 20 years, Snell built his practice into numerous connections and, in partnership with Mark Wilmer after 1938, into the Valley's largest law firm. Working for the cotton growers association and the power company, writing up incorporation papers for numerous businesses, and handling real estate such as John Lincoln's development of

the Encanto subdivision brought him valuable contacts. He added to these by his involvement and leadership in Kiwanis, the chamber of commerce, and the Arizona Club.

It had been Frank Snell whom Col. Hoyt contacted in the 1942 crisis and who had forced a resolution. For nearly the next 50 years Snell remained on call for various public concerns. He helped push the chamber to expand in 1945, served on the committee that hired Lew Haas as director, and arranged a crucial loan for the chamber. The bank agreed to the loan with one condition: that Snell remain as vice president. When a New York holding company had to sell Central Arizona Light and Power Company in 1945, Snell saw the importance of local ownership, and while Walter Bimson and Ted O'Malley negotiated the terms in New York, he organized the local investors. In 1952 he arranged the merger of this and several other power companies to create Arizona Public Service Co., for which he served as corporate counsel and board member. Throughout the coming decades Snell promoted economic development, shaped city government through the Charter Government Committee, and worked on various civic projects, like the Civic Center. He also contributed significantly to cultural and educational affairs, serving on the board of the Heard Museum, and for six years as chairman of the board of the American Graduate School of International Management, which he had helped organize.

(Far left)
Frank Snell (right) with Thunderbird President William Voris in 1986 — Snell's friend, Tom Chauncey, described him as "probably the most powerful man that ever existed in Arizona."
Thunderbird-The American Graduate School of International Management

Valley National Bank in the Professional Building at Central & Monroe, c. 1950
The Herb and Dorothy McLaughlin Collection, Arizona Collection, Arizona State University Libraries

"bossism" and vice did exist, but neither was as serious or deep-seated as critics contended, nor did they necessarily relate closely to larger problems of city government. Phoenix reformers in the late 1940s, like urban critics throughout the Southwest, borrowed the complaints of "bossism" and "corruption" made more accurately about larger, Eastern cities and which took most visible form in national congressional hearings in 1950-51. Though Doc Scheumack did have political influence, it was far less than his critics suggested. However, both he and his detractors found it useful to exaggerate his power. Accusations about the spread of vice were more legitimate, yet even those reports reflect not just social reality but also a revived concern about military business — and a powerful and useful political issue.

The political realities of postwar Phoenix were significantly more complex than these allegations suggest. Small businessmen and professionals had traditionally controlled city government. The 1942-1943 crisis had created a factional division in the commission which expanded after the war with the challenge from the Biz-Vets, an alternative coalition of businessmen and veterans. When critics pointed to the frequent replacement of city managers, they correctly identified a long-term trend and the product of political factionalism. But this had become a problem only recently, only when Phoenix had reached a size where the older political style and organization no longer worked. The issue, which the city's elite correctly identified, was how to manage a complex and growing city in order to encourage growth, and "growth of the right sort." Significantly,

Before World War II, the Phoenix leadership elite had focused on predictable, often short-term forms of economic development and had paid limited attention to politics and even less to cultural development. The war changed this pattern because the influx of soldiers made public morality and government honesty important issues, and the continuing squabbles with city politicians irked the political interest of the elite. The population boom that began during the war continued afterward, increasing the city's size and its need for jobs. And new economic opportunities occurred — in aviation, partly stimulated by the war, and in electronics, linked to aviation and military uses but increasingly important for consumer products. Promoting economic growth and expanding the city's size were interrelated issues, but both required a fundamental change in city government.

The structure of Phoenix government had been set in its 1913 reform charter: a mayor, with commissioners responsible for administering different city departments, and a city manager. Although it had initially functioned reasonably well, complaints grew louder during the 1940s that a political "boss" — Ward "Doc" Scheumack, manager of the Valley Paint and Supply Store — controlled the city. And when the military complained about the troops being led astray in 1942, critics charged that a corrupt city government tolerated vice. Both

a number of southwestern cities — including Dallas, San Antonio, Albuquerque, and San Diego — were experiencing the same problems and following almost an identical path.

In his successful campaign for mayor in the spring of 1946, Ray Busey promised to democratize city politics by revising the City Charter. (Ironically, Busey had been Scheumack's first employer in the Valley, but had fired him for alleged misdealings with city employees.) However, several recent attempts at charter revision had failed, so it was a pleasant surprise when he announced on October 23, 1947, a

Charter Revision Committee of 40 prominent citizens (including Frank Snell). As Busey later recalled, "These people were carefully selected to represent practically every facet of our social structure. Both major political parties and most of the religious beliefs were evident among them. Capital, labor, education, national and racial backgrounds, as well as industrial men were there." The group also included lawyers and judges, educators, and media representatives, as well as three former mayors. Working diligently from January to August of 1948 under the chairmanship of Charles Bernstein, a lawyer and head of the chamber of commerce, the committee adopted proposals drafted by Bernstein and Rhes Cornelius, of Phoenix Title and Trust Company. It recommended changing from a commission to a council form of government, eliminating the administrative duties of elected members; increasing the authority of the city manager and permitting the selection of a nonresident as manager; increasing the number of members to six; electing all members biennially at the same election; and continuing to elect members at-large in a nonpartisan election.

These charter amendments won approval from 69 percent of the voters in November of 1948, as a vigorous campaign by the committee and Pulliam's newspapers overcame the opposition of three commissioners, City Manager James Deppe and Doc Scheumack. Many citizens heaved a sigh of relief. But not for long. Transition to the new charter required appointing two additional council members, and when the reform forces led by Mayor Nicholas Udall could not muster a majority, opponents of the new charter appointed the new members. The new majority reapppointed Manager Deppe, effectively negating the aims of charter revision. Conditions worsened as factionalism divided the council and Deppe then fired various officials for political reasons. In March 1949 an audit revealed that lower revenues and higher expenses — some linked to poor administration — had put the city in a budget deficit, requiring a special election to approve a half-cent sale tax.

Anger at political conflict and misadministration reached the boiling point in July 1949 and fueled the organization of a citizens' committee to oust the existing political administration.

Alfred Knight, a businessmen who had previously lived in Cincinnati and knew about that city's reform techniques, roused the established business interests. Together with Dix Price, president of Young Democrats, and Ronald Webster, head of Young Republicans, Knight organized the Charter Government Committee (CGC) of some 100 members.

The committee began by selecting a slate of candidates for the November election. After some debate, the CGC accepted the request for support from two incumbents: council members

The *Arizona Republic*, November 6, 1949
The Reg Manning Collection, Arizona Collection, Arizona State University Libraries

Charles Walters and Mayor Nicholas Udall (son of former mayor John Udall, and the cousin of Stewart and Mo, later congressmen from Tucson). The other CGC candidates were charter members who had been very active in community organizations but had held no political offices, and who held various religious affiliations but a similar social standing: Hohen Foster, managing partner of the Barq Bottling Company; Frank Murphy, a successful insurance man; and Margaret Kober, one of several women on the CGC committee and the wife of a prominent doctor also active in civic affairs. After some jockeying, the final two slots were filled by Harry Rosenzweig, a prominent jeweler, and the friend he convinced to run with him, Barry Goldwater. Handsome, known for his photographs and movies of the state, and active in numerous groups, Goldwater apologized to his brother for abandoning the business to run for public office. "I couldn't criticize the government of this city if I, myself, refused to help," he said. And after noting their family's tradition of political service he added, "Don't cuss me too much. It ain't for life, and it may be fun." In fact, it turned out to be both.

The CGC faced a serious struggle. The Scheumack-Deppe slate included three incumbent councilmen with a fourth running for mayor. The mayoral contest was further complicated by the candidacies of two "independent" Deppe critics: Ray Busey and Jack Blaine, councilman and Biz-Vet leader. The well-financed, well-organized CGC forces mailed postcards to registered voters, ran newspaper ads, and "pressed the flesh" throughout the community. Udall and Goldwater operated as the leading spokesmen, and their statements carried a simple

underlying theme: the CGC was the "efficient and decent government which will cost you less" alternative to "vicious rule by a city boss." Bolstered by heavy support from the newspaper editorials, cartoons and opinionated news stories, CGC won in a landslide. Udall received 60 percent of the vote, the other council candidates averaged two-thirds of the vote while Goldwater won roughly three of every four votes. The CGC's victory rested on public interest, and turnout doubled from past elections to 41 percent of the eligible electorate.

Once in office the new council lost no time implementing the CGC platform. They fired manager Deppe and hired Ray Wilson, a professional city administrator from Kansas City, Missouri. Wilson quickly established his authority, taking politics out of city administration and personnel appointments — even surprising the council by retaining the police chief. Over the next 11 years Wilson reorganized and reduced the number of city departments, reformed budgeting and purchasing procedures, and improved and expanded city services. By the time he retired in 1961, Phoenix had twice won the All-American City Award.

The CGC Controls City Government

The day after the election the CGC chairman, Spencer Nitchie, announced that the group was disbanding as promised. But this announcement proved only partly true. Rather than disbanding, the group was essentially hibernating, for in two years and every city election for the next 25 years the CGC reappeared, dominating Phoenix government by nominating and electing candidates. After an election, only the CGC chairman retained formal office, but in the next election year he revived the organization by appointing an executive committee, and together they selected finance, nominating and campaign committees. The nominating committees picked people based on recommendations, not applications, and screened them for reputation and possible conflict of interest. They chose people active in service clubs and on city boards or commissions, but not politically ambitious — they had not held elective office before and, with a few notable exceptions like Barry Goldwater and Jack Williams, did not hold office afterward. According to Rhes Cornelius, the committee looked for candidates "who don't seek the job — they have to be sort of high-pressured into taking it"; people who could be "forced to do it as a matter of civic pride." Partly because of this relationship, the CGC financed and organized their campaigns, and they ran as part of a team.

Despite its name, the CGC did not represent a revival of the Charter Revision committee of 1947-48. In fact, many members of the earlier group opposed organizing the CGC, in part because it reflected a different approach to government. CGC slates looked diverse, including both Democrats and Republicans, a range of religious affiliations, at least one woman per council, and, beginning in 1953, a Hispanic candidate. More significantly, both the CGC and its candidates constituted a select element of the city's population. Rather than broadly and intentionally reflecting various groups within the city, the CGC represented a group of businessmen and professionals with citywide ties and name recognition who knew each other through civic activities, common association, and residence — the elite in which Snell, Bimson, and Pulliam were major forces. Equally important, their notions of government and politics played an extremely important role in shaping the city. Government, they believed, involved making broad policy decisions, based on nonpartisan, citywide standards — what was "good" for "all citizens," while "politics" was a four-letter word that meant the pursuit of self-interest or the benefit of a limited group. The public, or common good, would be achieved by allowing able people of good will and without personal or political agendas to decide the direction of the city; and leave the details to administrators.

In 1949 the CG slate won by a hefty margin, and that percentage rose still further during the 1950s, but two problems persisted. First, the CG did not enjoy uniform support across the city. In 1949 the CG ticket got only a third of the vote in eight of the nine south-central precincts south of Van Buren Street — the poorest areas of town; it won barely half in the next tier of precincts reaching to Roosevelt Street; but it averaged nearly 75 percent in the wealthy northwest precincts. The rising CG vote in subsequent elections increased these levels somewhat but did not change the basic disparity. And over the years voter turnout fell from the 1949 high of 41 percent to 25 percent of the electorate. Ironically, the dominance of the CG reduced the civic interest which it wished to encourage. (See appendix 1A)

Because CGC candidates ran as a slate, opponents had little chance of winning as individuals and, thus, found it essential to organize their own slate. In some ways they imitated the CGC

Members of the first CGC-dominated council included (seated, left to right) Hohen Foster, Margaret B. Kober, Frank Murphy, (standing) Charles Walters, Mayor Nicholas Udall, Barry Goldwater and Harry Rosenzweig. *The Goldwater Family Collection, Arizona Historical Foundation, Arizona State University*

strategy of balancing their ticket, especially in religion, but they differed in several important respects. Instead of being involved in citywide service clubs or on government boards, these candidates represented unions, local fraternal organizations, or veterans groups like the American Legion. They were also more explicitly political and partisan — in identification, in having worked for a party organization, or even in having held a government job. Most important, they were obviously less elite in occupation, wealth, status, or education. As retired railroad workers, bus drivers, beauticians, housewives and clerks, they lacked the citywide contacts, the name recognition, or the job-related skills necessary to win in citywide elections without political party help. Only the Phoenix Ticket in 1959 learned from past failures and avoided this problem. Besides a balance of party, religion and gender, its members were roughly equal in status to the CGC slate, and several had been active in community organizations. Their prominence and connections forced the CGC to run its most aggressive race since 1949.

(Far left) Nicholas Udall, Phoenix mayor 1950-1952 *City of Phoenix*

Hohen Foster, Phoenix mayor 1952-1954 *City of Phoenix*

City election campaigns of the 1950s largely replayed the campaign debates of 1949. The idea of electing council members from wards and on partisan tickets always remained just beneath the surface; several opposition slates specifically proposed it, and CG candidates denounced it at every opportunity. Grave warnings about the dangers of bossism, "patronage-hungry politicians," and vice gave these expressions emotional power. The last charge got the greatest play in 1953 when CG candidates warned that the opposition would be soft on crime. Adam Diaz alleged that the Economy Ticket intended to relax controls on vice; John Sullivan suggested that "Prostitutes ran wild when we were elected to office four years ago"; and Margaret Kober argued that since 1950 the city had eliminated prostitution and gambling.

In nearly every election, voters heard allegations that the opposition was trying to obtain support from the Democratic party. Opponents responded by labeling CGC nominees a "country-club council," claiming the committee was a clique that actually ran the city through the city manager's office and noting that the council members came from the same north-central area of town. Mayor Jack Williams, who had gained widespread public recognition as an announcer on KOY radio since 1929, responded with the familiar chorus, "There should be no north, no south, no east, and no west," and that ward elections would divide and weaken the council.

Although the basic question of the city government's efficiency revolved around the city manager — a perpetual issue, which echoed the conflict of the 1940s — more substantive and slightly less emotional issues became more prominent over time. In 1955 mayoral candidate Sam Levitin alleged that Phoenix spent more per capita than any other comparable city — an argument disputed by Councilman Wes Johnson, an accountant by occupation. In 1955 and 1957 the opposition complained about unfair or inadequate treatment of firefighters and police officers and noted the essential failure of the city bus service.

The most important discussions concerned taxes. CG officeholders consistently trumpeted their success in reducing property taxes by 25 percent in six years: from $2.28 per $100 in 1949 to $1.75 by 1955. But opposition mayoral candidates in 1957 and 1959 claimed that water rates had increased by one-third during this period, and those revenues were being

used for non water expenses. Sam Levitin made a more serious claim: that property taxes had fallen because the supposedly temporary city sales tax of one-half cent passed in 1949 remained in effect, and that otherwise property taxes would have been $3.09. Levitin noted correctly that increased sales tax revenues had been more responsible than government efficiencies for the city's economic health and its ability to expand services. He also accurately described both property and sales taxes as "poor man's taxes," recognizing that adding an income tax would have been a more equitable form. On balance, however, this policy made sense for the 1950s, for it spread taxation to include nonresidents, and, more important, it provided additional revenues crucial for the economic health of the city during a period of vital expansion.

Creating the New Economy

As they were taking over city government, the Phoenix elite also began pushing economic growth, aided by the booming national economy in the late 1940s and by people flocking to Phoenix in search of work. Chamber of commerce director Lew Haas led a calculated booster campaign, which included the monthly publication, *Phoenix Action*, and national advertising campaigns. While tourism and conventions comprised part of this strategy, the main emphasis involved the Industrial Development Committee's efforts to attract new businesses. Patrick Downey,

an executive at Valley National Bank, significantly assisted these efforts, periodically working directly for the chamber to visit and recruit larger firms. The chamber also brought businessmen to Phoenix, wined and dined them, then gave them "the hard sell," including offers to help them relocate.

Government support was crucial to this effort. The "cleaned up" city appeared more attractive to businesses and acted more vigorously to recruit them, contributing money to the chamber's ad campaigns, negotiating inducements for resettlement, and even sending officials like the mayor to recruit specific businesses. In 1949 the city government reduced taxes on manufacturing inventory and equipment, followed by state government action for manufacturing and warehouse firms. Together with a voter-approved Arizona right-to-work law in 1946, this created a pro-business climate that further encouraged businesses to settle in the Valley. Ultimately, though, the natural and labor climates had greater effect. Dry air helped manufacturing, and a supply of skilled labor, the ease of recruitment, and lower rates of absenteeism and illness were major attractions. Laws did not eliminate the labor movement — workers struck and unions organized — and their relative failure owed more to the types of employment and employees than the fulminations of newspapers or the plans of owners.

The economic expansion started in 1946 when the Aviola Radio Corporation bought the former AiResearch plant to produce radio components and the Reynolds Metals Company leased the aluminum extrusion plant. Reynolds bought the plant in 1949, expanded it, and by 1952 it had become the largest such plant in the world. The chamber's Industrial Development Department boosted its efforts in 1948, helped by the beginning of the Cold War. Within two years 50 new businesses with 1,750 employees opened in the Phoenix area. The Goodyear Aircraft company returned in 1949, building plastic pilot enclosures, wings for training planes and bags for blimps. (A decade later it would build support equipment for missiles and employ 2,000 workers.) Between 1950 and 1952 an additional 70 new firms opened, providing jobs for 6,680 workers. This included AiResearch, which relocated near Sky Harbor Airport in 1951 to build gas turbine engines, starters, pneumatic control valves, and (later) precision controls for missiles. By 1960, AiResearch

employed 3,800 workers. Other, smaller firms — like the 300-employee Phoenix Parachute Company — opened for the first time. The Korean War boosted military contracts to Phoenix plants, but military contracts throughout the 1950s paid for new and expanded plants as well as workers' salaries. Nearly all the major firms initially focused on aviation and electronics for military use, encouraged by the proximity to the U.S. Army electronics proving ground at Fort Huachuca. *(See appendix 1B)*

By 1960 manufacturing had more than doubled to nearly 20 percent of the workforce. The lion's share of this growth resulted from the 290 new manufacturers who had come to the Phoenix area since 1948, creating 23,583 jobs and with a payroll of $122 million. Only one in five of those new jobs stemmed from traditional employment in food, clothing, or building

materials, which grew partly because of the population increase. Three times as many jobs developed from aviation and electronics — many of them related to military contracts (as were jobs with "older" firms like Reynolds). These firms were attracted by and further stimulated the growth of subcontractors: tool and die companies, precision grinders, and other skilled machine and engineering firms. The large, important firms included Sperry Phoenix and General Electric, both of which came in 1957 and located in Deer Valley. By 1960 GE had 2,000 employees, and Sperry had 1,100. Above all, Motorola's strategy and growth shaped the Valley's future.

Begun by Paul Galvin in 1928, Motorola by the late 1940s had developed radio communications equipment and become a leading manufacturer of televisions. Its future, and that of all electronics firms, changed in 1948 with the development of the transistor. To pursue the possibilities of solid state electronics, Daniel Noble, the head of research for Motorola, convinced Galvin to establish a research lab. Favoring a Southwestern site because of the climate, Noble chose Phoenix because of its machine shops and transportation facilities and its strategic location between the atomic energy works in New Mexico and California. The lab opened in the winter of 1948, focusing on obtaining government contacts as one way to fund its research. The lab expanded rapidly, reaching 91,000 square feet in 1956, and in 1957 the headquarters of the military electronics division moved from Chicago to an additional plant of 192,000 square feet. Although war and the success of military contracts delayed some of the solid state research Noble had intended, by the mid-1950s they achieved a major advance in developing the first power transistor, which substantially improved the performance of industrial and consumer radios. In 1956 Motorola began a semiconductor products division with a plant of 40,000 square feet, which expanded fivefold by 1960. Thus, by mid-1960 Motorola had three plants and employed 3,800 workers. It began winning increasingly large government contracts, and its consumer products work was also expanding, indicating an even greater impact in the future.

continued on page 36

■Born on a Connecticut farm in 1901, Dan Noble spent his boyhood tinkering, and while in high school he built a science lab stuffed with chemical apparatus, radios and electric devices. Complaining of severe headaches and eye strain, Noble was advised by his doctor to stop reading for a year and develop himself physically — a prescription that led to his first experience in Arizona. In the spring of 1919 Noble moved to Prescott, where he spent his time hunting, trapping and working as a ranch hand. He later recalled that he even rode a wild horse — very briefly.

After a year, his headaches lessened, Noble returned home to attend Connecticut State College, and in 1923 the school's president hired him to teach math to engineering students. Noble continued his own education during the summers, completing his bachelor's degree in engineering in 1929 and doing graduate work at MIT.

Throughout these years Noble's early fascination with radios expanded, and he recognized the new medium's economic possibilities. Already in 1921 he had built a special receiver and after running an antenna from the church steeple to the town hall (which he had rented), he charged admission to hear a live broadcast of the Dempsey-Carpentier heavyweight boxing championship fight. In the 1930s he persuaded the university president to start an educational broadcasting station for the school, and he constructed a radio relay system to expand the signal. Always closely attentive to technological innovations, in 1936 he visited Professor Howard Armstrong at Columbia University to learn about his recent invention of FM technology. Impressed by Armstrong's presentation, Noble converted the Connecticut system into one of the earliest FM stations. Subsequently he designed mobile, FM communications systems for the state's forestry and police departments.

These successes caught the attention of Paul Galvin, head of the Motorola radio company, who attempted to hire Noble in 1940. Wary of leaving his academic position, Noble signed on only temporarily, but after only four months he made the arrangement permanent. During the next five years he developed FM "walkie-talkie" communications for the military, and after the war he worked on radios. Increasingly convinced that electronics companies should bolster their research, following the Bell Lab's development of the transistor in 1948 he persuaded Galvin that Motorola should start a research lab. Noble scouted sites in the West and decided on Phoenix in part because it was a growing metropolitan area and, he felt sure, people would like living there.

Noble was an efficient manager as well as an inventive scientist. One of his business strategies was to use the income from government contracts to subsidize research in semiconductors. "The government, with contracts, will constantly be working on the leading edge of the art," he reasoned, and, "technical information and techniques — and the general flow of information is relevant to your total movement in the field of electronics." He was able to begin work on semiconductors in 1951, and he continued to expand Motorola's involvement in the field. By the time he retired, Noble had served in many roles at Motorola: head of the Solid State, Electronics, and Communications divisions, head of the Semiconductor plant, and vice president for research.

Throughout his life Noble remained deeply committed to the importance of learning and educational institutions. When he moved to Phoenix, Arizona State College was only a small teaching school, but Noble saw its possibilities as a research institution, perhaps because it reminded him of conditions at Connecticut years earlier. Beginning in the mid-1950s and continuing for over a decade, he campaigned for improving the institution. Without this effort "[Motorola] could not expand and could not maintain leadership," he declared. "We could not hold our superior brain power here in the city." He also explained convincingly that the upgrade would benefit the Valley as a whole: "Phoenix cannot hope to compete with other areas in attracting the technical product industries, and holding them, without the development of engineering and science education and research at Arizona State University to a high level of scholarship and maturity." By articulating a vision of a research institution and a partnership between the university and the larger community, he contributed not only to developing ASU's science and engineering programs, but also to redefining the university's role in the Valley.

Noble also recognized the importance of a broad education, including moral and aesthetic values. He served as director of the Phoenix Symphony, the Phoenix Art Museum and the ASU Foundation. After many years as a "persistent sketcher" and occasional painter, in 1964 Noble decided to try a "research approach to abstract art" — a form he had harshly criticized — and he set out to paint 10 pieces to discover the motivation and purpose of this form. In just four months he completed nearly 60 works, and the experience changed his mind. While he continued to see some modern art as merely "decoration" or "a put-on," he concluded that many of them represented important principles of communication and representation. He was even more surprised when art critics found his work worthwhile. In 1966 the Phoenix Art Museum and the Stable Gallery of Scottsdale showed his paintings, followed by showings in Paris and San Francisco. In 1974 he published *Paintings and Pratings*, a limited edition of photoprints of 100 of his oils.

Still, it was as an electrical engineer that Noble won his greatest accolades. The holder of nine patents, he won the Western Electrical Manufacturers Association's Medal of Achievement, the Franklin Institute's Stewart Ballantine Medal, and the 1978 Edison Medal for his "exceptionally meritorious career." The award Noble seems to have prized most highly was his honorary doctorate from ASU in 1957. Thereafter, Noble referred to himself as "Dr." The title fit a man who devoted his life to learning and sharing knowledge. ■

(Above left)
Dr. Noble in his lab at Motorola, 1959
The Herb and Dorothy McLaughlin Collection, Arizona Collection, Arizona State University Libraries

(Above right)
By painting, Noble gained an appreciation for "communication and representation" in abstract art.
Department of Archives and Manuscripts, University Archives, Arizona State University

Motorola and Noble spearheaded the development of higher education in the Valley. To retain its employees and improve itself, Motorola needed its employees to have easy access to good university and graduate level training, especially in engineering and computer science. Phoenix College was only a two-year institution, and the University of Arizona was too far away, but Arizona State College in neighboring Tempe offered undergraduate degrees and had a booming enrollment. Noble

talked frequently with President Grady Gammage and engineering professor Lee Thomson, encouraging them to develop the school's engineering program, and in 1956 it began offering an undergraduate engineering degree. That year Noble began speaking publicly. Although admitting that the college's current standards were inadequate, he declared that it had the capacity to improve and that such a change was essential for the economic well-being of the Valley. "We must have adequate college level engineering and scientific training available at Arizona State College at Tempe." Executives at AiResearch and Goodyear voiced their support for Noble's ideas. A key factor in GE's decision to locate in Phoenix was concerns about ASC's programs in engineering and science. Encouraged by conversations with President Gammage and the new engineering degree, GE not only located in the Valley, it also donated a large computer to the school (its first) and established a center on campus where it worked on various computing problems.

The importance of education in this emerging economy reached a new level in the campaign to upgrade the institution. In 1958, following the combined efforts

of the college, high-tech employers, Phoenix boosters, and the Pulliam newspapers, the state's voters approved changing ASC to Arizona State University with the right to offer graduate degrees (a change the University of Arizona and a majority of Tucson voters opposed). By 1962 the undergraduate engineering programs were accredited, praised by outside reviewers, and attracting 10 percent of the university enrollment, including over 300 Motorola employees. The company had also created a program with ASU so its employees could pursue graduate degrees while still working, and more than 100 Motorola employees plus 200 employees of other Valley firms were following this path.

Growing Pains

In 1940 Phoenix was a modest-sized city of 65,414. Ten years later the population had grown to 106,818, and the city ranked 99th among U.S. cities. By 1960 the city had exploded to 439,170 people and ranked 29th. But these numbers obscure the larger story of population expansion throughout the Valley and the struggle by Phoenix to stay atop this wave of growth. The Phoenix leadership recognized that prosperity required jobs and an efficient government, and they worked effectively to create them. They also understood that urban expansion constituted an equally important part of their prosperous future, and that achieving this goal required a particular strategy.

In 1940 Maricopa County included Phoenix and only eight other incorporated areas, all of which were small, agricultural market communities with "one-street business districts." The West Valley was home to three towns. Glendale, which Dunkard farmers from the Midwest had founded in 1892 was

His Monument
By Reg Manning
Arizona Republic Staff Artist

the largest, and it incorporated in 1910. Wickenburg was small and too distant to be considered within the metropolitan area. The East Valley included the Mormon town of Mesa, the largest of its towns and the only one with any commercial district; Tempe, which included the Hayden Mill and Arizona State College; and Chandler, which boasted the San Marcos Hotel, an impressive resort but now overshadowed by the Biltmore and Camelback Inn. But in unincorporated suburban neighborhoods surrounding Phoenix lived an additional urban population twice the total size of these communities and two-thirds the size of Phoenix. By 1950 the incorporated West Valley had doubled (and several additional communities had organized); the East Valley had grown a bit more rapidly; and Phoenix had grown by two-thirds. But the unincorporated population expanded even faster, constituting about a third of urban residents in Maricopa County.

Home-building became a major industry in Phoenix after World War II, generating employment for workers, small business and architects, and providing opportunities for builders to acquire substantial wealth. Because it took relatively little capital to build one or two homes, many men with limited assets became builders. James G. Hart began in 1945 with $600, a car and a trailer. He got a subcontract for one house, arranged financing, and eventually built 31 houses in that subdivision. Seven years later he was building his own subdivision, Papago Village. A few entered the business because their fathers were contractors, and several, like Clarence Suggs, moved from insurance to realty, but most started without much help. More had come from another state — many from Arkansas, Oklahoma and Missouri. While some built custom homes, like Kenneth Rosing or Maxwell Dorne of Paradise Builders, most builders moved as quickly as possible into mass producing tract homes.

The ranch house became the primary kind of home built in the Valley after the war. This single-story structure usually made of Superlite block, had a low sloped roof and a carport. These ranch houses differed from prewar structures in several ways: they were larger — most had three bedrooms, or even four; the living room was near the back of the house; and as one observer noted, "the back yard is considered an extension of the living area," so that builders "often are including a terrace, or patio, with the right kind of fence screening needed for privacy."

Builders emphasized the ranch house's affordability. In 1953 the cheapest Phoenix houses cost roughly $8,000 to $9,000 for a house of 1,000 to 1,100 square feet; somewhat larger houses of 1,300 to 1,500 square feet listed for $12,000 to $17,500; and a house of 1,750 square feet would cost $20,000 or more. Commercial banks fueled this market, but

Population of Metropolitan Phoenix & Maricopa County 1940 to 1960

	1940	1950	1960
Phoenix	65,414	106,818	439,170
All urban areas (including Phoenix)	87,506	161,315	557,473
Unincorporated Phoenix	44,452	76,668	32,131
U.S. Census: Metro Phoenix	121,828	216,038	552,043
Other cities & towns	131,958	237,983	585,958
Maricopa County	186,193	331,770	663,510
Phoenix % of Maricopa County	35.1%	32.2%	66.2%
Phoenix % of urban areas	49.6%	44.9%	74.9%
Other cities & towns			
Glendale	4,855	8,179	15,696
Peoria			2,593
El Mirage			1,723
Tolleson	1,731	3,042	3,886
Avondale		2,505	6,151
Goodyear		1,254	1,654
Buckeye	1,305	1,932	2,286
Tempe	2,906	7,684	24,894
Mesa	7,224	16,790	33,772
Chandler	1,239	3,799	9,531
Gilbert	837	1,114	1,833
Scottsdale	[1,000]	[2,032]	10,026
Sunnyslope		[4,430]	na
Wickenburg	995	1,736	2,445
Gila Bend			[1,813]

NOTE: *Cities and towns are listed from the northwest, counter-clockwise around Phoenix, except the last two, which do not fit into this Salt River Valley organization. Populations are only listed when the areas are incorporated except for Scottsdale, Sunnyslope and Gila Bend.*

Mrs. Homeowner, 1956

Arizona Historical Society-Central Arizona Division

savings and loan companies and new entrepreneurial banks gained increasing shares of this business. By 1960 A.B. Robbs Trust Company handled 20 percent of the Valley mortgages, while Western Savings made over half of the growing number of loans from savings and loan institutions. Federal financing through the FHA or VA was a key part of this. Down payments could be relatively low, sometimes only eight percent, and John F. Long created a package involving no down payment.

Major innovations in construction techniques helped keep prices low. John Dolan built house walls on the ground and then raised them into place. Hugh Knoell owned a franchise from the Mobilhome company, and at his factory on E. Washington Street he constructed houses that he transported to the home site and placed on foundations. But John F. Long clearly stood out as the major innovator. He emphasized simple designs for open houses; he built his own cabinets and counters; and he used prefab trusses and walls, and plumbing trees. As a result, Long could boast that his prices were at or near the lowest, and he provided relatively good quality structures. In using mass production techniques, Long resembled other successful builders across the country, but he did even better in emphasizing scale. FHA standards encouraged this trend, recommending that builders construct larger numbers of fewer home models for the sake of economy and predictable housing values. The president of the Arizona Home Builders Association expounded

on this change in 1954, telling the public that builders no longer constructed single homes; instead, home owners were buying "an integrated unit of the community. The home builders in your city are really community builders." Although the community building aspect was questionable, builders were developing increasingly larger subdivisions, rising from about 30 to about 180 houses. Furthermore, builders produced homes more rapidly — some built 70 to 100 houses per year.

But Long operated in a different league, constructing 350 houses per year by 1954 and increasing that rate to 1,000 per year by 1956. Even more important, Long initiated the shift from home building to community development. In 1953 he hired Victor Gruen, a noted architect and planner from Los Angeles, to design a community west of Phoenix that Long named Maryvale after his wife. The design included places for shopping and employment, schools, recreation and hospitals. The models opened in 1955 to huge crowds; at $7,950 for a three-bedroom house, Long was selling 125 houses a week.

The availability of inexpensive housing outside the city, and particularly the shift to community development, posed a growing problem for Phoenix because these areas might feel self-sufficient and want their own government. To avoid the kind of suburban strangulation then becoming evident in Midwestern and Eastern cities, and to become the dominant city in the Southwest, Phoenix had to persuade these new

John F. Long opened Maryvale, the Valley's first whole-community of homes, in 1955.
John F. Long Properties, Inc.

areas to be annexed. This task took careful planning. The installation of charter government had erased the city's image of corruption and mismanagement, but significant issues remained.

The city paid close attention to services during the 1950s, and their improvement, expansion and efficiency contributed greatly to the city's overall success. Adequate funds coming through property and sales tax revenues, bonds and federal funds, as well as effective management made these improvements possible. The city built, paved, and extended streets and installed nearly 15,000 street lights. It obtained water from the Salt River Project, built a filtration plant, and bought out private water companies supplying well water. Further, it expanded the sewage treatment system and reduced the use of cesspools. Phoenix also reorganized, expanded, and equipped its fire and police departments. The city overcame a significant hurdle in 1957 when voters endorsed a $70 million bond issue to fund a variety of urban needs identified by the Phoenix Growth Committee, a citizens' committee of 464 people formed by Mayor Jack Williams. While half of these funds went to fix the water system, other monies went to expand the airport, build a new library, fund new parks and playgrounds and build a new municipal building.

Soon after his appointment in 1950 as city manager, Ray Wilson ordered a study of the surrounding "fringe" areas and a comprehensive plan for annexation. In 1953 he hired John Burke as director of annexation. Public attitudes and city budgets initially limited the city's activities, but first cautiously and then more aggressively by 1957 the city moved to encompass the surrounding

areas. It began by providing some services to certain surrounding areas — water to 60,000 nonresidents in 1957; sewers to Sunnyslope and Maryvale; and police and fire service to other neighborhoods. This "creeping annexation" showed people the benefits of belonging to the city. In overt public campaigns city officials explained that annexation would bring even more services, and that taxes would cost residents less than what they already paid for services. The city also sought support from areas with businesses as well as residences. Eliminating the city's inventory taxes and a special sales tax on manufactured goods, as well as revising city zoning, building, and planning ordinances in 1959 cleared the last objections to annexation from major businesses.

The city's major problem was that a fringe area might seek to incorporate itself; the city's protection was that both pro-annexation and pro-status quo residents would oppose incorporation. This scenario occurred in Sunnyslope, the area immediately north of the city. Five times — in 1949, 1953, 1955, and twice in 1958 — those residents defeated proposals to incorporate variously defined communities. The last effort had been primarily defensive, to prevent annexation, but after that initiative failed, Phoenix annexed the community in April 1959.

Resistance also sprouted in South Phoenix, an area south of the Salt River. In February of 1953 an incorporation effort there failed. To circumvent continuing opposition there, the 1960 annexation effort linked South Phoenix with Maryvale, an area overwhelming in favor of annexation. A law suit failed to overturn this action, and a 1961 law made incorporation of adjacent urban areas virtually impossible.

The final threat to Phoenix's growth was annexation by a neighboring community. In 1945 Phoenix was six miles from Glendale and from Tempe, but the growth of all three brought them into competition. Phoenix worked out an amicable division of territory with Glendale, but it fought with cities to the east. When Tempe attempted to encircle an area of adjacent territory, Phoenix successfully protested in court. More serious conflict involved Scottsdale, which incorporated in 1951 with 2,000 residents and sought to expand to the west. When the courts overturned a pre-emptive annexation by Scottsdale in 1961, Phoenix quickly annexed much of the same area. The two cities finally resolved the division of territory in 1964.

The measure of its success is, first, that in 1940 and 1950 Phoenix had comprised only a third of the county and half the urban population; in 1960 it made up two-thirds of the county and three-fourths of the urban area. Annexation provided most of this change: three-fourths of the 1960 population lived in areas annexed since 1950 (just like Tucson) and half in areas annexed since 1958.

A Dramatically Different Place

By 1960 Phoenix had achieved national recognition. It had become the leading city in the Southwest, the 29th-largest city in the nation, and the fastest-growing city of its size. It was a dramatically different place than it had been a mere two decades before. While its prosperity and expansion represent part of a larger story of Sunbelt growth — national migration, the expansion of aviation and electronics linked to national defense spending, and suburbanization — Phoenix achieved its position through determined effort and planning, and it did so more successfully than other competitors in the region. The city succeeded because its leadership elite recognized that economic and population growth depended on an effective government. The economic strategy was not unusual for the period or area, but Phoenicians did particularly well in realizing it. Perhaps the city's greatest danger came from the spreading population and the possibility of suburban strangulation. The annexations from 1958 to 1960 eliminated that threat, more than doubling the city's population and providing it with relatively free fields for future growth to the north and south.

But in 1960 Phoenix also faced a future with different issues and problems. Encompassing an area literally 20 times larger than it had in 1940 and with roughly five times the population, the nature of its population and leadership had also changed. Personal connections in such a community were more difficult, and interests were becoming increasingly divergent, based on neighborhood, income, culture and race. The burgeoning population had begun to create issues of sprawl, downtown decay, traffic and air quality. More amorphous but no less real, the city's identity was coming into question.

Reg Manning,
the *Arizona Republic*,
September 11, 1955
*The Reg Manning
Collection, Arizona
Collection, Arizona State
University Libraries*

Washington and 1st
Avenue, c. 1956.
*Arizona Historical Society-
Central Arizona Division*

The view of Phoenix from South Mountain, 1965
Arizona Historical Society-Central Arizona Division

Building a City
1960-1980

By 1960 Phoenix had begun to achieve the kind of national visibility that local leaders

had first dreamed of in the mid-1940s. An expanding city in the nation's most

dynamic region, Phoenix benefitted from its Western location, but it also began

contributing substantially to the area's growth, prosperity and prominence. National

evaluations of urban fiscal policies and the provision of city services needed to

chapter two

consider the strategies and successes of Southwestern cities, particularly Phoenix. Discussions about the future of the country's cities included urban decay, suburban sprawl and special purpose suburbs, all of which existed in Phoenix. Urban politics had a particular flavor in the Southwest, and charter government continued its overwhelming dominance. The economy also represented a continuation of trends begun earlier and a regional pattern of development. By 1980 Phoenix had emerged as one of the most important Western cities. (*See appendix 2A*)

Phoenix and the West

Dramatic expansion characterized the entire West, and especially the Southwest, during this era. Before World War II the larger region had been home to only one in 10 Americans; 20 years later that proportion had doubled, and by 1980 more than a quarter of the U.S. population lived in the West. Although people settled throughout the region, the greatest influx came to the Southwest, from Texas to Southern California. This burgeoning population concentrated in cities, and almost as if "urban population watching" were a spectator sport, Westerners cheered as their cities rose rapidly in the national rankings. By 1960 three cities in Texas and one in California had joined the older centers of Los Angeles and San Francisco in the top 18 cities, with Seattle and Denver retaining their status in the top 25. By 1980 those Texas and

California cities had risen still higher in population and rank, joined by Phoenix at 9th and San Jose in 17th place.

Western cities also gained prominence because their form seemed to represent the modern American city: a sprawl of suburbs. Los Angeles and Houston were extreme cases, but most cities in the region spread over large areas. Half of the geographically largest cities in 1960 were Western, and those grew even larger in subsequent years. Like Phoenix, these cities considered annexation a necessary way to avoid being strangled by suburbs, and they relentlessly gobbled newly developed subdivisions. They grabbed adjoining vacant lands also, but because Western cities attracted population so rapidly, houses and malls soon sprouted in those undeveloped areas, too.

The speed and style of this expansion meant that Western cities had much lower population densities than America's "older" large cities. In 1960 the largest Eastern cities from New York to Baltimore averaged roughly 14,000 persons per square mile; the big, industrial Midwestern cities, from Cleveland to St. Louis, had about 12,000, (with 7,000 for smaller cities in that region); but the density of Sunbelt cities was only 2,300 to 4,000. In 1980 the same pattern held except that declining inner city populations reduced the density in the older cities.

From a distance Phoenix looked like any Sunbelt city, but a closer view showed important differences. Between 1940 and 1960 Phoenix had grown more rapidly in population than any other city in the mountain states, and only Denver remained larger. By 1980 Phoenix had passed Denver, Seattle, San Francisco and San Antonio, trailing only San Diego, Dallas, Houston and Los Angeles. Phoenix grew even more rapidly in area: in 1960 it was the ninth largest city with 187.4 square miles; in 1980 it held 324 square miles, ranking fourth in the nation (excluding a few odd cases). Thus, by 1960 Phoenix had become the model of sprawling cities: large and growing rapidly, it ranked last among major cities in population density (listing only 2,343 persons per square mile in 1960 and 2,437 in 1980).

Up to 1980 Phoenix's economic development generally reflected regional, especially Western urban patterns. The city's shift to manufacturing, particularly in electronics and aerospace industries, mirrored developments across the region, as did the rise of financial services,

The Phoenix Ramada Inn
on Van Buren Street, c.1960
*Arizona Historical Society-
Central Arizona Divsion*

tourism and construction. The increased national importance of these sectors — compared with steel and automobile manufacturing — helps explain the city's prosperity.

But the growing attraction of an outdoor lifestyle drew people to Arizona and fueled the economic expansion. The city also grew as a regional retail market and distribution center. Furthermore, Phoenix served as one of the federal government's regional centers, housing federal employees from numerous government agencies both common and specific to the region, like the Bureau of Land Management. As the state capital, Phoenix had an employment advantage over its closest southwestern competitors because it provided employment to a growing number of government workers. All of these elements fueled an impressive expansion during the 1960s and 1970s, but the Valley also struggled to build an economic infrastructure and to overcome a boom-bust tendency of its economy.

Phoenicians considered charter government fundamental to their city's growth. They believed that CGC had fulfilled the promise it made in 1949 to develop an efficient, scandal-free city government and manage the city's expansion effectively. They applauded the successful recruitment of businesses, the annexation of new areas and the distribution of city services. The key elements of charter government's philosophy were relying on a self-appointed, civic-minded group of businessmen and professionals to choose nominees for mayor and city council; retaining a system of non-partisan, at-large elections; emphasizing issues of economic growth; and focusing on broad public policy issues while leaving the "details" of government management to a city manager.

Phoenicians described the struggle in the 1940s and the events of the 1950s as dramatic, defining times in the city's history. Much of this was true, but the story makes greater sense as part of a broader movement. As Amy Bridges explains in her study

The Arizona Republic,
December 10, 1961
*The Reg Manning
Collection, Arizona
Collection, Arizona State
University Libraries*

By 1960 some Phoenicians had begun to recognize the fundamental limitations of CG's approach to government and politics. The group's stranglehold on power made elections uneven contests, reducing public interest in government and diminishing the character of public debate over the issues. The great emphasis on expansion overshadowed other issues, particularly the flight of businesses from the downtown area and the spreading blight of slums in the central city. Throughout the 1950s and into the 1960s, CG ignored serious housing problems on the south side, which resulted from residential segregation, ineffective housing inspection and insufficient construction of private or public housing.

Although the city had generally succeeded in providing services to new areas, not all neighborhoods were treated equally or had the same needs, and the city bus system was a general and increasing failure into the 1970s. Neither economic expansion nor public schools offered adequate opportunities for persons at the lower end of the economic scale, and minority groups faced the additional burden of racism. Finally, the success of Charter Government's vision of growth carried the seeds of subsequent dilemmas — traffic snarls, significant air pollution, rapidly escalating crime, and sprawling, low-density development that threatened much of what Valley residents considered attractive.

of municipal reform in the region, growing cities across the Southwest like San Antonio, Albuquerque, San Diego and San Jose organized remarkably similar campaigns and adopted virtually identical systems of government. Rising to oppose "machine politics," political action groups in these cities too had revised their city charter to institute the same nonpartisan, at-large system of elections and give city managers increased authority. As a result, during the 1950s these cities had followed essentially the same strategies involving economic expansion, annexation and the proliferation of suburbs. By the 1960s, however, they also encountered a number of problems that threatened to undermine the entire system.

All Southwestern cities faced these issues and difficulties in the 1960s and 1970s, but each city made its own choices about handling them. Phoenicians struggled with these problems, and in the process they changed important aspects of politics and government; but they retained their fundamental belief that the city could grow its way out of difficulty. This touchstone belief in growth came amidst evidence of growing prosperity, but it was countered by the reality that personal connections and the character of the Valley were being changed forever.

A Different Kind of Machine: Charter Government and Politics of the Center

The Charter Government Committee was essentially a political machine, but its supporters vehemently rejected this label. Mayor Jack Williams insisted in 1959 that the CGC "does not offer in any sense the possibility of the development of a political machine." Its upper-middle-class composition clearly distinguished it from the stereotype of a lower class, ethnic-based

organization run by "ward heelers" and cigar-smoking bosses, but "middle-class machine" was not an absurd term. Such organizations dominated other Southwestern cities at this time, and over the previous 60 years they had periodically controlled other cities in the Midwest and East. A political machine is simply an organized effort to control political power. The CGC fits the definition because it was an organized, self-perpetuating group that chose candidates, planned their campaigns, and financed them.

The main difference from ordinary machines is that both explicitly and intentionally the CGC preached a model of "selfless" civic participation and denied the legitimacy of interest group politics. Volunteer groups like the Valley Beautiful Committee in 1963 represent a highly visible example of such participation. Other groups provided even more important opportunities: roughly every five years the mayor appointed a large committee that proposed policy and spending priorities for the city — choices that were largely followed. Championing the virtue (and possibility) of a "common" urban purpose, CG remained adamantly committed to citywide elections for city council, and it convinced voters in referenda held in 1967 and 1975 not to establish a ward system. Mayor Williams explained that another "of its iron-clad rules is that it will not select anyone as a council candidate who has expressed a desire to become a member of the City Council," and it enforced term limits on its nominees. This approach ultimately failed because city growth changed the demands of officeholding, repelling some people and attracting others. Equally important, the notion that governance was simply implementing logical choices ignored fundamental conflicts in values and goals. In reality, CG's policies did favor certain groups, a bias its critics fully understood. Clear policy differences emerged in the 1960s, and conflicts over political leadership expanded throughout this period. By the late 1970s CG was defunct, yet it had succeeded for 25 years because it understood the crucial elements of politics and acted in ways that any political boss would have approved.

CG was effective because it occupied the political center, but that opened it to attack from the left or the right and required flexibility. After the increasingly predictable challenges of the 1950s, CG faced a different type of campaign in 1961, when its opponents managed to set the agenda. In January a local Baptist minister, Rev. Aubrey Moore, originally from Mississippi, collected 10,000 signatures on a petition opposing the city's housing code, ultimately driving the city council to repeal the code. This provided a springboard for Moore, who delivered regular radio addresses, to become the leading spokesman in the fall for a slate called the Stay American Committee (SAC). Like prior CG opponents, the SAC wanted to elect councilmen from wards, reduce the city manager's power, and hire a local person for that job; it differed dramatically in its main goal — fighting a "communist conspiracy" to destroy city government. Denouncing zoning, housing codes, and land use planning as steps toward confiscating all private property, they lambasted urban renewal and the purchase of private water companies as other elements of the red menace. Their primary allegation concerned the National Municipal League, which they generally referred to in semi-secretive fashion as "1313," the building number of the League's Chicago headquarters. The SAC charged the league (to which Phoenix and most cities belonged) with directing a conspiracy of experts to eliminate all other local entities and establish a "Metro" government as part of a "dictatorship under a socialistic U.N. one-world system." No aspect of city life escaped their purview. They denounced the collection of money by city children for UNICEF, and they claimed that "the inexcusably snarled traffic conditions in Phoenix, the ill-timed and repeated tearing up of streets are part of the announced plan of those who would rule the world by planning confusion for the people."

Refusing to debate publicly with CG candidates, the SAC issued press releases, bought TV ads, delivered radio addresses and campaigned to small groups. Normally, CG campaigns boasted of their accomplishments, but here they were on the

Tear Down The Building?

The *Arizona Republic,* October 29, 1961 *The Reg Manning Collection, Arizona Collection, Arizona State University Libraries*

defensive, forced to respond to the SAC's charges with lengthy rebuttals — describing the SAC's misrepresentations of taxes and city government, arguing that the housing code and urban renewal program no longer existed, and explaining that the city belong to cooperative, professional organizations, none of which had been cited by Congress as suspicious or dangerous. CG strongly defended the National Municipal League and (its trump card) noted that conservative icon Senator Barry

Goldwater was one of its regional vice presidents. The SAC blithely replied that Goldwater was obviously ignorant of the group's purpose and offered to educate him.

The league was not part of a plot, but the SAC belonged to a semi-secret national movement begun three years earlier in Dade County, Florida. Its mimeographed "fact sheets" and conspiracy theories also reflected its close association with the ultraconservative John Birch Society, to which at least its mayoral candidate, Buck Hanner, belonged. Hanner also revealed that his group intended to spread its campaign to other Arizona communities and then to the nation. The SAC's charges and tactics appalled and frustrated Mayor Mardian, and he wrote to warn other Western mayors, many of whom had already encountered similar groups. The CG's campaign included endorsement statements from former city officials and community figures as well as newspaper ads with lists of supporters. The crisis also had the unusual effect of bringing liberal critics of CG to its defense. In the end, CG won handily with nearly three-fourths of the vote, but voter turnout fell to 19 percent, the lowest level since

before 1949. Also disturbing was the location of the SAC's votes: four of the six precincts it won were in southern Phoenix, and it won 49.6 percent of the vote in the newly annexed South Phoenix area — a sign of continuing resentment there.

Two years later CG faced a more critical struggle: a minor challenge from the right and a vigorous threat from the left — an attack that boosted voter turnout to one-third and forced CG into its first run-off election. In September 1963 the Action Citizens Ticket (ACT) challenged CG with a different type of slate and set of issues. As its mayoral candidate the ACT chose Richard Harless, a widely known, three-term Democratic congressman. Its diverse slate for city council included socially prominent individuals like Ed Korrick, scion of the department store family, and Bob Aden, a wealthy restaurateur and theater manager. Also included were Lincoln Ragsdale, a mortician, insurance agent, and leader in the NAACP, and Manuel Pena, owner of an insurance and realty company and, among various community activities, a board member of the Phoenix Urban League. Building from a strong base in South Phoenix, especially among Democrats, the ACT picked up an informal endorsement from local labor unions. The ACT discussed familiar topics while pledging to "destroy the invisible government control exerted too long by a few individuals," It criticized the condition of various city services, noting especially the city's high crime rate and proposing a shift in taxation. The ticket also raised new issues, attacking CG's failure to pursue land-use planning, construct freeways, or to deal with the problems of unemployment and slums in the downtown and south Phoenix areas.

A third, conservative Republican slate appeared late in the campaign and complained about poor street planning, inadequate services in newly annexed areas, and the Planning and Zoning Commission's "dictatorial attitudes." This group received relatively little attention and few votes but influenced the outcome in two ways: by holding CG council candidates below 50 percent of the votes, thus forcing a run-off election; and by endorsing the ACT candidates in the run-off election. CG ran a traditional campaign, touting its 14 years of governance and using its incumbent status to solicit position papers from the city manger's office to defend that record. Dismissing charges of improper influence, CG increasingly followed the attack of Pulliam newspapers, claiming that ACT was "dictated to by the liberal-labor element" and would raise taxes. CG's mayoral candidate, Milton Graham, owner of a distributing company and member of numerous civic groups, narrowly won in the primary election, and its council candidates succeeded by only a small margin in the run-off contest, with Korrick running ahead of the other ACT candidates slate and nearly winning.

While the ACT lost the election, its efforts reshaped city politics. Mayor Graham and CG moved to the left to address the ACT's concerns, and by 1965 its support of civil rights and efforts to obtain federal urban funds had won wide approval. Furthermore, CG's nomination of two minority candidates — Dr. Morrison Warren, an African-American educator, and Frank Benites, a Mexican-American labor leader from South Phoenix — confirmed an arrangement to obtain ACT's support for the CG slate.

Two years later a conservative slate ran against CG, but it mistakenly shifted from criticism of city services to less popular complaints about downtown improvement, most notably a civic center, and CG won by a two-to-one margin. The only suspense in the entire race came early in the campaign when Mayor Graham broke with CG tradition and requested endorsement for a third term. After considerable debate, the CG Nominating Committee endorsed Graham and ensured victory in the election. But when Graham sought a fourth term in 1969, the CGC refused, and Graham's decision to run as an independent set the stage for a major political battle.

The CGC rejected much more than just Graham's candidacy. Following a conservative national trend, it decided to shift policies from social reform to law and order. To do so it abandoned all incumbents (as they also abandoned it) and nominated an entirely new slate of candidates — all Republican men active in service groups like Kiwanis and Rotary — and their campaign emphasized crime control and freeways. Of the departing, two-term councilmen, Warren and Benites ran for re-election on Graham's slate, while John F. Long retired and endorsed Graham. One of the single-term council members dumped by CG also endorsed Graham, while a second, Dorothy Theilkas, ran for re-election as an independent. The social turmoil of those years also attracted other council candidates. CG's emphasis on crime and fiscal conservatism was matched by the council candidacies of four members of George Wallace's American Independent Party, who also opposed freeways and favored a ward system.

CG's mayoral candidate, John Driggs, whose family owned Western Savings and Loan, benefitted from a hefty campaign fund and fervent newspaper support to defeat Graham with a slim majority of 51 percent, while the 20 candidates for council forced a run-off election between the CG and Graham slates. As in 1963, Ed Korrick ran ahead of his colleagues (on the Graham slate), but this time the slates were so close that he managed to beat the lowest CG candidate and become the first non-CG candidate to win election in over 20 years. A final complicating factor in this election, reflected in the unusual number of blank mayoral ballots and in two independent women candidates, was the outrage felt by numerous women that neither major slate had included a woman. Given the 20-year record of women serving on the council, and the general political importance of women candidates, this omission seemed particularly insulting.

During the next four years that Driggs was mayor, CG remained largely in control of political developments. In 1971 it added Ed Korrick to its slate, and it rectified its previous mistakes by nominating an African-American accountant, Calvin Goode, and a woman, Margaret Hance. Two years later Timothy Barrow won an easy victory to replace Driggs as mayor, and only two independent candidates ran for council, but one of them won — Gary Peter Klahr, a maverick whose lawsuit forced reapportionment of the state legislature in the mid 1960s and who had being running for city council since 1967.

CG's end came suddenly in 1975 when one of its own broke ranks. Councilwoman Margaret Hance, connected by birth and marriage to the CG establishment, differed from

continued on page 51

the honorable

lorna c. lockwood

■In Arizona, politics has often been a family business. The importance of heredity and connections shows in the repeated names of officeholders, family names like Udall, DeConcini, and Babbitt. Sometimes prominence in law and judicial office has also followed the lines of family and kin, and Phoenix has seen the repetition of names like Stanford, Struckmeyer and LaPrade. It is understandable, then, that the child of a state Supreme Court Judge might achieve important positions in Phoenix's legal and judicial system. Lorna Lockwood's political success in Phoenix, and even more her elevation to serve as an Arizona Supreme Court Justice (1960-1975), like her father Alfred Lockwood (1925-1942), began with her family ties. But her personal merits outweighed the importance of kinship, since Lorna had to overcome what was a serious "disability" before the 1970s: she was female.

Growing up in southern Arizona, Lorna was influenced by her father, a judge, and by his law partner, Sarah Herring Sorin, the first woman to practice law in the state. Lorna became one of the first female students at the University of Arizona's School of Law, but after graduating with a fine record she could only find work as a legal stenographer. Going to Phoenix when her father moved to the Supreme Court, she worked with two groups that shaped her career: a political party and a woman's organization.

In 1929 Lorna moved into high party councils as a member of the Executive Committee of the Democratic State Committee. In 1938, recruited by the Business and Professional Women's Club and with substantial party support, she won election to the state House of Representatives and was re-elected in 1940. Working as an assistant to Congressman John Murdock in 1942-43 further burnished her political credential, and she won a third legislative term in 1946. With her political connections and legal expertise, Lorna became an influential legislator, serving on the important Rules Committee and chairing the Judiciary Committee in her third term.

Lorna began practicing law in 1939, and from 1945 to 1948 worked as a partner with her father and her brother-in-law,

Z. Simpson Cox. Her growing reputation in Phoenix resulted in her appointment to the city's Charter Revision Committee in 1947. Three years later she made state history as the first Arizona woman to be elected a Superior Court Judge, and she served on the Maricopa County bench until 1960. From 1954 to 1957 she served as the juvenile court judge, building a reputation as a thoughtful and sensitive jurist. Her accomplishments and prominence on the bench of the most populous county encouraged Governor Paul Fanin to appoint her to the Arizona Supreme Court in 1960.

During her tenure on the bench, Lockwood became the first woman in the United States to served as chief justice of a state supreme court, an honor she held in 1965 and 1970 (the post rotated among justices). Though rumored as a possible U.S. Supreme Court nominee in the 1960s, Lockwood remained on the Arizona bench until her retirement in 1975. Her influence on the court was substantial, and a tribute to her service emphasized her "strong support of the rights of the poor, the uneducated and the indigent."

Lockwood advanced the role of women in society, law and politics. The most obvious connection is with Sandra Day O'Connor, another Arizona legislator and state judge, whom President Reagan appointed to the U.S. Supreme Court in 1981. Lockwood cherished her role as a judge, but she also emphasized political action and liberal values. As one reflection of this, in 1968 she taught a class at the YWCA in practical politics for women. And it is not surprising that the following year, political action and family ties combined when one of the women running for city council in the 1969 election was Charlotte Cox, Lorna Lockwood's sister.■

previous women on the city council by working outside the home as a writer-producer of tourist television programs. Hance grew dissatisfied with the CG's refusal to select persons interested in an office and experienced in city government, and when the CGC chose political novice Lyman Davidson for mayor, Hance opposed him. With six additional candidates for the office, Davidson garnered only 23 percent of the vote, while Hance won 57 percent, becoming only the second woman in the country to be elected mayor of a major city. (Lila Cockrell of San Antonio, elected a few months earlier, was the first.) CG's electoral debacle was equally impressive in council races as only two of its candidates won (coming in fourth and fifth), while Rosendo Gutierrez and Calvin Goode, whom the CG refused to renominate, finished first and third. In 1977 CGC met to endorse several candidates, but for the first time in 25 years it did not nominate a slate. While those who had identified with CG remained an influential voting bloc and an important source of campaign funding, the organization passed into history.

Charter Government died primarily because the city in which it had been created no longer existed. Over its 25 years, the city had grown to 10 times its 1950 population. Time and the influx of new residents meant that many people had no memory of the political circumstances of the 1940s that had originally inspired the movement. Furthermore, as John Driggs reminisced in 1978, Phoenix had changed "from a little city where the people who influenced commerce and industry here could almost all be found at a service club luncheon" to a large metropolis with a diverse and dispersed leadership. The aging and death of the older generation of leaders made it harder to achieve a consensus. CG's ideals of a volunteer, disinterested leadership had decreasing relevance where increasing responsibilities meant that by the early 1960s being mayor was becoming a full-time job and by the late 1960s councilmen were working

(Far left)
Timothy Barrow, Phoenix mayor 1974-1976
City of Phoenix

Margaret Hance, Phoenix mayor 1976-1984
*City of Phoenix,
Photo by Bob Rink*

20 to 30 hours per week. (Like most Southwestern cities, Phoenix paid its elected officials poorly, but by the 1970s salaries had risen to adequate levels.) The increased size, political interest, and activity of minority populations also changed electoral dynamics. Finally, Phoenicians generally developed different ideas about politics, favoring open selection of leaders and debate over issues, because the city was more diverse, consensus on its proper direction was diminishing, and political issues of the 1970s were less amenable to simple solutions.

Taxes and Revenues

Some things about Phoenix politics remained the same during these two decades. While less constant than death or taxes, debates over taxes came close. And with good reason: taxes tied to revenues and strategies for dealing with them were central to the city's basic goal of growth.

CG's bedrock political strategy was holding the line on property taxes, and CG candidates repeated that pledge religiously at every election. This strategy proved politically popular, especially with businesses, but it also created serious problems in financing adequate city services. City government escaped some tax responsibilities during this time because school boards determined taxes and spending for education (within legislated limits), and after 1957 the county had sole responsibility for public health in the city. Funding some services in existing neighborhoods, such as paving streets and installing sewers, came through "special improvement districts" where those who received the new services were taxed to pay for them. The city did provide some services without fee — garbage and trash pickup, for example, and unlike some cities it did not charge for use of sewers.

Perhaps the most vital service, the water system, operated differently and was frequently a prime issue in election campaigns. In essence, the city charged for water usage and to finance steady expansion of the water system. This involved buying private water companies and providing water to newly annexed

In 1970 the Washington Hotel was demolished to make room for the 35-story Valley National Bank Building between Central and 2nd St. and Van Buren and Monroe.
The Herb and Dorothy McLaughlin Collection, Arizona Collection, Arizona State University Libraries

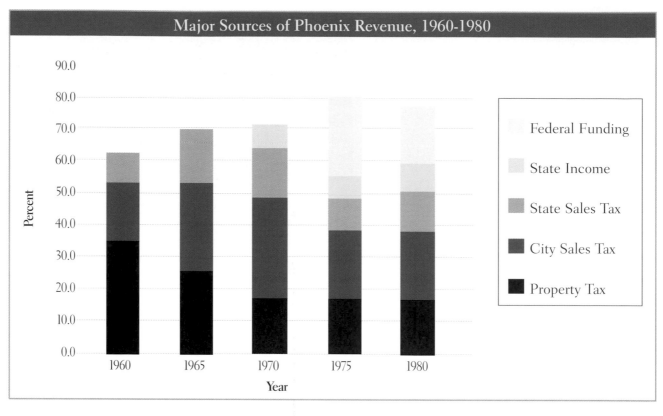

Major Sources of Phoenix Revenue, 1960-1980

Federal Funding

State Income

State Sales Tax

City Sales Tax

Property Tax

Percent

90.0
80.0
70.0
60.0
50.0
40.0
30.0
20.0
10.0
0.0

1960   1965   1970   1975   1980

Year

areas (more cheaply than before annexation). It also included partially paying for construction of major facilities like filtration, pumping, and sewage treatment plants. By the 1970s water rates had tripled, but city officials contended that these were fees for necessary services, not taxes. More important, the system provided an adequate supply of good water — and at a price lower than what most Southwestern cities charged.

During the 1960s Phoenix chose to boost its sales tax rather than raising property taxes to deal with growth and the expanding demand for services. A sales tax would grow with prosperity, and it enabled the city to tax both nonresidents and winter visitors. In 1969 the city added a "sin" tax on tobacco and liquor sales, but this proved unpopular. Phoenix also relied on several types of state revenues during the 1960s. The state sales tax (those revenues increased over 500 percent) and reallocated state gas tax revenues (which quadrupled to $4 million by 1970) provided vital funding for streets and roads.

The city's revenue problems worsened during the 1970s, but this was not an uncommon situation. Like other cities across the country, from St. Louis to Atlanta to New York, Phoenix suffered from growing expectations and from inflation

averaging over 10 percent annually. In 1972 the state government agreed to share 15 percent of its income tax revenues with cities, but in 1975 necessity finally compelled the city to abandon its pledge and raise property taxes by a third.

Federal Dollars

Phoenix would have needed to raise taxes much more had it not received money from the federal government. Initially reluctant to accept federal funds, city leaders adjusted their attitudes as the city's goals and problems changed. In addition, federal government spending grew dramatically and changed in character during this era, creating opportunities that Phoenix could not afford to ignore. From 1950 to 1960 federal grants to cities — mainly for capital projects like building programs for airports, city services like sewers, roads, public housing and hospitals — grew from $2 billion to $7 billion and increased to 44 grant-in-aid programs. By 1964 the number of programs jumped to 115, while spending rose to $24 billion in 1970 and $43 billion in 1974. The new programs included money for construction but also for people, including job training, educational assistance, urban renewal programs, model cities programs and law enforcement.

Jack Williams, Phoenix mayor 1956-1960, Arizona Governor 1968-1972
City of Phoenix

Thanks to Barry Goldwater's efforts in 1965,
the summit of Camelback Mountain belongs to the public and not private developers.

Photo by Jeff Kida

In the immediate postwar era Phoenix sought federal money as it had during the war years, as a crucial means for building the city's prosperity. In 1958 Mayor Jack Williams wrote to Congress in support of these programs, saying that "We feel that certain Federal grant-in-aid programs in which the City of Phoenix is participating are very vital to the future of the community. These include urban renewal, public housing, airport construction, and urban highway construction. Without Federal participation in these programs, the City of Phoenix alone would not have sufficient financial resources to undertake the programs." *The Arizona Republic* and the *Phoenix Gazette* were always cautious about these programs (and critical of others), but during the 1960s they and others raised strong objections to accepting federal money or participating in federal programs.

Mayor Sam Mardian, a conservative Republican and part owner of a family construction business which built numerous commercial and public buildings during the 1950s, began the shift. In January of 1961 he reversed his previous position, declared federal aid unacceptable, and rejected a $10.5 million urban renewal project the city had been pursuing for four years. Several years later the city indirectly solicited federal funds for poverty programs, but when it applied for job training funds in 1967, the newspapers denounced the decision. By contrast, the subsequent use of federal funds for law enforcement, specifically to hire more police, received far more support than criticism.

During the 1970s, attitudes about federal monies changed again. The city's expanding needs, its revenues reduced by inflation, and continuing resistance to increasing local taxes forced Phoenix politicians in an uncomfortable position. Mayor Driggs, a banker by occupation (in the family's Western Savings and Loan), could read the balance sheets and actively pursued federal moneys for various programs, even for the city's bus service in 1973. The latter support roused some opposition, but most considered it a necessary response to a real problem. Coming into office in 1976, Mayor Hance warned about the dangers of accepting federal funds, especially to pay city operating expenses. Her attempted economies included cutting the limited local spending on antipoverty programs and instituting

The *Arizona Republic*, October 22, 1965 *The Reg Manning Collection, Arizona Collection, Arizona State University Libraries*

Life Buoy For A Drowning Camel
By Reg Manning   Arizona Republic Staff Artist

hiring freezes, but she refused to contemplate raising city taxes. She pursued federal funds as the only reasonable alternative — and did so successfully: Phoenix's share of that dangerous lucre increased to $89 million in 1978.

Federal funds in this era continued doing what Mayor Williams had previously described: allowing Phoenicians to do what they otherwise could not. A prime example is the preservation of mountain land within the city. Following his defeat in the presidential election of 1964, Barry Goldwater returned to Phoenix as a private citizen and headed an effort to prevent additional development of Camelback Mountain. He solicited private donations, cajoled property owners to sell or give up their land, and, when private sources had been exhausted, he swallowed his objections to federal government action and successfully solicited federal funds in 1968 to achieve public ownership of the mountain's summit. Five years later Phoenix voters supported spending local money to purchase additional mountain land to create the Phoenix Mountain Preserve, but again federal funds were crucial to acquire the necessary area.

Pursuit of federal dollars roused less opposition during the 1970s because of two changes in President Richard Nixon's New Federalism policy: revenue sharing and block grants. The Revenue Sharing program began in 1972 and granted money to cities and states based largely on population. With no real federal oversight or restrictions, most cities used the money to pay for existing rather than new services. This permitted them to avoid raising taxes or even to lower them, as Phoenix did in 1973 when it repealed the unpopular tobacco and liquor taxes and replaced the lost revenues with revenue sharing funds. (In the 1980s the Reagan administration first reduced revenue sharing funds and then ended the program in 1986.) The Community Development Block Grant program of 1974 made federal money easier to obtain and more palatable by combining seven urban-related grant programs (such as Model Cities, urban renewal, or water and sewerage systems) into a single program. It required an annual application, but the process was undemanding and 80 percent of the funds were granted based on a formula involving population, poverty and housing. As a result, Phoenix enjoyed a jump of 689 percent in these block funds by 1978, the third highest increase among the nation's major cities. Thus, the city's increased need for revenues combined with fewer restrictions and less oversight to make federal money an increasingly attractive source of revenue during the 1970s.

What's a City to Do? Providing Services

CG's emphasis on low taxes related to its second theme: emphasizing efficient and effective city services. Phoenix city government rated very well in cost effectiveness. Besides having low taxes, the city consistently had near the fewest number of employees per capita population of any city near its size. (Its closest competitors were also Southwestern cities — San Diego and San Antonio). But this statistic did not represent efficiency in every department. The Phoenix Fire Department, for example, was understaffed and ill equipped. Compared to other cities its size, Phoenix had proportionately fewer firemen, fewer stations and less powerful equipment. Until the mid-1970s national insurance regulators ranked the PFD near or at the bottom. While the city did hire additional firemen, the proportion increased only 20 percent during this period.

In 1961 Mayor Mardian declared that "the most important single item of business" was improving streets. By 1980 the city had made substantial progress regarding "local and collector" streets. The mileage doubled and the proportion that were "improved" rose from only half to nearly all. But Phoenix failed to provide enough major arterial streets. Although the mileage of such streets nearly doubled to 212 miles in 1980, it was less than half of the estimated necessary mileage. Predictably, the accident rate increased (up 39 percent) and the average speed on streets declined (from 28 to 24 miles per hour), which meant that trips took longer and were more expensive, and air pollution increased enormously. The explanation was simple. The city had grown very rapidly, and traffic had increased twice as quickly as expected. Inadequate revenues also hampered the city: the state increased the gas tax only slightly in 1963 and 1965, it gave no revenues to the city from 1971 to 1974, and it did not reapportion the gas tax revenues to help urban transportation needs until 1975.

Phoenix Police Department patrol car, 1961
Phoenix Police Museum

The real problem was the conflict between dream and reality. Phoenicians loved their low-density city, but this lifestyle depended on cars. City officials were understandably not eager to challenge this preference, but they failed more obviously and less pardonably in not providing either mass transit or freeways. After ending the streetcar system in 1948, city officials struggled for a decade before selling the municipal bus system to a competing private line. As average daily ridership plunged from 58,000 in 1957 to 31,000 in 1960, the city remained unconcerned, but the continuing decline (down to 14,000 in 1970) seemed more serious as traffic congestion worsened noticeably. Furthermore, many of the poor could not afford cars and depended on public transportation. In 1969 the city began subsidizing the bus system, in 1971 the city took it over, and starting in 1973 it began supporting the system with federal mass transit funds. By 1983 ridership had tripled to 43,000, but this had little effect on the growing snarl of traffic.

Freeway building proved even more complex, disastrous and political. In 1949 the city developed a street and highway plan, which it updated in 1960, partly to accommodate the planning and funding

of the U.S. Interstate Highway Act of 1956. The city then had a mere seven miles of freeway, the Black Canyon Freeway, on the west side of town. The plan proposed reasonable use of the city's grid system of streets, a cross-town expressway south of McDowell Street connected to a north-south route along 20th Street (the Papago Freeway), a freeway on the southern boundary of the city (the Maricopa Freeway), which continued south to Tucson (as I-10), with another highway (the Superstition Freeway) splitting to east and running south of Tempe and Mesa. Despite city endorsement and the availability of federal highway money for the interstate portions, nothing happened because of cost and resistance from merchants who feared losing customers. In January 1969 the council decided to build the cross-town Papago Freeway route as the extension of I-10. Seeking to deflect the objections that the highway would divide the neighborhood, the design called for a roadway elevated to heights of between 25 and 100 feet. Proponents believed this would provide a unique landmark; critics felt it would a horrible eyesore. Besides objecting to the expense, a growing number of Phoenicians worried that building freeways would simply encourage still greater urban sprawl. Finally, others criticized the specific route location as unnecessarily destructive of historic buildings and archaeological sites. The result was a complex political battle, involving the impassioned opposition by Pulliam (and his newspapers) and three city votes, all of which delayed construction for over a decade. As a result, by 1980 the Valley still contained only 35 miles of freeway.

Despite the seriousness of the traffic situation, Phoenicians during this era worried more about crime. The problem began receiving significant public attention in 1963, when the Uniform Crime Reports indicated the crime rate in Phoenix ranked very high. In the election campaign of that year, the ACT slate made crime a major issue, and at his inauguration Mayor Graham declared that it was the city's top problem. Later that year a Citizen's Task Force recommended hiring more police, providing better equipment, reorganizing the department, and collecting more and better data.

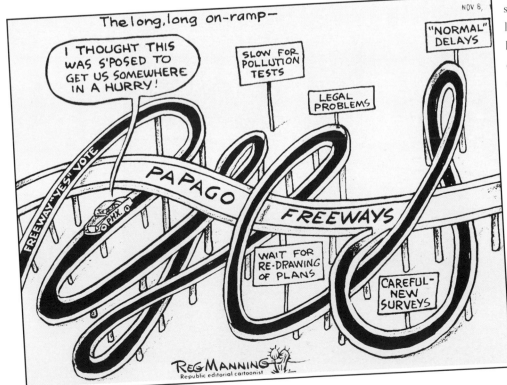

The long, long on-ramp—

NOV 8,

I THOUGHT THIS WAS S'POSED TO GET US SOMEWHERE IN A HURRY!

SLOW FOR POLLUTION TESTS

LEGAL PROBLEMS

"NORMAL" DELAYS

FREEWAY "YES" VOTE

PAPAGO FREEWAYS

PHX. O.

WAIT FOR RE-DRAWING OF PLANS

CAREFUL— NEW SURVEYS

REG MANNING
Republic editorial cartoonist

The city implemented most of these proposals but with little apparent effect, as the crime rate continued to worsen. In 1967 Phoenix ranked as the third-most crime-ridden city among U.S. cities of its size, and in 1973 and 1974 it experienced the largest increases in major crimes in the nation. In combatting crime, Phoenix did not wish to be too frugal, and it boosted the number of personnel and spending at a substantial rate throughout this period — aided after 1968 by federal funds, which provided a quarter of the city's police budget by the late 1970s. (This increase differed from the status-quo policies of San Antonio and San Diego.)

Various factors besides an inadequate number of police explain this increase in crime. Such rises were a national phenomenon and one of the top domestic political issues. Crime grew more rapidly throughout the West. It also related to the city's higher proportion of youth, and discussions of juvenile behavior and delinquency were rife during this era (although in 1970 Phoenix was the only city over 500,000 without a juvenile division in the police department). Increasing levels of affluence and proportions of households with no one home during the day also provided greater opportunities for crime. Although criminal behavior was rising, some of the increase reflected major improvements in reporting, and many increases concerned relatively minor crimes. As Police Chief Lawrence Wetzel noted in 1974, "Twenty-four percent of the larceny crimes are under $10 yet they count the same as a murder in the F.B.I. statistics; 65 percent of burglary crimes are under $50, yet they count the same as a grand theft in the F.B.I. totals."

Other serious factors also contributed to the problem. Nationally, social analysts argued that poverty and racial discrimination contributed to the increased crime rate and that the solution would involve more than simply increasing the number of police. Mayor Graham came to accept this perspective and adopted programs seeking to address the problems. Certain types of crime also appeared more commonly and scandalously in Phoenix and the Valley. Like many booming areas, they attracted swindlers, con men, and organized crime.

Land fraud in the 1960s inspired wags to label Arizona "The Tainted Desert." Increasing instances of fraud and corruption, highlighted by a series of newspaper articles in 1974, led the police department to pay more attention to such activities. The trial and conviction of land swindler Ned Warren brought some of the worst aspects of this culture into clear public view. A handsome ex-convict connected to various mob figures who were also moving to Arizona, Warren created numerous corporate fronts to fleece investors in phony land schemes. He sought to associate himself with politically influential Arizonans, and although these contacts were mostly innocent, his scams depended upon the bribes he paid to a state real estate commissioner, Fred Talley. As the prosecution of Warren finally moved forward in 1975, Warren's former partner, Edward Lazar, was murdered on the day after he testified about their bribery of Talley. Lazar's murder shocked the public and created further delay, but Warren was eventually charged with bribery, fraud and extortion. In 1977 he pled guilty to 22 felonies and died in prison in 1980.

The initial exposure of Warren in the late 1960s resulted from stories by *Arizona Republic* reporter Don Bolles, who wrote numerous stories on organized crime and government corruption. On June 2, 1976, Bolles was fatally injured by a car bomb. A massive investigation ensued, involving Phoenix police, reporters from the *Arizona Republic* and a team of reporters from around the country, which demonstrated that three men carried out the murder. The leader, Max Dunlap, a Phoenix contractor and land developer, organized the execution, apparently at the request of Kemper Marley Sr., to whom he owed $1 million.

(Left photos)
On June 2, 1976, *Arizona Republic* crime reporter Don Bolles was mortally injured by a car bomb, a hit meant to stop his investigation of organized crime in Phoenix.
June 3, 1976,
The Arizona Republic,
Photo by Ray Cosway

A wealthy liquor dealer and rancher, Marley was infuriated by stories Bolles had written which undercut Marley's nomination to the state racing commission. The three conspirators were first found guilty in November 1977, but legal complications resulted in a series of retrials that did not end until 1995. Marley was never charged. The massive publicity damaged Phoenix's image, but it invigorated local and state efforts to prevent and prosecute fraud. Phoenix police created an organized crime bureau, and the state legislature was forced to pass a series of important anti-crime bills.

Social Issues and City Politics

Like other cities at this time, Phoenix struggled not only with traditional political problems like city services but also with broader social conflicts. On the eve of World War II, Phoenix had constructed three housing projects, and the housing shortage after 1945 pushed demands for additional units. After considerable debate, including opposition from the Chamber of Commerce, in the spring of 1950 the council finally approved the construction of 500 units near existing public housing sites, and in 1958 it authorized additional units to be built near downtown. Despite the growing need for additional low-income housing, the city refused to build any additional units. After 1960 the public continued to endorse a form of federal housing aid — but only the federal support for middle class homes readily available through FHA and VA loans.

Phoenix followed a similar path in connection with federally funded slum clearance and redevelopment programs. As part of its initial involvement with this process, the city passed a nominal housing code in 1956. The following year it established an Urban Renewal Department and received $200,000 to plan a slum clearance project in the downtown area. In 1959 the city submitted this plan, but federal officials rejected it because the housing code allowed slumlords to prevent housing inspectors from examining properties. The newspapers and Reverend Moore then began denouncing the city, and a fearful council repealed the code in February of 1961, leaving the city with no minimum standards for housing. Two years later a new council passed a new housing code, but at a special election on May 21, 1963, a slim majority of voters rejected this code. Three years later, after the Phoenix Junior Chamber of Commerce gathered 30,000 signatures and attempted to pass a housing code by referendum, voters again rejected a code. Not until 1970 did the city council finally adopt a code which voters did not overturn. And only after that point could the city obtain federal funds from the Model Cities program.

Martin Luther King, Jr. and Rev. Ralph Abernathy at ASU's Goodwin Stadium in 1964 with Phoenix religious leaders and ASU President G. Homer Durham *Department of Archives & Manuscripts, University Archives, Arizona State University Libraries*

The debate over the housing code involved matters of private property, but it also overlapped with the growing public issue of civil rights. Beginning in the 1950s the city began addressing this issue, prohibiting overt discrimination by government in various forums. It banned discrimination at the (municipal) Sky Harbor Airport restaurant in 1952, desegregated public schools in 1953 and 1954, and theaters in 1954, and forbade discrimination in public employment in 1955. Though helpful, these actions did not address the underlying nature of discrimination or the problems of inequality. On February 3, 1962, the U.S. Civil Rights Commission held a one-day hearing on conditions in Phoenix as part of a nationwide investigative effort. Mayor Mardian addressed the commission and provided a seven-page evaluation of conditions in the city. He concluded that substantial progress had been made recently; that Indians, Asians and Mexican Americans faced no discrimination or problems; and that African Americans faced difficulties in only some areas of private employment and in buying or renting homes. Although he acknowledged that federal laws had provided some benefits, he claimed that voluntary action was preferable and recommended that "minority groups should take advantage of this situation and obtain these gains gratefully."

Mardian's description misrepresented the conditions in Phoenix and ignored the larger problems minorities faced. The most basic difficulty was securing the right to vote. Although Mardian's claim that minorities faced no discrimination in voting was literally correct in terms of government officials, significant hindrances arose from the voting system and the accepted actions of private individuals. Discrimination was less blatant than in the South, but Arizona law placed two obstacles to voting: registration at the county courthouse and English literacy, a requirement established in 1912 to reduce Mexican American

voting. Even past those hurdles, minority voters faced intimidation. Conservative Republicans attempted to prevent voting by "unqualified voters," and in the early 1960s they intensified their efforts in a program called "Operation Eagle Eye." One tactic involved mailing letters that demanded an answer by mail to registered minority voters. Those who did not respond were challenged at polling places as not residing at that address. More commonly, observers demanded that voters read from the Constitution and challenged the qualifications of any person whose responses were considered inadequate. Years later several election officials remembered that one young attorney, William Rehnquist, was particularly aggressive. He asked numerous questions, challenged the residency and qualifications of many voters, demanded that they interpret the Constitution, and created long lines at the polling booth. His obstructive behavior finally got him thrown out of polling places at the Bethune School by Manuel Pena and at Southminster Presbyterian Church by Rev. George Brooks. In 1965 Congress outlawed literacy tests and other forms of voter intimidation, but Arizona did not formally repeal this provision until 1972.

Issues of employment, residence and public treatment also generated controversy. Various African American groups, including the NAACP, Congress of Racial Equality and the Urban League, with leaders like Rev. George B. Brooks, Representative Clovis Campbell and Lincoln Ragsdale, increasingly pressed for redress of these grievances. In conjunction with a public march on July 26, 1963, the Maricopa NAACP produced a booklet on "Equality in Employment," which presented a different view of conditions for minorities than Mayor Mardian's. It noted that the vast majority of African Americans holding government jobs were laborers, and that, for example, they held only six of more than 600 positions on the police force. Private employers hired few African Americans, and virtually none for clerical, sales or skilled positions. Schools remained functionally segregated, fewer African Americans held teaching positions than 10 years previously, and all of the elementary teachers taught in schools that had mostly or only African American children. Half of the motels and hotels surveyed refused to accept African Americans, as did various restaurants. Finally, discrimination in housing meant that all public housing units were racially segregated, and that African Americans were unable to purchase homes north of Van Buren Street.

This information reinforced the message being presented by the Community Council, a coalition of community organizations focused on community social problems. Beginning with their studies of 1960 census tract information about South Phoenix and following through other investigations, programs and conferences, the council began talking about the "Inner City," identifying these problems as related but not restricted to race. In this regard the council fit a national trend. After a decade of seeing the nation as the "affluent society," Americans — including Phoenicians — rediscovered the existence of poverty. Reinforced by efforts of the Phoenix Human Relations Commission (appointed in July 1963), the Community Council appointed an Inner City Committee in December and began working with newly elected Mayor Graham. Recognizing both the serious issues and the fact that South Phoenix had voted strongly for the ACT slate, Graham invited numerous community leaders to meet with the city council on April 15, 1964. Impressed by the high turnout and the evidence of citizen interest, Graham appointed a private commission, Operation "LEAP" — Leadership and Education for the Advancement of Phoenix — to work on various community issues, funded with $50,000 from the city and the obligation to obtain $25,000 from private donors.

LEAP rapidly outgrew the initial, limited expectations of it, primarily because of the federal government's War on Poverty. Within a year it had successfully applied for and was administering federal funds of over $1.5 million and local funds of about $250,000. It had organized various neighborhood councils; it operated a small business loan program; and it administered the Head Start and Youth Corps job programs. It also had plans for numerous additional projects and had already applied for some of them. Because of this success and Mayor Graham's growing interest in the inner city, LEAP became a department of city government in January 1966 and continued to handle social programs.

The city adopted a public accommodations ordinance in July 1964; the state passed a civil rights law in January 1965, banning discrimination in employment, voting and public accommodations; and in 1968 the city banned discrimination in housing. But progress was slow, erratic and incomplete. Frustration exploded in riots July 25-26, 1967, near one of the African American public housing projects, but this ended relatively quickly due to the involvement of Rev. Brooks and a curfew lasting until July 31. During the 1970s African Americans made gradual gains on a variety of fronts, but the core problems remained. A key to the progress that did occur, and itself a matter of success, was the growing power of African American politicians such as Calvin Goode in the city council (1972-1994), and Cloves Campbell and Art Hamilton in the state legislature.

Mexican American political activity occurred in two phases. Beginning in 1941 a chapter of the League of United Latin American Citizens (LULAC) represented their interests. Mexican Americans shared many of the same conditions as African Americans — poverty, segregated housing and schooling — but partly because their population was larger and

Phoenix Head Start is one of a wide variety of social services programs started by LEAP in 1964.
City of Phoenix, Photo by Bob Rink

Chicanos por la Causa
started in 1969 in the face
of the city's unfair
treatment of Chicano
students in the public
schools. Today, CPLC
serves more than 75,000
men, women and children
a year through wide-ranging
and comprehensive human
services, development
programs and housing.
Chicanos por la Causa

because of American racial attitudes, more were able to live outside of the south Phoenix area and to achieve greater economic success. As a group, Mexican Americans faced equally severe political obstacles, but individual leaders more quickly won political recognition on the city council, including Adam Diaz (1954-56), Val Cordova (1956-1960), and Ray Pisano (1962-66).

In the late 1960s several new groups organized and important new political figures emerged. Frank Benites, a labor leader with links to South Phoenix, was influential on the city council (1966-70). Rosendo Gutierrez, a civil engineer, was active in numerous community groups, including the Urban League and the Community Council, and had chaired Operation LEAP in the mid-1960s. Nominated by CG for city council in 1973, he ran successfully without its endorsement in 1975. Serving as vice mayor in 1976, he conflicted strongly with Mayor Hance and challenged her, unsuccessfully, in the 1977 mayoral election. Alfredo Gutierrez, who served in the state senate (1972-86), began his political career in 1968 at Arizona State University by helping organize the Mexican American Student Organization to protest discrimination against Mexican American workers there. The following year he joined with Joe Eddie Lopez to help organize Chicanos Por La Causa (CPLC).

That organization's first major activity occurred in October of 1970, when it organized a month-long boycott of Phoenix Union High School over issues of violence and educational failings, especially directing Mexican American students into vocational tracks instead of toward college. With initial funding from the Southwest Council of La Raza, the Ford Foundation and the federal government, CPLC became an effective community development corporation, led first by Ronnie Lopez and then by Tommy Espinoza. Initially focused on referring people to social service agencies, CPLC began developing its own services involving housing, education, job training, health care and a credit union.

By 1980 city politics in Phoenix looked different than it had 20 years before. CG's controlling structure, agenda and leadership was gone, but what had replaced it was unclear and unformed. Old CG leaders were appalled at the loss of "common purpose." As Harry Rosenzweig complained, "[in] the last 10 years or so, they gotta have a Mexican, a Negro, gotta have somebody from Maryvale, somebody this and that, and everybody's now getting interested like [Rosendo] Gutierrez, a nice guy, but he's trying to form a power base for himself. He wants to go further in politics."

The observation about Gutierrez's ambitions was somewhat ironic, of course, since Rosenzweig was a major Republican power broker, since he had helped Barry Goldwater into the city council and then directly into the U.S. Senate, and since other city government leaders had also moved to other offices. But Rosenzweig correctly observed a changed attitude, and the

When Frank Benites won his seat on the city council in 1966, both labor and South Phoenix neighborhoods gained a voice in city affairs.
The Herb and Dorothy McLaughlin Collection, Arizona Collection, Arizona State University Libraries

In the 1960s and 70s, Phoenix remained a city of single-family homes and had the lowest population density of any U.S. city.

City of Phoenix, Photo by Bob Rink

responsibilities of representatives differed vastly by 1980 from what they had been when Rosenzweig served in 1950. Promoting economic growth remained a goal, but it required somewhat less attention than before, while the problems of economic growth, in terms of lifestyle and the fundamental structure of the city, demanded greater and more creative responses.

More People, More Spaces

Phoenix continued to grow rapidly after 1960. The population increased by one-third in each decade, and newcomers fit a pattern. The largest number came from California (one of eight) and Illinois (one of 10), while overall, half came from the Midwest and a quarter from the West. But the city's population was extremely mobile. Between 1965 and 1970, for example, Phoenix gained roughly 35,000 people, yet four times that number had left the city (California was the most popular destination) and had been replaced by additional immigrants. Surveys identifying the reasons for migration showed that roughly one-third (depending on the economy) came for employment, and most of them came with a job. Another 10 percent came to retire in the Valley. Climate and lifestyle attracted a growing share of immigrants (rising over time to one-fifth), while fewer people came to relieve health problems (their proportion dropped to one of eight). Finally, migration to the Valley resembled sustained migrations throughout American history in that many people came to join relatives who had come previously.

In 1980 Phoenix ranked ninth in population and fourth in geographic size, and consequently it had the lowest population density of any large U.S. city. The preference of Phoenicians — and of local developers — for detached ranch homes laid the foundation for this sprawl, but other factors also contributed. The absence of effective city or county planning or zoning encouraged "leapfrog" development where builders sought land on the outskirts or outside of the current city boundaries. Such land cost less, and the "wide open spaces" allowed developers to use mass production building techniques to the fullest extent, reducing the cost of construction. It also enabled developers to design entire communities, and area amenities often played a crucial role in attracting buyers.

Phoenix continued to move rather quickly to annex these newly developing areas, especially in the north and northeast. Unlike its actions in the late 1950s, these caused little controversy. Settlement of the annexation dispute with Scottsdale

Population of Metropolitan Phoenix and Maricopa County

	1960	1970	1980
Phoenix	439,170	584,303	789,704
Suburbs	119,862	300,457	597,207
All Urban Places	559,032	884,760	1,386,911
MARICOPA	663,510	971,228	1,509,175
Phoenix: % of Urban	78.6%	66.0%	56.9%
Other Cities/Towns			
Mesa	33,772	63,049	152,453
Tempe	24,894	63,550	106,919
Glendale	15,696	36,228	96,988
Scottsdale	10,026	67,823	88,364
Avondale	6,151	6,626	8,134
Buckeye	2,286	2,599	3,434
Chandler	9,531	13,763	29,673
El Mirage	1,723	3,258	4,307
Gila Bend	1,813	1,795	1,585
Gilbert	1,833	1,971	5,717
Goodyear	1,654	2,140	2,747
Guadalupe			4,506
Paradise Valley		6,637	10,832
Peoria	2,593	4,792	12,251
Surprise		2,427	3,723
Tolleson	3,886	3,881	4,433
Wickenburg	2,445	2,698	3,535
Sun City		13,670	40,664
Sun City West			3,741
Sun Lakes			1,944
Youngtown	1559	1886	2254
Carefree			986
Cave Creek			1,589
Fountain Hills			2,771
Litchfield Park		1,664	3657

Arizona State University
*Arizona State University
News Bureau,
Photo by Tim Trumble*

of them ranked among the fastest growing U.S. cities of over 100,000: Mesa held second place, and Tempe ranked ninth. Aggressive annexation contributed substantially to suburban growth. The three major east valley cities of Mesa, Scottsdale, and Tempe totaled less than 15 square miles in the late 1950s; they spread to over 100 square miles by 1970 and over 200 in 1980. Tempe's development owed much to ASU's quadrupling in size to nearly 40,000 students, making it one of the largest universities in the nation. The city also successfully pursued manufacturing firms, especially electronics companies, for industrial parks along its western boundary. The pace and extent of growth in Mesa threatened to overwhelm its traditional identity as an agricultural and Mormon settlement. Its new territories included various distinct subcommunities, and among them were several retirement communities like Leisure World. Mesa's economic focus changed substantially with the addition of facilities operated by major industrial and manufacturing firms — Motorola's integrated circuit factory, a McDonnell-Douglas helicopter plant, and Talley Industries, a defense contractor and manufacturer of propellants. Scottsdale's claim to be "The West's Most Western Town" lost meaning as the western style of the older area was rapidly overwhelmed by the spread of typical suburbia, by a proliferation of upscale resorts and residential areas that did not employ a western theme, and by carefully cultivating the arts. The agricultural focus of West Valley communities continued as numerous smaller towns and cities from Avondale to Tolleson grew steadily. Only

in 1964 fixed a clear boundary between the two cities. Annexing the northern subdivisions came at the request — not against the wishes — of residents, since those neighborhoods were essentially built to be annexed and existed separately for only a brief period. Moreover, a state law of 1961 prohibited the incorporation of towns within six miles of Phoenix, without the city's permission. However, in several cases Phoenix moved more aggressively and competitively, using "strip annexation" in the west and southeast to prevent Avondale, Tolleson and Tempe from annexing territory it intended to claim later. Thus, despite leapfrog settlement, the city's rapid annexation of surrounding territory meant that much of the land within the city was vacant: 63 percent of Phoenix Planning Area in 1972, down to an estimated 40 percent in 1980.

The *Arizona Republic*,
August 25, 1957
*The Reg Manning
Collection, Arizona
Collection, Arizona State
University Libraries*

The Changing Suburbs

The growth rate of Phoenix from 1960 to 1980 was very impressive by most standards, but it paled compared with Valley suburbs, which burgeoned by more than 500 percent during this period. In the 1970s two

Glendale advanced at the East Valley's pace, as did the unique retirement community of Sun City.

Unlike the suburbs in some metropolitan areas, the larger of these cities existed as more than "bedroom suburbs," partly because their existence predated Phoenix's expansion. They retained and generally increased their industrial firms, providing an important source of employment for some residents. Commercial business grew even more rapidly, as shopping malls spread across the entire Valley, most notably Fashion Square (1962) and Los Arcos (1969) in Scottsdale, and TriCity Mall (1968) and Fiesta Mall (1979) in Mesa. Nevertheless, important changes became evident by the 1970s. Expansion ended the clear physical separation between and among Phoenix and these communities. Rapid suburbanization also created an increasingly common environment, a metropolitan mindset, and a decrease in the distinctiveness of each community. Each struggled to determine, with varying degrees of success, an identity and role in the larger metropolitan area.

By the time Metrocenter opened in 1973 as "Arizona's first two-story mall," indoor, air-conditioned shopping had become the norm, nearly destroying retail shopping downtown. *WestCor*

Planned Communities

Planned communities emerged as another and increasingly attractive response to suburban sprawl. By the mid-1970s various companies were developing the 25 communities in different stages of planning and building. These communities resembled some conventional subdivisions in that they provided recreation for residents, almost always lakes and golf courses, and a careful blend of housing types. But these communities went beyond subdivisions in being much more self-reliant — including shopping and entertainment facilities, churches, schools and libraries, other public or governmental services, and some employment. In addition, they had rules that proscribed various behaviors, activities or structures.

Charles Sargent, an ASU geographer, described three types of planned communities evident in the Valley as being planned suburbs, special-purpose developments, and quasi-new towns. In 1956 John F. Long had begun the Valley's first planned suburb, Maryvale, but this form proliferated in the 1970s and included Ahwatukee (Phoenix), Arrowhead Ranch (Glendale), McCormick Ranch (Scottsdale), and Dobson Ranch (Mesa). American Continental Homes planned and built Dobson Ranch, which hosted a city park and police substation, and its neighborhood association regulated housing codes, managed recreation centers, and negotiated with the city for services. The category of "special purpose developments" included a few desert communities like Carefree but greater

continued on page 67

(Left photos) In 1960, Del Webb's Sun City introduced the concept of "adult living." Thousands of people showed up for opening day and 272 homes sold the first weekend. *Del Webb Group*

del e. webb

Del E. Webb,
TIME magazine,
August 3, 1962
*Del E. Webb
Group*

■One of the few Arizonans to grace the cover of *TIME* magazine, Del Webb made his fame by following his boyhood skills and interests: building and baseball. Born in Fresno, California, Del took after his father, a contractor and baseball player. Del quit school early to work construction and play semi-professional baseball. He grew to be 6'4" and over 200 pounds, and while not a Walter (or a Randy) Johnson, he was a fairly talented pitcher. His baseball career was cut short in 1926 when, sliding into home plate, he cracked some ribs and tore ligaments in his pitching arm. The following year he nearly died from typhoid fever, which confined him to bed for a year and left him weighing only 99 pounds. As he recovered, in 1928 he decided to move to Phoenix for his health.

Working for a contractor who went bankrupt while building a grocery store for A. J. Bayless, Webb asked Bayless to make good on the contractor's check. The owners agreed, provided he take over the job. So Webb started his "company" with a few wheelbarrows, picks and shovels. Despite the Depression, Webb found sufficient work building commercial buildings, and in the mid-1930s opened a second office in Los Angeles. As the United States prepared for war, Webb landed numerous war contracts, rebuilding Fort Huachuca, constructing Luke and Williams fields, and building other military structures, hospitals and relocation camps. Webb's success stemmed from his ability to calculate jobs, his hard-driving attitude toward suppliers and, as Ted O'Malley observed, his affable wooing of government leaders in Washington.

By 1945 Webb had become wealthy and made connections with the rich and famous. While golfing with Dan Topping and Bob Hope, Topping suggested that he and Webb buy the New York Yankees baseball franchise. Webb jumped at the chance. It permitted him to reconnect with a sport he loved, but it also provided another money-making opportunity. By selling off company land in Newark, Webb quickly made back most of his investment. When he sold the team in 1965 to CBS, Webb made a substantial profit, but he had also had the pleasure of owning the most successful franchise in baseball history during its most successful era.

Webb's company flourished during the 1950s, building Vandenberg Air Force Base in California, numerous other military sites, factories in over 20 states, banks and shopping centers. In Phoenix he constructed Uptown Plaza and three of the major office buildings in the Uptown Business District.

Webb's influence and fame owe most to his decision to build Sun City — which put him on the cover of *TIME* magazine in 1962. Webb grew increasingly attached to this development, attending various ceremonies, and some people equated the man and the community. The truth, as a company president explained, was more prosaic: "He didn't personally create the world's most famous retirement community. He did establish an organizational framework with freedom of others to do so under his direction."

By the 1960s Webb was wealthy (worth over $100 million) and nationally prominent but not equally respected in Phoenix. Some people complained that he had treated subcontractors roughly. A more serious complaint came from certain community leaders who felt that he displayed too little of the civic responsibility they cherished. In fact, Webb had never been a civic leader. Harry Rosenzweig felt that Webb had focused on making money, that he gave virtually nothing to local charities, and that he had essentially ignored his local friends. Ted O'Malley also found that Webb became more isolated.

When Webb complained about his public image, Tom Chauncey advised him to "get out in this community and give some of those millions away that you earned. You can get into the boys clubs and the girls clubs and the United Way and the Community Council. ...You could build some housing for the poor. You could give some parks." And Chauncey especially chastised him hiring a public relations firm to improve his image, saying "You're supposed to do good, not have somebody make you look good."

Webb did listen to Chauncey and others. Chauncey observed, "he did change before he died." He worked actively for the National Boys Club, serving as a director of the organization. He also gave more substantially to local charities, and especially important he established a foundation that provided important grant funds for Valley causes. But his greatest and lasting influence was the creation of Sun City and its heirs.■

numbers of retirement communities. The first of these, Youngtown, began in 1954 in the West Valley, but Sun City, which started in 1959, created the market and inspired the spin-offs and imitators that appeared in the 1970s.

By the 1950s the Del E. Webb Corporation had become a successful national builder. Webb saw the need for additional building opportunities, and Webb partner L.C. Jacobson decided to investigate constructing a retirement community. The key to success, the company concluded, was designing the entire community, providing substantial amenities, and completing them before selling the homes. DEVCO, the subsidiary responsible for Sun City, envisioned the community as a relatively inexpensive settlement for retired persons — a Maryvale or Levittown for the elderly. It quickly discovered that the community was very popular (272 homes were sold in the first weekend) and that many buyers had more money than the planners had anticipated (half the buyers paid cash). After a few years sales for the original models (priced from $8,000 to $11,300) slowed, and in 1965 DEVCO began offering more expensive models with more amenities, which led to another boom in sales. This shift expanded in 1968 with Phase II of Sun City and housing prices ranging from $16,000 to $32,000. With a population of over 40,000 in 1980, Sun City was the fifth-largest "city" in the Valley, but since it was not incorporated and had no municipal government, it was not formally a "city."

Although it was widely and national touted, by the 1970s some observers criticized Sun City as an isolated, sterile enclave because it was homogeneous in population (white) and politics (conservative Republican). More specific criticism concerned Sun City's opposition to rasing taxes for the neighboring Peoria school district, as their votes defeated every bond measure for 15 years. Peorians faulted Sun City residents for avoiding a basic social responsibility, while the retirees complained that they had purchased homes with the expectation of lower taxes and no school taxes. A partial settlement developed in 1975 when Sun City managed to secede from the Peoria district. Most residents dismissed the "enclave" criticism and considered the community successful because it provided a wide range of

recreation opportunities and services, and it encouraged residents to remain active: already in 1962 residents had organized over 90 clubs and organizations, and numerous people worked as volunteers in various community projects. Other retirement communities started in the following decade, including Leisure World (Mesa), Sun Lakes (south of Chandler), and Sun City West.

The third form of planned community was a new, separate community. Litchfield Park began in an unsystematic way in 1919 when it started offering housing to officials of Goodyear Farms (named after Goodyear chairman Paul Litchfield). In the early 1960s, with agricultural profits declining and Goodyear looking for ways to diversify, the company hired community planner Victor Gruen (who had designed Maryvale) to develop an ambitious master plan for a hierarchical, structured community of up to 100,000 people. The inspiration for this, according to Litchfield Park's director of marketing, was that "Our cities just happen, sprawling into ugly asphalt jungles with mishmash zoning, the monotony of row upon row of look-alike tract housing, streets congested with traffic, slums and ghettos. In short, America the ugly. Goodyear wanted Litchfield Park to be different."

But Litchfield Park struggled. First, the housing market slumped, then infrastructure costs ran much higher than anticipated so Goodyear could not prepare industrial sites. As a result, the town generally failed to attract businesses, and the absence of employment reduced Litchfield Park from a separate town to largely a bedroom suburb. The plan suffered another blow when the state legislature killed a proposed branch campus of Arizona State University that the University and the Board of Regents had accepted. Finally, the extension of I-10 to Los Angeles, which had been planned for completion by 1971, was delayed by a decade. Consequently, the community fell far short of its ambitious goals.

David And Goliath — By Reg Manning, Arizona Republic Staff Artist

Metropolitan Problems

The growing interaction between different Valley communities created new problems and increasingly required intercity cooperation on important issues involving growth.

The report of the Phoenix Forward Task Force (1970) advised city leaders to "discourage urban sprawl" and push for "optimum usage of land." In 1972 an investigative team of the American Institute of Architects warned about the dangers of sprawl and recommended creating a greenbelt around the metropolitan area. The transformation of agricultural and desert land into residential areas and the loss of open space affected all Valley residents, as did positive steps like creation of the Phoenix Mountain Preserve.

Traffic problems also troubled the entire Valley. In December of 1962 a spokesman for the Maricopa County Health Department dismissed the findings of a national study that Phoenix ranked "among the top five cities for dirty air," but a sample of public opinion done the previous year showed that 99 percent of the people felt that air pollution was a problem. Leonard Huck, a member of the Valley Beautiful Citizens Council expressed a common view in 1965: "Phoenix averages more hours of sunlight than any other city in the Western hemisphere, but this God-given treasure will be rendered useless if a smog cover precludes the inhabitants from enjoying it."

Despite the passage of several laws in the late 1960s, the Phoenix Forward Task Force announced that pollution was "the greatest immediate threat to the community." It recommended state action to obtain industry compliance with clean air guidelines, and it recognized that automobile emissions were fouling the air. In truth, auto emissions produced over 80 percent of the Valley's air pollution, a fact that led to mandatory auto emission inspection in the 1970s. After suffering through foul air alerts, hearing reports of worsening health problems, and seeing the smog cloud, the majority of Valley residents supported efforts by the Environmental Protection Agency to force compliance with the Clean Air Act.

Perhaps the most surprising problem for this desert metropolis was flooding, but 10 times during this era the Valley suffered major flooding. Growth affected this problem directly and in several ways. Some damage occurred to buildings erected in the flood plain, especially in the West Valley. More important, the amount of building and paving in various areas channeled all of the periodic high rainfall into washes, creeks and rivers, instead of allowing it to disperse over a wider area. The problem became more disruptive because growth integrated the Valley and increased traffic across the Salt River. Floods prevented people from driving across the river bed and forced them to use bridges, but still higher water closed some bridges. This created gigantic traffic jams. One response, which helped a little and encouraged thinking about different traffic solutions, involved temporarily using the frieght railroad line between Tempe and Phoenix for a commuter train. But the loss of time was not the main problem: floods destroyed bridges and homes and killed at least seven people. Solving the crisis required the cooperation of numerous communities.

Downtown

By the early 1960s downtown had become an economic, social and visual blight. Responsible for over half of the city's retail sales in 1948, the area handled only half that amount a decade later. By the early 1960s sales figures fell by another 50 percent, and a third of the sales were for lunches. The decline reflected the city's growth, but even more strikingly the automobile revolution. Cars and malls spelled an end to downtown shopping. The Uptown Plaza at Central and Camelback marked the first new approach to shopping in 1955. A few years before, Ralph Burgbacher had purchased the Central Avenue Dairy at Central and Osborn, which he began transforming into a very large residential and business development called Park Central. The opening of Park Central Mall in 1957 included two department stores, a Goldwater's and a Diamond's; and the opening of five additional Phoenix malls by 1963 drew away more downtown stores. By 1968 every downtown department store except J.C. Penny's had left. The major problem, in the eyes of downtown merchants, was the lack of parking, and they lambasted the city's unwillingness to help create a solution. But with Eugene Pulliam thundering against the socialism of public parking garages, the city refused to act. In fairness, however, Phoenix was not unique in its inaction; in 1960 few cities its size had built public parking structures. Moreover, the problem went far beyond this. It involved driving cars, not just parking them; it included urban sprawl, inadequate freeways and public transportation, air-conditioned interior space, and a different style.

To a large extent, the decline of downtown represented a problem that was generally American, not uniquely Phoenician. Still, several developments accentuated this decline. Beginning with the construction of the Guaranty Building by David Murdock in 1960, an Uptown Business District including five buildings of over 16 stories developed in an area from Thomas to Indian School Road, and from 7th Avenue to 3rd Street. A second business district, the Camelback Corridor, emerged in the mid-1970s, stretching from 20th Street to 44th Street. Two public recreational structures were built — the Municipal Stadium (1963) and the Veterans Memorial Coliseum (1965) — both outside of the downtown area. Finally, the worsening economic conditions downtown resulted in the degeneration into slum status of the "Deuce" neighborhood, which stretched from 1st Avenue to 6th Street, and between Jackson and Washington streets.

At its low point in the early 1960s the downtown remained the governmental, legal and financial center of the city. Construction of the Municipal Building (1963) and the Maricopa County Complex (1965) enhanced this, but building Civic Plaza and Symphony Hall provided a much greater lift. It enabled slum clearance of the Deuce and provided a new basis for retail businesses, restaurants and new hotels: the Adams Hotel (later Phoenix Hilton) and the Hyatt Regency (1975). At the same time each of the major banks constructed a new office building downtown — the First Interstate Bank (1972), Valley National Bank (1973) and Arizona Bank (1976). Creation of Patriots Park (1974) also changed the complexion of the area. By 1980 the prospects for the area provided some reason for optimism.

Given the serious problems facing downtown, it is somewhat surprising that through the 1960s the city's planning focus remained on suburbs and expansion. The Valley Beautiful

By the mid-1960s, loss of retail businesses had changed the "Deuce" neighborhood (bordered by 1st Avenue and 6th Street, Jackson and Washington) into a Phoenix eyesore.
City of Phoenix, Photo by Bob Rink

Citizens Council provided one means of addressing issues, but while its membership included major local figures such as Walter Bimson and Daniel Noble, it remained an unofficial, voluntary group. An intriguing effort appeared in 1969 after several architecture classes at ASU created Rio Salado, a model for developing the largely dry and unused Salt River bed into a recreation area. In 1971 the city's Planning Department began shifting its focus with the Central Phoenix Plan. Though largely accepting the existing division into Central and Uptown Business Districts and proposing to link them, it represented an effort to think constructively about the city's development. The Comprehensive Plan-1990, a plan for the entire city produced in 1972, also endorsed existing patterns of development, but it too stimulated further planning efforts, especially

Civic Plaza's opening in 1972 brought crowds back to downtown for the first time in a decade.
Arizona State Archives

Tempe Lake, 2000
Arizona State University News Bureau, Photo by Tim Trumble

obtaining reactions from neighborhood groups. A major shift occurred in 1975 when the city council endorsed a new approach to planning. This urban village model organized the city into nine areas, or villages, and encouraged each area to develop relative self-sufficiency in everything from housing to employment. This decentralized approach aimed at developing community and neighborhood identification,

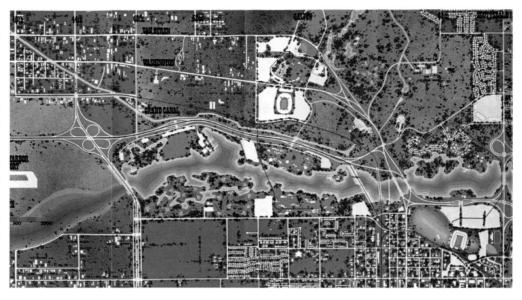

(Left and below)
In 1969 several ASU architecture classes created this model for developing the largely dry and unused Salt River bed. The plan, called the Rio Salado Project, became a Tempe reality in the late 1990s. *Department of Archives & Manuscripts, University Archives, Arizona State University*

as well as reducing various urban ills such as traffic and pollution. Formally described and adopted in 1979, it brought Phoenix national attention — and helped bring the city its third "All American City" award.

A Maturing Economy

The Phoenix economy continued to expand at an impressive rate. The chamber of commerce continued advertising, with striking success, the advantages of working in or visiting the Valley. Business relocations to the Phoenix area increased from 1961 to 1964 above the previous high level, with 473 new businesses arriving. In subsequent years the chamber and other private groups still encouraged businesses to relocate, but the efforts dealt mainly with larger companies, for smaller firms found sufficient incentive in the Valley's booming economy. The Best Western Motel chain moved its headquarters to Phoenix in 1966, as did Greyhound in 1971. Major expansions included Western Electric's building the largest telephone-cable plant in 1968, while American Express completed a regional center for its credit card division in 1970.

High-tech firms like Digital, Honeywell, Intel, GTE, and Litton added to the Valley's existing strength in this burgeoning field, but Motorola's enormous expansion completely overshadowed all of the other firms. By 1974 the Government Electronics Division Plant in Scottsdale had increased to 713,00 square feet and 4,000 workers, and it produced important products in navigation and missile guidance. The main semiconductor plant on 52nd Street expanded to 1.2 million square feet, while a Mesa plant opened in 1966 housed the world's largest integrated circuit facility in the world (752,000 square feet). Together with its additional sites in Tempe, Scottsdale and Phoenix, Motorola employed 22,000 people, which was one-fourth of the Valley's manufacturing workforce. The continuing expansion of other firms in electronics and aerospace, including AiResearch, GE, Goodyear Aerospace, and Sperry Rand, kept the numbers of manufacturing workers increasing and their proportion of the Valley's workforce at roughly 20 percent. (*See appendix 2B*)

Other elements of the economy also remained relatively constant. Retail sales continued to grow rapidly by about 80 percent each decade. That figure represented only about half the rate seen in the 1950s, but it reflected a fairly stable 60 percent of the sales in the entire state. One important and somewhat troubling change in retailing involved the disappearance of locally owned department stores. Goldwater's, Diamond's, and Korrick's were sold to corporations headquartered outside the Valley. Beyond the economic consequences, observers worried about the broader effects, since the Phoenix owners had traditionally been prominent in civic affairs.

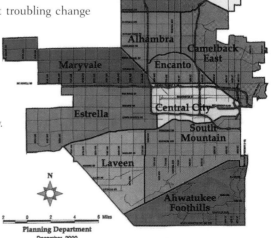

Urban Villages

Phoenix 2000

Planning Department
December, 2000

In finance, as in retailing and manufacturing, the Valley and especially Phoenix dominated the state. The three largest banks — Valley National, First National, and Arizona — held over 80 percent of Arizona's bank deposits. Despite their strength, competition emerged in the 1960s. Investors organized numerous banks, some in Phoenix, most notably Guaranty, Continental, and Thunderbird banks. Identifying special areas of activity and sometimes merging to join resources, most prospered. Savings and loan associations were similarly concentrated in Phoenix and dominated by a few institutions — Western and First Federal (which later merged into Merabank). Although smaller than the banks (with roughly one-quarter the resources), they grew very rapidly in this era.

The Ups and Downs of Building

Construction remained a prime source of income and employment, averaging roughly eight percent of the workforce, and value of the construction burgeoned in Phoenix and the major suburbs. However, the fortunes of this industry fluctuate, and the Valley experienced more gyrations than most places. The first collapse occurred in the early 1960s when the national economy was booming and other sectors of the Phoenix economy were vibrant. The number of homes constructed plummeted by 80 percent from 1960 to 1963, and employment dropped by a third. Whether higher interest rates or overbuilding had caused the problem, the consequence was striking and personal: the number of home builders fell from 80 to 20 by 1965. Those who survived devised various strategies to deal with the crisis. Some pursued commercial and industrial contracts, though competition was stiff. Others built apartment buildings, but that market also dried up. Glen Hancock shifted from building to remodeling homes. John F. Long began producing mobile homes for residential as well as commercial and industrial use.

A final case is that of Travis Williams. Like many builders, he and his brother Daremon, had begun working in the late 1940s, but their firm played a unique role in the history of Phoenix housing. Their father, D.W. Williams, and uncle, J.S. Jones, working as the Williams and Jones Contracting company, had begun building homes in South Phoenix during the early 1940s. To help meet the severe need for decent housing for African Americans after the war, a group of African American investors in 1946 created the Progressive Builders Association, which purchased 160 acres at the southwest corner of 24th

Street and Broadway. Daremon worked for his father's company, as did Travis, while completing his education at ASU. When their father decided to move to California in 1950, the brothers took over the firm and renamed it the Williams and Jones Construction company. Besides developing the Broadway tract and other South Phoenix properties, the firm built homes in Scottsdale and Sunnyslope.

When conditions declined in the early 1960s, Travis earned a real estate license and began handling the sale of their homes. Finally, having laid off nearly everyone else, the brothers decided that Travis should find another job. Having served on a Community Council task force, he was asked to work for the council in planning and developing programs. As Operation LEAP expanded, in 1965 he created a Small Business Development Center. After several years the economy had rebounded, and Travis decided to return to the family construction firm, but LEAP offered him a job as a program planner. After talking with his brother, he agreed to take the job. He continued in this field until he retired in 1989, becoming director of LEAP in 1970 and director of the Human Resources Department in 1977. Throughout these years he remained a resident of South Phoenix. His commitment to neighborhood and social action was shared by his son, Cody, who served on the city council in 1994-2002.

The construction industry took several years to recover from the economic disaster of the mid-1960s, but from 1968 to 1973 building was brisk. The next crash, from 1974 to 1976, saw a 50-percent drop in employment and a three-fourths decline in housing. In July of 1974 unemployed construction workers totaled 9,500 and comprised half of all persons seeking unemployment compensation. By 1977, as the city's population growth began to accelerate, the housing market recovered and soon reached new heights, but the skyrocketing interest rates of 1979-1980 greatly reduced the building of single-family housing. The construction industry was an important part of the Phoenix economy, tied to income, employment and banking. Short downturns were expected; but longer crashes, like that of the early 1960s, posed a more serious threat to the larger economy.

The fluctuations evident in the construction industry were only slightly mirrored in other economic sectors. Tourism continued to grow rapidly, and by the 1970s it had replaced agriculture as the second leading economic sector. New resorts were built, especially in northern Phoenix and Scottsdale, and older resorts were remodeled, air-conditioned for summer use, and expanded. One such change involved the Arizona Biltmore Resort, one of the Valley's landmarks, which the Wrigley family sold to Talley Industries in 1973. When a fire caused extensive damage, the architects at Frank Lloyd Wright's Taliesin center designed an overhaul, and over the next five years the resort doubled its accommodations.

The convention business also expanded, tripling after completion of the Civic Plaza. Although in 1981 Phoenix ranked only 26th nationally in convention business, this represented an important direction for future growth. Both tourism and conventions relied on air travel, and traffic at Sky Harbor Airport continued to expand at a stunning annual rate of 11 percent. Terminal 2 opened in 1962, and a much larger Terminal 3 followed in 1979. Airline deregulation in 1978 brought three more airlines and so much more business that the planned destruction of Terminal 1 was postponed.

A More Complex Valley

By the end of the 1970s an era seemed to be ending. Numerous little signs added to the larger sense that the focus, direction and management of Phoenix was changing. The Phoenix Chamber of Commerce, so dominant through the 1940 and 1950s, faced stiff competition from suburban chambers and even challenges to their authority from interests within the city. The dramatic increase of suburban populations and the growing interdependence of all the Valley's communities meant that Phoenix could no longer make unilateral decisions about many important issues. The proliferation of business interests and communities meant that business no longer spoke with a single voice. The end of Charter Government opened the political system, but a city the size of Phoenix needed structures and procedures to enable ordinary citizens to participate.

Eugene Pulliam's death in 1975 represented both a real and a symbolic shift. It removed an active, aggressive and powerful voice for clear, simple tradition. For three decades Pulliam had dominated the news — both in reporting it and making it. His strong beliefs shaped what his papers said and influenced what the city did. His papers provided crucial support to CG and virtually transformed public opinion on certain issues, like the initial design for the Papago Freeway. In the 1970s alternative voices began to emerge: the *New Times* started in 1970, and Cox Enterprises bought the *Mesa Tribune* in 1977, later uniting it with Tempe and Chandler papers. Diversity and changes in public opinion also limited the options of Pulliam and other members of the Phoenix elite. Shortly before he died, Pulliam organized the Phoenix 40, a group of civic leaders who demanded a strong attack on crime, especially organized crime. Although this approach offered some advantages in dealing with a serious public issue, efforts to perpetuate the group led to significant public outcry at its perceived elitist composition and approach, revealing how much attitudes had changed.

As the 1970s came to a close, Phoenicians remained generally committed to economic and demographic growth, yet they were increasingly concerned about the consequences of what they considered "unmanaged" growth. At a minimum, the problems of traffic, smog and crime needed specific and immediate policy solutions. But the larger questions — about community, size and sprawl, and establishing or defining a larger Phoenix identity — hovered in the background, soon to force their way into active public debate.

Central Avenue, 1981
*City of Phoenix,
Photo by Bob Rink*

Mural artist Roberto Delgado created this wall mural at the McDowell Road/Squaw Peak Parkway overpass. The imagery depicts an aerial view of the prehistoric Hohokam Salt River irrigation system combined with streetscape elements of the surrounding neighborhood.
Phoenix Arts Commission, Photo by Bob Rink

Metropolitan Complexity
1980-2001

chapter three

Looking back from the early 1990s on the development of Phoenix during his lifetime, Frank Snell mused that he "liked Phoenix best when it had about 400,000 people." His friend Tom Chauncey, another Phoenix power broker, also expressed regrets, judging that "we've grown too fast." But Barry Goldwater expressed a different view, claiming that "You can't complain about progress. My God, in 20 to 25 years this is going to be

the fourth biggest city in the U.S." Other Phoenicians in the 1990s lauded the transformation of downtown. That mixture of pride and concern, of enthusiasm and nostalgia, runs through the city's recent past like desert silt in the flooding Salt River — and raises similar concerns about society's ability to control the flow of events.

Growth brought distance and separation, complexity and diversity to Phoenix. The sheer scope of the city — the miles it encompassed, and the numbers of people — made life within its boundaries vastly different than even a few decades before. The interrelationships also shaped a different type of life. In the earlier Phoenix, the physical proximity of shared neighborhoods and common shopping brought people together. Growth and

expansion ended much of that, but they also brought a rich diversity of groups and interests, and a burgeoning of economic and social opportunities. Furthermore, people learned ways of dealing with and thinking about the city. Rather than thinking about the sprawling metropolis as a whole, they focused on a limited number of places they actually encountered. Such mental maps made the city comprehensible and accessible.

At the same time Valley resident also created a new range of connections — shared frustrations with traffic, a common concern with air pollution or water usage and a sense that solutions required metropolitan agreement. Most troubling was the possibility that the engine of growth which had propelled change — much of it good — would continue, uncontrolled and uncontrollable, consuming the qualities which had originally attracted people to the area. By the 1990s a sizable majority of Valley residents agreed with Tom Chauncey's evaluation that the city had grown too fast, but what lent credence to those who worried about the future of the area is that half of the population said they would leave if they had an opportunity.

The Proof of Status

The city's promotional activities for the 2000 census started with the new year. Public officials vividly remembered when preliminary 1990 census results had shown the Phoenix population at

983,403, ranking eighth and narrowly ahead of Detroit. Elation quickly turned into concern, however, when Detroit Mayor Coleman Young alleged that his city's population had been undercounted and rallied volunteers to find residents who had been missed. Although final tabulations kept Phoenix ahead, city officials determined to avoid any repetition. In January 2000 they began asking residents to be counted. Starting in April a steady barrage of newspaper stories, media ads, and even balloons and billboards at intersections stressed the importance of being included. When former Phoenix City Councilman Rosendo Gutierrez suggested that Latinos boycott the census to protest a raid by Mesa Police and the INS, the *Arizona Republic* quickly warned that an undercount would "mean fewer services geared toward Latinos."

(All photos) A complete and accurate census count in 2000 was critical to the city's ranking and funding. By April, reminders to complete the census appeared on nearly every major street corner. *City of Phoenix, Photo by Bob Rink*

This time no one contested the census count, which confirmed a significant change in the city's status and self-image. A leading Western city by the 1960s Phoenix began to emerge as a national city by 1980, rising from the 20th to ninth largest city in the country. However, its population still lagged far behind that of the highest ranked cities, and having comparatively few suburbs, the metropolitan area ranked only 24th largest. In the 2000 census Phoenix had climbed to the sixth-largest city in the country. The city's population of 1,321,045 had grown by two-thirds since the last census, the most rapid expansion of any big city and third among the 50 largest cities. Even more dramatic, the metropolitan area jumped to 14th, reflecting a 170 percent increase in the suburban population.

These population numbers generally reflected "more of the same," with one major exception: the proportion of Hispanics (largely Mexican but including other Latin Americans). From 1940 through the 1980s that population had kept pace with city growth, remaining about 15 percent. But during the 1990s Hispanic immigration increased dramatically. Social conflict and violence south of the border, combined with U.S. prosperity fueled both legal and illegal immigration. As lawmakers debated legal standards and conditions for permanent residence, native and immigrant Hispanics in great numbers worked in agriculture and construction, as domestics and factory laborers and in service industries.

Hispanics had historically concentrated in South Phoenix. In the 1990s their proportion there had increased but also spread: by 2000 they comprised over half the population in an area stretching north to Thomas Road, and from Tempe in the east to 43rd Avenue in west Phoenix. The core of this area was also the most impoverished in the city, with over half the residents living below the poverty level. Development, particularly the expansion of Sky Harbor Airport, disrupted some older Hispanic neighborhoods and displaced the residents. The poorest neighborhoods were plagued by gangs, violence and inadequate services.

Older agencies like Friendly House continued to provide vital assistance, as did new groups such as Centro de Amistad, started in 1977, provided physical and mental health programs, while the Valley Interfaith Project helped organize the communities to press for better community policing and neighborhood centers. However, Chicanos por la Causa (CPLC) remained by far the most important organization, despite severe reductions in federal support in the early 1980s which shrank the program by half. During the 1990s money from various public and private sources revitalized the organization, raising the budget to $10 million in 1996. Its wide range of programs included economic development and assistance, housing, health and others geared toward

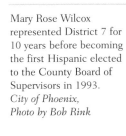

Mary Rose Wilcox represented District 7 for 10 years before becoming the first Hispanic elected to the County Board of Supervisors in 1993. *City of Phoenix, Photo by Bob Rink*

As of the 2000 census, 34 percent of the city's population is Hispanic.

Scottsdale Convention & Visitors Bureau, Photo by Paul Markow

families. Many of its projects succeeded, but some did not, like the investment with Fife Symington into the Mercado market area in downtown.

Important progress occurred within the Hispanic community in these decades. Although elementary and secondary education caused great concern, with low test scores and underfunded schools, more high school students graduated, and Hispanics made up a growing proportion of college students. By 2000 the proportion of Hispanic students at ASU had risen significantly, to 11 percent, aided by efforts like the Hispanic Mother Daughter Program. More than one third of the Hispanic community in 1993 had at least some college education, although this figure dropped in subsequent years due to the influx of large numbers of poorly educated immigrants.

Increasing numbers of Hispanic citizens joined the middle class, particularly in business and the professions, as evidenced by groups like the Hispanic Chamber of Commerce and the medical association. In 1993 one-third held white collar jobs, and 17 percent of the households had an income over $50,000. Hispanics achieved greater prominence in politics, particularly with the election of Ed Pastor to Congress in 1991, and with leaders in the state legislature like Armando Ruiz, and Mary Rose Wilcox in city council and then the Maricopa County Board of Supervisors. Spanish became a more audible presence in the Valley — on the streets, on 10 radio stations and two television stations (KDRX and KTVW) by 2000 — and, increasingly through the 1990s, employers sought workers fluent in both English and Spanish, frequently offering higher pay.

Use of the language also became an increasingly divisive political issue. In 1988 Arizona voters passed an initiative declaring English the state's "official language." Although struck down in federal court in 1990 (and finally by the state Supreme Court in 1998), it reflected growing concern about whether Hispanics were "melting" into the American population or remaining separate. The issue re-emerged in 2000 when state voters passed another language law, this one to prohibit bilingual education in favor of English immersion instruction. Although the courts will rule on this measure, the increasing number of Hispanic immigrants ensures that the issue will not disappear.

Other minorities did not experience the same population boom. African Americans remained roughly five percent, while Native Americans increased slightly to two percent. The latter group became more visible in the Valley because suburban sprawl touched against nearby reservations. Even more importantly, government decisions during the 1990s allowed gambling on reservations, which created a much needed economic stimulus and opportunities. The conditions facing African Americans in this period remained substantially what they had been during previous decades. The population remained concentrated in South Phoenix, restricted more by income rather than overt discrimination. Although the levels of poverty and unemployment in Phoenix fell slightly below national norms, the problems of inadequate housing, education and employment continued. Progress occurred as greater numbers of African Americans appeared in middle class occupations and neighborhoods, as well as students at ASU and community colleges.

Community organizations remained strong, and African Americans served important political roles in the city and state legislature. Calvin Goode and Cody Williams pushed programs to advance South Phoenix and to build the downtown area.

Councilman Calvin Goode served District 8 from 1972 until his retirement in 1994. *City of Phoenix, Photo by Bob Rink*

Growing representation and upward mobility has given Hispanics a greater voice in Phoenix politics. *City of Phoenix, Photo by Bob Rink*

African Americans and civil rights supporters mobilized during this era in a conflict over establishing the birthday of Rev. Martin Luther King, Jr. as a public holiday. Gov. Bruce Babbit first declared the holiday in May 1986, but the following year his successor, Evan Mecham, rescinded the order. For the next five years the state struggled through a confusion of laws and conflicting referenda. Cities established a paid King holiday, starting with Phoenix and by 1991 including Glendale, Tempe and Scottsdale. Despite polls showing clear majorities favoring such a law, particularly in Phoenix, not until 1992 were Arizona voters able to vote on a single state law creating a King holiday. They passed the measure overwhelmingly, the only state to create the holiday by popular vote.

Boom, Bust and Change

The Phoenix economy grew rapidly but unevenly during these years. In the early 1980s the economy sputtered before revving up: unemployment began at eight percent before dropping, while employment leaped from 623,300 in 1980 to 913,800 in 1987. During the next four years the economy sagged, with unemployment spiking at eight percent, slow job growth, and limited increases in income. Beginning in 1992, however, the economy boomed: unemployment dropped under three percent while the number of jobs jumped nearly eight percent annually, rising to 1,631,200 in 2000. Per capita income

increased by more than one-third in only five years after 1993.

But while all economic sectors expanded, some grew more rapidly than others. After four decades in which manufacturing led the economy's advance, this sector lost some of its share of the area's employment, dropping steadily from 18 to 10 percent. Most of the larger manufacturing firms remained important employers. The largest private employer in 2000 was Honeywell, the manufacturer of aerospace equipment which merged in the 1990s with Allied Signal. Its workforce of 16,994 in 2000 equaled the total workforce of both companies in 1989. The second largest firm, Motorola, employed 15,000 — a large group but down by a quarter during the late 1990s from the workforce of roughly 20,000 it had employed since the early 1970s. These reductions reflected Motorola's ill-fated Iridium cell phone network, but also some weaknesses in the high-tech industry.

Other high tech firms in the Valley remained fairly healthy during this era. Intel, the major semiconductor manufacturer, arrived in 1979, by 1989 it had 3,100 workers and, after building a major plant in Chandler, employed 10,000 people in 2000. Other semiconductor or circuit manufacturers employing over 1,000 workers included Microchip Technology (another Chandler firm), Texas Instruments, STMicroelectronics and Sanmina. Despite the importance of these manufacturers in the Phoenix economy, as a high tech center the Valley ranked near the middle of Western cities and just below the top 10 high-tech cities in the nation. The Valley did experience major gains in marketing high-tech equipment, with local firms like Avnet and Insight achieving success. But the high-tech downturn occurring at the end of this era also had local casualties: major distributor MicroAge was forced into bankruptcy in 2000.

All other economic sectors held their own over time except services, which leaped from one-quarter to one-third of the employment market, making up for the slower rise in manufacturing. Telecommunications companies expanded, particularly Qwest (previously US West) with 7,500 employees. Although financial services generally expanded, a 1989 tax law encouraged a dramatic expansion of credit card operations in the Valley: by 2000 a dozen companies employed some 10,000 people.

Equally dramatic, a local start-up firm became one of the major companies in the Valley. Taking advantage of airline deregulation and sensing the continuing expansion of travel to the Valley, in August 1983 a group headed by Ed Beauvais began America West Airlines with three planes and 280 employees. Expanding at a tremendous pace, by 1986 the new firm had 46 planes and 4,500 employees, and by 1989 it employed 5,700 people. Unfortunately, the company expanded too rapidly and, faced with stiff competition for the Valley market from no-frills Southwest Airlines, in 1991 America West filed for Chapter 11 bankruptcy protection. Reorganized and under new leadership, in 1994 the company emerged in a surprisingly vibrant state, and by 2000 employed 9,700 workers and ranked as the nation's eighth-largest airline.

America West had its headquarters in Tempe, but it affected the entire Valley. Similarly, Phoenix owned and operated Sky Harbor Airport, but its fortunes also reflected and influenced the entire area. Passenger traffic increased at a frenzied pace, rising over 500 percent between 1980 and 2000. Much of the increase was connected to American West and Southwest, but by the mid-1980s all of the major national carriers flew into Phoenix. Tourism and conventions continued to grow dramatically: between 1981 and 1992 Phoenix rose from 28th to 10th in national convention bookings, with roughly 15,000 conventions and a direct economic impact of $600 million. The huge increase in traffic made the addition of Terminal 3 in 1979 insufficient, and Terminal 4 opened in 1990. A third runway, torn up when Terminal 3 was built, was added in 2000 to accommodate the increased traffic.

Not everyone appreciated the increased activity. Tempe regularly complained about noise, and beginning in the 1980s some critics proposed a regional airport between Phoenix and Tucson. Most Valley residents, and especially Phoenicians, rejected the idea and only partly because of cost. An urban airport offered numerous advantages to travelers and significant economic opportunities for Phoenix. But by 2000, with talk of a fourth runway, major terminal expansion, and huge expenditures, other voices suggested sending some air traffic to surrounding airports.

Other options existed. Since the 1950s the city had maintained the Deer Valley Airport, and as the base for 1,210 general aviation aircraft by 2001, it led the nation. Other Valley communities emulated this strategy. On the westside, Glendale began an airport in 1985. In the east, Mesa had retained Falcon Field after World War II, and by 2001 it hosted nearly 275,000 arrivals and departures annually, and 17,000 people worked in or associated with the airport. Chandler Airport was nearly as busy, but neighbors opposed its expansion. The most ambitious effort concerned Williams Field. Decommissioned in 1993, the Air Force gave many of its buildings to ASU, to the community college and to a flight school. The three runways and terminal went to Mesa, in its bid to create an economic center and a minor passenger airport to relieve Sky Harbor.

Higher education played an increasingly important role in economic development. The ASU East Campus at Williams housed the College of Technology and Applied Sciences and supported Mesa's interests in economic growth. ASU's second campus had begun on the Phoenix-Glendale border in 1984 after some years of ASU offering classes at a variety of West Valley locations. ASU West developed a particular strength in its MBA program. The main ASU campus continued to grow — even when planners attempted to keep it from going above 40,000 students. The engineering program, an established strength by the early 1960s, continued to expand, including specialized facilities such as the Semiconductor Materials Research Lab. The College of Business expanded even more rapidly, and by the mid-1980s its enrollment totaled one-fourth of the university. Its Real Estate Center and the Han Center for Entrepreneurship and Innovation produced valuable work for businesses, and the L. William Seidman Research Institute

(Far left)
ASU East

(Center)
ASU Research Park

(Below)
ASU West

Arizona State University News Bureau, Photos by Tim Trumble

In 1980 the city
introduced drivers to the
"reverse lane" concept in
an effort to relieve rush
hour traffic congestion.
*City of Phoenix,
Photo by Bob Rink*

generated research reports that guided public policy makers as well as businesses. An even more direct connection was the ASU Research Park, established in 1984. Modeled after the tremendously successful Stanford Research Park, it created a campus-like environment for businesses and opportunities for business-university cooperation.

Construction, Land Development and the S&L Crisis

During this era, as always, construction proved the most variable part of the economy. It directly employed seven percent of the workforce, but it influenced the employment of more than twice that number. The connection of construction with real estate development and finance not only influenced employment but in this era also led to economic disasters, with far-reaching effects on Arizona's economy and institutions. While Phoenix builders had always been optimistic, during the 1980s their motto became "If we build it, they will come." Unlike previous economic slowdowns when real estate followed a declining economy, in the 1980s real estate caused the decline.

After the economic and construction slump of 1980-82, the recovery involved unprecedented amounts of construction. Even more unusual, the activity raced past existing demand. By 1986 commercial space in the Valley was vastly overbuilt, with vacancy rates for offices (30 percent) and apartments (13 to 17 percent) well into the danger zone. A glut of residences also accrued by this time. Commercial foreclosures ran to $1 billion in 1986 and $2.5 billion in 1988; nearly half of all residential closing were foreclosures. Home building, and especially apartment building, collapsed.

Several factors fueled this situation and reflected forces outside the Valley. Between 1977 and 1986 the number of builders in Arizona increased seven-fold. Many came from Texas, fleeing the collapse of that state's building industry, and the strategy they and others followed was "build to maintain a market share." Tax benefits justified some construction, but the 1986 Tax Reform Act removed those advantages and destroyed the strategy. The final and most important factor was the 1982 deregulation of savings and loan institutions while continuing to insure their deposits. S&Ls, which traditionally loaned money for single-family homes, now began handing out money for many types of real estate development, and this shift greatly affected the Valley's economy. Without adequately funded government regulation, S&Ls would pay grossly inflated land prices, or would fund proposals with virtually no investment by the developer and split the expected profits. According to Bill Crocker, later brought in to clean up Security Savings, "This institution, like many savings and loans in Arizona, was run like a venture capital company."

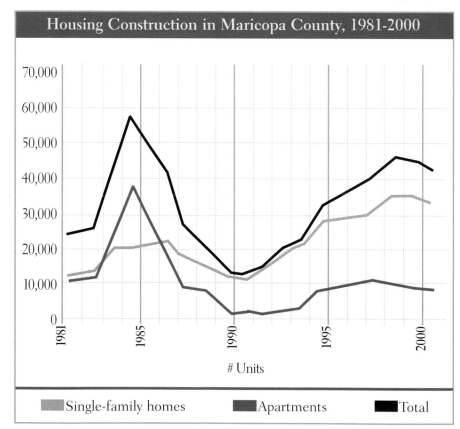

Housing Construction in Maricopa County, 1981-2000

Units

Single-family homes   Apartments   Total

Some actions just involved terrible judgment, but in other cases, especially when economic conditions worsened, the individuals engaged in fraud. The most egregious instance involved Charles Keating, who came from Cincinnati in 1978, created a financial and development empire, and made himself, ultimately, the biggest S&L swindler in the nation. Keating used a Phoenix financial services company, American Continental Corp., to buy Lincoln Savings and Loan in Irvine, California. He then used Lincoln's assets to fund his Arizona developments, and when conditions worsened, he misled and defrauded investors to stay afloat. Ultimately, even this money could not sustain his lavish spending on the Phoenician resort, and in building his planned community of Estrella, intended to be a morally controlled city of 200,000 persons about 15 miles west of Phoenix. American Continental filed for bankruptcy in 1989, but federal authorities charged Keating with bilking Lincoln Savings out of $1 billion. Paying off the Lincoln creditors cost taxpayers $3.2 billion, the most expensive such disaster in the country. Keating himself was convicted in 1993 on 73 criminal charges.

Although far less costly to taxpayers, the activities of Fife Symington also involved fraud and revealed the failure of the system. The beneficiary of "sweetheart deals" from Southwest Savings, on whose board of directors he had served, Symington attempted to shore up his endangered developments by obtaining loans from various investors based on fraudulent information. Although Symington's resignation as governor and his criminal conviction had greater political significance, in economic terms the combined action of the S&Ls caused more damage.

The ultimate tally is hard to believe. In two years after February 17, 1989, nine of Arizona's 10 S&Ls (two from Tucson) failed, costing taxpayers over $5 billion. Federal regulators filed civil charges against directors and officers of six thrifts and criminal charges against three. Even more incredible, the crisis could have destroyed more institutions. In 1985, acting in advance of new federal rules, Arizona legalized interstate banking. Banks in New York (Chase Manhattan and Citibank) and California (Security Pacific and Bank of America) immediately purchased four of Arizona's six largest bank at for premium prices. Unfortunately for the purchasers, Arizona banks also had made ill-advised loans, and as the economy declined, their losses mounted. They differed from S&Ls most importantly in not engaging in fraud but also because the two largest and Arizona-owned banks — Valley National and First Interstate —

plus the out-of-state banks had sufficient resources to withstand the serious losses (Security Pacific lost $1.1 billion in 1989).

As Arizona's S&Ls and a number of its small banks began folding in 1989, larger banks, especially the Bank of America, bought their assets. By 1992, as health returned to the economy, a wave of bank mergers took place, prompting one observer to suggest "putting up bank signs with Velcro." A final round of mergers occurred in 1998-99. As a result, three out-of-state banks controlled 90 percent of all bank assets in the state. Many people criticized this concentration of economic power, one further reflected by the declining number of banks in the state from 53 in 1985 to 29 in 1996. Surprisingly, just as the concentration reached its greatest extent, a counter-trend emerged: a dozen banks organized from 1996 to 2000, with the prospect of more to come. Often calling themselves "community" banks, these institutions aimed to offer the style of personal banking that the large banks were abandoning.

This pattern of concern and out-of-state ownership also characterized other economic areas. In home construction, Quail Homes went bankrupt and Bowen Homes filed for Chapter 11 bankruptcy protection, Cardon Homes and Hamon Homes left the Valley, while Knoell Homes sold to California-based Shea Homes and Del Webb eventually sold to Pulte Homes. Within a few years an influx of grocery store chains — such as Albertson's and Fred Meyer's — led to further re-shuffling and the disappearance of local stores (Lucky's, ABCO, and Smitty's) and the takeover of others, like Fry's. Wal-Mart stores entered the Valley like a tornado, setting up megastores that eliminated competition and reshaped areas, and provoking major public protest. By 2001 Wal-Mart was the fourth-largest employer in the state. Besides the issues of declining entrepreneurial opportunities and wealth leaving the state, community activists

During the 1980s and 1990s, construction encroached on the surrounding desert at a rate of "an acre an hour," and pride in the city's growth mixed with worry about urban sprawl. *Arizona Office of Tourism, Photo by John Trotto*

worried if transplanted managers of national chains would commit their time and money to the community as had those persons who owned Phoenix institutions.

The business community's efforts to direct the economy reflected a continuing private-public partnership, but also recognized a new metropolitan context. The Phoenix Chamber of Commerce, once the dominant influence on the city's planning, struggled with changing conditions. In 1977 it had transferred the promotion of tourism and conventions to a Valleywide agency. In 1983 it started calling itself the "Phoenix Metro Chamber" but abandoned the title after a few years, reflecting the growth and independence of suburban chambers. And over the next several years its membership declined by roughly half. The Phoenix Economic Growth Corporation, a mixed public-private group started in 1985 to plan the city's economic future, carried greater influence. Its role was soon overtaken by economic crisis, however, and Mayor Goddard responded by gathering a summit of business, civic and political leaders from the Valley. While not eliminating the East Valley Partnership, which had organized

in 1982, it provided a Valley-wide, public-private forum for discussing the Valley's future.

Of Mayors and King-Makers

When Margaret Hance defied the CGC and ran successfully for mayor in 1975, she contributed greatly to breaking the influence of this political machine. But her action, and the proliferation of city council candidates in that year (a total of 26 people), also reflected changing public attitudes about political power and the role of elites. But how to construct an alternative political system which provided greater political access for citizens as well as capable candidates? The limitations of the new regime quickly became apparent: the number of council candidates fell, competition diminished and in 1981 voter turnout dropped below 20 percent. The problem was that campaigning in a city with three-quarters of a million people and spread over more than 300 square miles was too difficult and expensive for all but a few persons. Those with name recognition, with sufficient money of their own or able to raise campaign funds, had an enormous advantage. Ironically, CGC continued to influence the process by endorsing candidates.

Frustrations with this system strengthened the long-standing effort to elect council members from districts. With polls showing that two-thirds of the public favored such a system, the Committee for District Representation organized a petition drive which forced the city council to schedule a popular vote on the plan in December 1982. The proposal faced numerous, important opponents: Mayor Hance, her Charter Review Committee, the Charter Government Committee, the Phoenix 40, the Chamber of Commerce and major business interests. They raised all of the familiar arguments about the dangers of ward politics, calling it "old-fashioned," and the *Arizona Republic* denounced it as a plot "to concoct a mechanism that ultimately will enable union bosses to seize control of city hall." More sober critics worried about excessive localism and competition between districts, but offered no solutions to the problems with at-large election. The District Committee's leading spokesman, Terry Goddard, described the elite's united opposition as a reason to change the system. "Under the present system, a small group of self-appointed manipulators control who is elected to the City Council. These men have operated under the assumption that they and they alone know what is best for the city." By contrast, a district system could provide representation for diverse communities and interests. Despite a well-financed campaign of opposition,

continued on page 86

Holsum Bakery, which was established in Phoenix the same year the city incorporated, baked and served the city's 100th anniversary cake in 1981.
City of Phoenix, Photo by Bob Rink

■Old-time residents remember the flower gardens by South Mountain as a spectacular sight. Their rise and disappearance is the story of a few families and the broad forces of change.

In 1928 Kajiuro Kishiyama moved his young family from California to Arizona, finally settling in Phoenix in the mid-1930s. Leasing land just north of South Mountain Park on Baseline Road, he grew vegetables and flowers. He also assisted a neighbor's relatives, the Nakagawa family, to relocate from Utah by hiring them for six months. In 1938 he sent his 10-year-old son, George, to be educated in Japan, but World War II trapped him there until 1947. Responding to fears and rumors after Pearl Harbor, in May 1942 the government ordered most Japanese Americans (in the Valley this included those living south of Grand Avenue and Van Buren Street) to internment camps. The Kishiyama and Nakagawa families were interned at Camp Poston (built by Del Webb), but after 11 months the Kishiyamas were released when John Martin and John Massero vouched for them. Returning home, they discovered that equipment and household goods left in the haste of their departure had been stolen.

After the war Kajiuro decided to focus on raising flowers, as did the Nakagawas. Sensitive to a previous law which forbid aliens from owning land, Kajiuro bought 26.5 acres of land in the name of his 20-year-old daughter, who was a citizen. Complaints that his daughter was not the actual owner led police to arrest and jail them. Z. Simpson Cox, a lawyer in partnership with Alfred and Lorna Lockwood, bailed them out of jail and got the charges dropped. With this land and additional leased acreage, in 1946 the family began the business of growing flowers and supplying them around the state. They were joined by the Nakamuras family — distant relatives and former neighbors in Japan — who worked for the Kishiyama family until 1948, when they leased their own land, becoming the third Japanese family to raise flowers commercially.

In 1947 the Kishiyamas began selling flowers outside the state. The condition of Sky Harbor Airport and the capacity of the airplanes defined the scope of their business. In 1947 the planes flying into the airport were DC3s, which meant they could ship fresh flowers as far as Houston or Chicago. The introduction of DC6s and DC7s meant flowers could be sent further, to Detroit, and when Phoenix entered the "jet age" in 1957-58, Phoenix flower growers began shipping all over the country.

After George Kishiyama returned from Japan in 1947, he attended school and worked on the farm. Drafted in 1951, he went to Korea, and when he returned, George joined father as partners in the South Mountain Flower Garden. They had acquired an additional 10 acres of land in 1952, and as business expanded, they leased still more land.

The Japanese community expanded during the 1950s and 1960s, and flower farming boomed. The Watanabe family, which had been farming in nearby Laveen, bought land on Baseline in 1951. The Mariyama, Sakato and Iwakoshi families (Kajiuro's daughter and son-in-law) also began farming, and by 1960 these families were cultivating over 400 acres and shipping flowers to 230 outlets across the nation. On weekends Baseline Road was filled with cars of people admiring field after beautiful field of flowers.

Conditions began changing in the 1970s. The energy crisis dramatically increased certain costs — especially fertilizer but also seed. Flower farmers, like all farmers, had precious little profit margin to begin with, so George Kishiyama and others were forced to reduce their workforce and limit production. Joe Conroy, a flower wholesaler, first developed a new market with lower transportation costs in selling to grocery stores — first Smitty's, then other area grocery stores. This could not avoid, however, a larger problem. Ironically, by the late 1970s, faster air travel now proved the flower growers' nemesis — even faster air travel meant that buyers in the Midwest or on the East Coast could buy fresh flowers cheaper from growers as far away as Mexico, Columbia and Ecuador. By the 1980s competition spread to producers in Europe and Asia.

By the 1980s most of the original growers were thinking about retirement, but as Kenny Watanabe observed, "I don't think any of the other young people in other families want the business. They've gotten better educated and got better jobs." At the same time, developers began buying up land in the South Mountain area, farmers could sell their land for a handsome profit. By 1990 only three families still grew flowers and on only 60 acres. When George Kishiyama finally decided to sell and retire in 1997 he was startled to discover that Phoenix, in hopes of retaining the original character of South Mountain had zoned his land only for agriculture. For the next three years he struggled to get the city to rezone his property. He succeeded, and in 2001, having planted his last crop of flowers, he was ready to sell. ■

(Above left)
During World War II, all Japanese-Americans living south of the Grand Avenue-Van Buren perimeter were removed to internment camps outside the city. Those living north of the perimeter could stay at home but could not move freely about the city.

(Above right)
Phoenix's Japanese flowers gardens reached their commercial peak in the 1960s.
Arizona Historical Society-Central Arizona Division

It's rising to the left, I tell you! The sun is rising to the left!!

Honestly, Mayor Hance, aren't you reading a bit much into Goddard's victory?

the district forces triumphed with 51 percent of the vote and voter turnout above the level in the city's previous general election.

With the new system in place for the 1983 election, different political forces came into play. Mayor Hance decided not to seek a fifth term, which leveled the field considerably. Her mantle of the traditional CG policies of supporting business, economic growth and expansion was taken up by Pete Dunn, a conservative Republican and three-term state legislator. His opponent was Terry Goddard, a young Phoenix lawyer previously active in opposing the Papago Freeway route. Goddard benefited from considerable name recognition, since his father was chairman of the state Democratic Party and a former Arizona governor, but Terry's performance during the district fight had also won him recognition and respect. Goddard was also articulate, ebullient and an effective campaigner. Labeling Dunn "the henchman of the status quo" and denouncing the Phoenix 40, he called for a more open government and suggested balancing quality of life concerns with a drive for development. Although voter turnout doubled over the 1981

election, the result closely resembled the voting for the district system, with Goddard winning a solid 53.8 percent of the vote.

Goddard's tenure as mayor (1984-1990) marked a distinct shift in city governance, policy and politics, but with some continuities. He supported economic growth, recruiting new business and annexation, policies which surprised some opponents from 1983 and helped win the support of the city's newspapers and some key economic leaders. He helped to create the Phoenix Economic Growth Corporation, a public-private group to advance economic development, and when the Valley's economy weakened in 1989, he stimulated the development of the Greater Phoenix Economic Council. He also supported the arts, adding public art and an historic preservation program.

Goddard inherited an able city administration, which he later likened to "a race car usually kept in the garage with the motor idling." He decided to take it out for a spin — or two. He increased the city's focus on zoning, planning and infill growth, although that was hampered by urban competition and the drive for sales tax revenues. More importantly, he combined a commitment to revitalizing downtown, an interest in major projects and a willingness to propose additional taxes. He supported the Rio Salado project to develop the Salt River bed, proposals for highways and mass transit systems and city funding for a downtown baseball-football stadium. Voters rejected some of these proposals but supported many others, including major downtown construction projects. Goddard also encouraged thinking about Phoenix as a desert city, and sought to preserve clean air and open spaces.

Goddard's tenure as mayor ended in 1990, when he resigned to seek his father's old office as governor. (He narrowly lost a run-off election to Fife Symington.) His replacement was Paul Johnson, also a Democrat and young (31), who had owned a construction company and attended ASU part-time. He had won election to city council three times, initially with Goddard's help and subsequently without opposition. Acknowledged as an extremely hard-working council member, Johnson skillfully out-maneuvered more senior and better-known colleagues to win the council's election as interim mayor, holding the office until the next general election. During that period he compiled a huge campaign fund (reportedly $200,000) which, combined with his effective actions as mayor, discouraged anyone from contesting his election in 1991.

When the economic downturn began affecting city revenues, Johnson postponed spending rather than raise taxes. His balanced support for economic development and the environment, including protection of the mountain preserve and expansion of the city's recycling program, resembled Goddard's approach. So too did his interest in becoming governor. In March of 1994 he resigned as mayor to compete with Goddard for the Democratic nomination for governor. (In an acrimonious campaign, both men lost to grocer Eddie Basha, who lost in the general election to Governor Symington.)

Johnson's favored successor was a friend, councilman Skip Rimsza (Johnson was best man at Rimsza's wedding), a Republican and owner of a realty company who was first elected to the council in 1989. The council chose Thelda Williams as interim mayor, but Rimsza won the public election the following fall, and a year later (when he defeated Williams), and a third race in 1999, all by the same comfortable margin. As a councilman Rimsza had pressed for infill development and for requiring developers to pay substantial fees. In his mayoral campaigns, Rimsza focused more on crime, proposing to hire additional police, form special police units and encourage neighborhood action. In 1997 he proposed a modest program to expand the city's desert preserve and he supported efforts to create a more vibrant downtown.

City Council and City Government

The political environment for council members changed with the new election system in 1983, and the new direction offered by Mayor Goddard. CGC had declined since 1977, but the district system provided the final blow, since the organization had existed to create citywide slates. The new system changed the electoral dynamics. A total of 51 candidates sought the eight council seats, including four of the six incumbent council members, and only incumbent Calvin Goode won election outright. In all other districts the top two candidates competed in a run-off election. In the end, two of the other three incumbents won. The most notable upsets caused by the new system involved two former councilmen — Rosendo Gutierrez and

Gary Peter Klahr — who changed residence to run in District 4; both lost.

Fewer candidates ran in subsequent elections; usually a couple of districts saw minimal or no opposition, but most had at least two candidates. Nevertheless, incumbents enjoyed a major advantage: three elections were held before any incumbent lost (in 1989) and in the next decade only three more suffered defeat. Even more unlike the CGC era, council members after 1980 remained in office for longer, some for numerous terms: Howard Adams, a conservative pro-growth Republican sat on the Council from 1978 to 1990; John Nelson represented West Phoenix from 1984 until his retirement in 2000; and Calvin Goode from South Phoenix had the longest tenure — 22 years — which ended when he retired in 1994. Obviously, few people used this office as a springboard for higher political rewards.

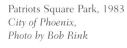

Skip Rimsza, Phoenix mayor, 1994-present
City of Phoenix,
Photo by Bob Rink

Patriots Square Park, 1983
City of Phoenix,
Photo by Bob Rink

Mayor Johnson digs into the Central Avenue Beautification Project, 1992.
City of Phoenix,
Photo by Bob Rink

Instead, the office attracted persons interested in serving their neighborhoods. These campaigns also encouraged a discussion of issues, particularly as related to the districts' interests. However, money made a difference; incumbents acquired much larger campaign funds, which partly explains their success.

City council service changed appreciably after 1983. Previously, the council had been assisted by two aides and met two afternoons a week, "a very part-time job," as Mayor Goddard later noted. He pushed a more active agenda, increased council meetings and provided each council member with an office and an aide. The district system encouraged citizens to contact their representatives, and it "increased the volume of traffic dramatically," according to Goddard. As a consequence, council members reportedly spent at least 30 and as much as 70 hours per week on their duties. This obviously limited who could hold the office. John Nelson may have been the only person during this period who worked a full-time job; many held no outside job. The problem for most people, then, was salary. In 1983 voters increased council salaries from $12,000 to $18,000, but in 1987 and 1991 they rejected proposed pay hikes. Finally, in 1995 voters boosted the salary to $34,000 (and to $36,000 in 1999), which represented the median income for Phoenix residents. Holding office might still mean

some economic hardship, but it would not be prohibitively burdensome for most people.

Opponents of the district system had worried about city-wide planning and policy making, but parochialism did not weaken city government. To a great extent — and unlike the experience of previous decades — the revenue sources, spending needs and functions of city government remained stable. Government revenues and spending did increase, but adjusting for inflation and population growth, the figure was only slightly over 10 percent. The city faced a problem when the federal government eliminated revenue sharing in 1986, but a slight boost in the city sales tax maintained its overall revenues. City government continued to grow, but at the same rate as the population, and this also held true for the police force and its share of the city budget. (*See appendix 3A*)

As in other cities, crime remained an important political issue throughout this period. During the 1980s and early 1990s the city's crime rate increased, especially the rate for violent crimes, but these rates were lower and increased less than rates in other Southwestern cities. However, when these rates began falling in the mid-1990s, those other cities experienced more rapid declines. This contrast, and especially Phoenix's higher property crime rates, prompted demands for improvement.

(Far right)
Phoenix City Hall, 1993

Historic Phoenix City Hall

*City of Phoenix,
Photos by Bob Rink*

Most other decisions also reflected a general concern about city development: support for expanding the desert mountain preserves, parks and libraries or creating a historic preservation program (1985) to preserve important structures reflected a general awareness of need. Differences did exist, but they ran more along ideological than geographical lines; consensus appeared more often than conflict. The responsiveness of council members to their constituents increased because of districts and because, by the 1990s, numerous neighborhood associations had developed throughout the city. Their proliferation was evidenced by their web pages, and the city's support was apparent in its "how-to" instructions for organizing such groups. Their functions varied greatly — some functioned as block watches, patrolling for crime while others sought to solve neighborhood problems. At a minimum they attempted to encourage some sense of community and connection between residents; at their most assertive level, they supported the city's urban village model. But although this scheme was nationally touted by urban planners, it never functioned fully as intended. Many residents never knew about the villages or what village they belonged to — partly because the "community" had no institutional or historic basis. A more fundamental weakness concerned the inability to develop substantial areas of employment or a compact "downtown." But even if independent and self-sufficient communities did not develop, the model provided clear justification for including citizen participation in planning for their community.

Building the City

If the failure to create multiple "downtowns" was a serious weakness in the urban village model, a more basic flaw was its neglect of the original downtown. Some defenders of decentralized, low-density Western cities, especially in the 1980s, considered downtowns outdated and not viable. Mayor Goddard argued that downtown belonged to all city residents, and that they could and should provide public functions. Private efforts helped to stimulate downtown growth, first through the Phoenix Community Alliance and then the Downtown Phoenix Partnership, but the focus and vision of Mayor Goddard drove the development. More than anything else, the passage in 1988 of an excise tax and a major capital spending bond initiative, which included money for downtown projects, sparked the area's rebirth in the 1990s.

The Arizona Science Center in Heritage Square
City of Phoenix,
Photo by Bob Rink

The Phoenix Museum of History in Heritage Square
City of Phoenix,
Photo by Bob Rink

The initial step involved private construction, the first in over a decade. Following completion of the condominium units at Renaissance Park in 1986, the Renaissance towers, the Arizona Center and the Mercado opened to provide shopping, restaurants and office space, while the America West Arena (1992) attracted concerts and sporting events and a multiscreen movie theater attracted additional audiences. Public buildings, a traditional component of urban life, also proliferated during the 1990s, including a new city hall, a municipal courthouse, and the Sandra Day O'Connor U.S. District Courthouse (2000).

The construction of educational and cultural facilities transformed the character of the area and greatly encouraged the arts and education. The Museum of Science and Technology and the Phoenix Museum of History completed a block already occupied by Heritage Square, a collection of 10 historic buildings relocated to create an historic district. The Herberger Theater Center, the refurbished Orpheum Theater, The Dodge Theater together with a new library, Little Theater and an expanded Art Museum vastly enhanced the city's cultural

Squaw Peak Parkway
construction
City of Phoenix,
Photo by Bob Rink

facilities. Bank One Ballpark drew crowds and created additional opportunities for new restaurants. The Collier Center, housing the Bank of America and Phelps Dodge Center, expanded the city's office space, while additional hotel space (Embassy Suites and the Marriott) was also being constructed. Finally, a series of housing developments were constructed — the St. Croix Villas and the Lorna Park Estates — but the most ambitious project involved redeveloping an area south of the Margaret Hance Park, which would make a serious dent in the Downtown Partnership's goal of 5,000 housing units.

Observers could note that the larger area still contained numerous dilapidated buildings, it lacked a substantial residential base, and it contained very few opportunities for shopping. Moreover the city had failed to attract some key sporting events, like the NCAA basketball finals, largely because of a lack of hotel rooms. However, the presence of so many cultural, educational and recreational facilities provided a significant attraction for Valley residents, with an estimated nine million visitors. Passage of a bond election in 2001 promised additional facilities, including a Phoenix Family Museum and a Valley Youth Theatre, repairing Symphony Hall, expanding the Art and Science museums and completing the main library.

Annexation

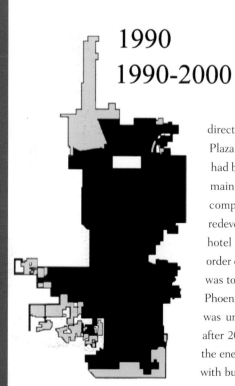

1990 ■
1990-2000 ▢

In 2001 debate over the city's future direction involved a major expansion of the Civic Plaza. Proponents contended that Phoenix facilities had been surpassed by those of other cities, and that maintaining its convention business, let alone competing for larger conferences, required a costly redevelopment. This would then stimulate additional hotel construction. Critics complained that the order of development was wrong and that the project was too costly and unrealistic. Although supported by Phoenix voters, the project required state fund's, which was unlikely in the state's weakened economic state after 2000. Yet whatever the outcome, it is evident that the energetic development in this area now compares with building activity elsewhere in the Valley.

Still More Annexation

In 1980 Phoenix contained 325.2 square miles of territory, making it one of the largest cities in the nation. Although it abutted the Gila Indian Reservation on the south and several cities on the east and west (to a large degree), during the next two decades the level of annexation actually increased, mainly by moving north. By adding another 152.4 square miles by 2000, the geographic city became larger than Los Angeles. But unlike many previous annexations, these actions conflicted with the goals of neighboring cities and roused opposition within Phoenix itself.

The city added some land in Laveen, to the southwest and west, after deciding that it was not vulnerable to storm waters flooding down South Mountain, but the main opportunities after 1980 lay to the north. At that initial point the city's northern boundary was Pinnacle Peak Road, some 17 miles north of downtown. In December 1984 the city annexed an irregularly-shaped, 27.5 square-mile, section in the north-central part of that area, extending north to the Carefree Highway. This quickly led to the most serious annexation struggle that Phoenix had faced in 30 years.

Several weeks after the Phoenix action, Peoria suddenly annexed a strip of land to its north and connecting to a large parcel which ran east to the Black Canyon Freeway. Two days later Scottsdale scheduled debate on a surprise proposal to complete a complementary move to annex a thin strip of land running far north, beyond Carefree, and then west to Black Canyon Freeway. If implemented, these measures would have set a finite limit to Phoenix's expansion and made it land locked — exactly what it had sought to avoid since the 1950s. Acting quickly, Mayor Goddard and Councilman Korrick persuaded Scottsdale to postpone any action on this plan. With the looming threat of state legislative intervention, Scottsdale and Phoenix agreed, after some months of discussion, to a division which largely extended their existing boundary further north.

The dispute with Peoria took longer to settle and involved overlapping and competing annexations. That city's 1985 annexation action was rescinded, but conflict over the territory re-emerged in March 1987 over New Town, John Long's proposal to build a large desert community in that area. While Peoria again proposed to annex the section extending to the Black

Canyon Freeway, Phoenix announced a much more ambitious plan — to annex west to the Agua Fria River and north to Lake Pleasant. Ultimately both proposals were scaled back, but allowing Phoenix to extend its western boundary to 67th Avenue. In the mid-1990s both cities expanded north. Peoria reached up to Lake Pleasant and Yavapai County, and Phoenix continued annexing north along the Black Canyon Freeway, and preserving the prospect of still more expansion in the future. In April 2000 Phoenix again proposed annexation in the area (of 50 square miles), but this time it included negotiations with Peoria as part of the process. By contrast, throughout the 1990s the city remained in conflict with Cave Creek.

Opposition to Phoenix's northern annexations also came from within the city. A growing and increasingly vocal group complained about the consequences of growth for Phoenix and the Valley. By the late 1980s and even more during the next decade, members of city council raised objections: Mary Rose Wilcox and Linda Nadolski argued that annexations were becoming too costly and unnecessary; Thelda Williams and Duane Pell argued that additional acquisitions delayed needed services for areas already in the city. And several members complained that further annexations detracted from efforts to encourage in-fill development. In 1985, even before the additional annexations, 30 percent of the city's buildable land area lay vacant.

Annexation supporters claimed that both the vacant land and the areas needing services were heavily concentrated in the recently annexed outskirts, and that time would resolve some of those issues. A more direct response from a continuing majority on the council, including mayors Goddard, Johnson, and Rimsza, argued that growth was inevitable, that expansion

need not prevent growth within the city, and that with proper planning annexation made sense. In 1989 Goddard reiterated that "many cities in the country have become surrounded by suburbs and choked to death," but he also explained that the

Metropolitan Phoenix Population Changes 1980-2000			
Area	1980	1990	2000
Phoenix	789,704	983,403	1,321,045
Suburbs	597,207	1,027,088	1,612,174
All urban places	1,386,911	2,010,491	2,933,219
Maricopa County	1,509,175	2,122,101	3,072,149
Phoenix: % urban	56.9%	48.9%	45.0%
OTHER CITIES & TOWNS			
East Valley			
Mesa	152,453	288,091	396,375
Chandler	29,673	90,533	176,581
Tempe	106,919	141,865	158,625
Gilbert	5,717	29,188	109,697
Sun Lakes	1,944	6,578	11,936
Guadalupe	4,506	5,458	5,228
North Phoenix			
Scottsdale	88,364	130,069	202,705
Fountain Hills	2,771	10,030	20,235
Paradise Valley	10,832	11,671	13,664
Cave Creek	1,589	2,925	3,728
Carefree	986	1,666	2,927
West Valley			
Glendale	96,988	148,134	218,812
Peoria	12,251	50,618	108,364
Sun City	40,664	38,126	38,309
Avondale	8,134	16,169	35,883
Surprise	3,723	7,122	30,848
Sun City West	3,741	15,997	26,344
Goodyear	2,747	6,258	18,911
El Mirage	4,307	5,011	7,609
Buckeye	3,434	5,038	6,537
Wickenburg	3,535	4,515	5,082
Tolleson	4,433	4,434	4,974
Litchfield Park	3,657	3,303	3,810
Youngtown	2,254	2,542	3,010
Gila Bend	1,585	1,747	1,980

Main Street, Scottsdale
*Scottsdale Convention &
Visitors Bureau,
Photo by Paul Markow*

The annual Glendale
Glitter & Glow Festival,
downtown Glendale
Glendale Tourism Division

city had reduced the cost of annexation to residents by increasing water and development fees. Finally, annexation was competitive, driven by cities' excessive dependence on sales tax revenues and illustrated by the 1996 annexation of 12 square miles which housed an outlet mall.

The majority also recognized that annexation provided one method for controlling the nature and direction of that growth. Developers kept one eye on city policy, and, for example, the aggressions by Scottsdale and Peoria in 1985 were partly stimulated by efforts of Atlanta developer Harrison Merrill to find a favorable hearing for his plans to build in the disputed territory. An alternative approach involved coordinated planning by the various cities and the county, plus assessing land use and development fees, but coordination was hard to achieve, and county controls were particularly lax.

Suburbs and Subdivisions

Phoenix's growth stood out among the nation's largest cities, and even most urban centers, but the Valley's other communities posted the most impressive growth rate (170 percent). During the 1980s Mesa grew faster (89 percent) than any other city in the country over 100,000, with Glendale (14th) and Scottsdale (18th) close behind. In the 1990s Gilbert topped the national list with a phenomenal 276 percent increase; Peoria and Chandler also scored in the top 10; with Scottsdale and Glendale "trailing" at 15th and 19th respectively. The five largest suburbs now contained nearly as many people as Phoenix did. Having annexed even more territory than Phoenix during the previous two decades, and with much of that land still vacant, they expected to continue growing rapidly. Although the Valley's other communities remained relatively small, they grew at double the rate of the other five suburbs, and they annexed over 600 square miles of territory. Reading their future from the Valley's past, they now anticipate a third wave of migrants and settlement in the area.

Rapid suburban growth prompted debates about the forms and consequences of housing. The trends of the 1980s, accentuated by the housing crash and the builders' desire to return to profitability, led to spreading visual and social blight during the

continued on page 95

The annual Renaissance Festival, Mesa
Mesa Convention & Visitors Bureau

john f. long

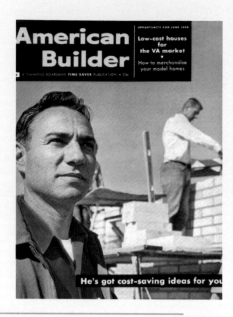

■John F. Long spent his life building homes and breaking new ground. The area's leading builder for many years, Arizona AFL-CIO named him Labor Man of the Year in 1958. The leading vote-getter for city council in 1967, he retired from public office just three years later because "it took so long to get things done," but several times thereafter he planned initiatives so voters could determine some important public policies. More than anyone else, Long helped develop the West Valley, but his ideas about community and life in the desert affected the entire area.

Born in Phoenix in 1920, he graduated from Glendale High School and then served in the Air Force in World War II. Returning home, he married, and after receiving a great offer on a house which he and his wife had built for themselves, Long began building for profit. Beginning on individual houses, he developed techniques for speeding up the construction and lowering costs. Moving next a tract of 30 homes, and then one of 134, he perfected his methods and began his characteristically self-sufficient approach to building: designing homes, testing and using plastic pipe, using trusses instead of rafters. By 1954 he decided to build an entire community because it would allow economies of scale and he could add other elements besides homes. He read about the Los Angeles planner, Victor Gruen, in a trade publication and asked him to design the community. He bought nearly 70 farms and he got financing from California lenders who liked the master plan concept. The community, named Maryvale after his wife, was composed of relatively inexpensive homes and proved hugely popular with homebuyers.

In Maryvale, in other smaller areas and in various projects he planned, Long built affordable homes and developed whole communities. He constructed a full range of services and amenities for residents and insisted on green spaces between developments. And over the years Long continued to support Maryvale and the larger West Valley through numerous donations, especially of land for public use. As he noted in 1977, "a large city has advantages and disadvantages; a person seems to lose his identity in a city. I guess basically that's why I created one." Twenty years later he proudly noted, "We provided a way of life for families who otherwise wouldn't be able to afford it."

In the early 1970s, as the oil embargo increased the cost of gas, Long began thinking about transportation, energy-efficient homes and conserving water. By 1980 he had developed a solar home which produced excess electric power, and he proposed selling electric cars which could run on that energy. Besides the larger environmental concerns, he also wanted to reduce energy costs in order to maintain the affordability of housing. He built Solar I, a West Valley subdivision of 20 solar-energy homes, but he also proposed a much larger development near Lake Pleasant, which was not built.

Long's interest in water conservation showed in the homes he built, which relatively early included lower water-use toilets. More generally, Long objected to the misuse of water in the Valley. In the late 1950s he began complaining about the inefficient use of effluent or treated water, and his dissatisfaction finally boiled over in 1986. Upset by the state legislature's failure to regulate the spreading use of water in artificial and decorative lakes, Long promised to finance an initiative drive to prohibit the use of fresh water in such lakes, and instead use treated water for lakes, parks, and golf courses. Polls showed that

huge majorities favored such a law, but that developers — except for Long — did not. Long's actions worked, in part and the legislature passed a regulatory measure the following spring.

During the 1990s several of Long's actions significantly affected the future of the West Valley. Although he stopped building houses in 1992, focusing instead on commercial developments, he continued to plan communities, particularly a solar community near Lake Pleasant. He also remained the leading proponent of bringing sports facilities to the West Valley. In 1986 he offered land for a major league baseball stadium, and later for a football stadium. Those offers bore no fruit, but another proposal, including 59 acres (about $10 million) and a loan of $10 million, produced a Maryvale spring training stadium, which opened in 1998. Shortly after that, Long put a more ambitious project into motion. For years he had been disturbed by the barren, cement-lined bed of the Agua Fria River and had imagined it as a recreation corridor. When he heard that the Maricopa County Flood Control District was thinking of better ways to use the land, he quickly responded. He called together the parks directors of the cities through which the river runs to plan improvements. By the spring of 2001 the Army Corps of Engineers had given Avondale and the Flood District $5 million to restore the river's last five miles to a natural state. Glendale was building trails, and it seemed probable that the Central Arizona Project would begin that fall to release hundreds of millions of gallons of water into the northern Agua Fria river bed, as part of a project to recharge the groundwater in the West Valley. While Long's vision of 47 miles of trails and parks still required major effort and expense, it was now a vision shared by many in the West Valley. ∎

continued from page 92

1990s. Homes and subdivisions were relentlessly uniform, an ocean of stucco and red tile as far as the eye could see. Home style obstructed community development and casual social interaction. The demand for larger homes and the rising cost of land resulted in narrower lots and two-story homes, with their most prominent street feature being garage doors. Many builders argued that consumers wanted this, but critics cited the success of some modest-priced custom home builders, noted the significant affect of building regulations and pointed to the deleterious consequences of the existing pattern. In 1998, hoping to alleviate these conditions, the Phoenix City Council adopted new design standards. Other jurisdictions also sought to address the issues by regulating lot size, but larger lots meant lower density and more sprawl. One alternative gaining popularity was the "New Urban" architecture, with narrower streets and house fronts dominated by porches and doors, not garages.

Another suburban variant, the retirement community, remained very popular. The separate jurisdictions of Sun City West and Sun Lakes added roughly 35,000 residents during this era, and an additional seven communities developed within Mesa. More restrictive and expensive subdivisions — "gated communities" — appeared in greater numbers, especially in the northern and southeastern parts of the Valley, while the range of community attractions broadened, with one neighborhood built around a waterskiing lake. The most significant aspect of suburban development has been the growing popularity of master-planned communities. Driven by consumer demand for ready built amenities and reflecting the rapid sprawl of population, over 40 percent of the homes sold in the metropolitan area during 1998 were located in planned communities. Such communities have frequently been "leap-frog" developments, located at some distance from other subdivisions or towns. This can, of course, be a complication. The community of Estrella, begun by Charles Keating, had failed in part because of its remote location. Purchased and reopened by another developer in 1994, it benefited from escaping Keating's debts and from the western spread of the metropolitan area.

Clearly the most important, elaborate and popular planned community was Anthem. Developed by the Del Webb Corporation, it sits in the far north Valley, well beyond city boundaries and any other development. The planning and construction reflect lessons the company learned in building its West Valley retirement communities. Beginning construction in 1998, the company spent over $180 million before the first resident moved in, having built not only the housing infrastructure but also a wide range

of recreation amenities (a lake, a golf course and a community center) and a school, fire station, health center, water treatment facility and basic stores. When the models opened in March 1999, it proved wildly popular. Almost 1,000 houses were sold in the first week; by July 2000 1,600 homes had been sold, and the community had added a bank, hotel, Blockbuster Video store, McDonalds and a U-Haul facility. By the following July the population reached 5,100 — a rapid move toward the planned 30,000 people.

The community's most basic requirement was water. Situated outside the area for water from the Salt River Project or any municipality, the Webb company concluded a 100-year arrangement with the Ak-Chin Indian Community to purchase part of their allocation of Central Arizona Project water. Being far from any other community meant that Anthem required its own basic services, which the builder provided. What the community lacked was employment. Although connected to I-17, it is 38 miles and roughly 45 minutes (depending on traffic) from central Phoenix. The Webb company and community supporters suggested that employment opportunities would emerge nearby, pointing to the new facility built by USAA, a major insurer of military personnel. Whatever does happen, it is clear that Anthem represents a victory of microplanning over area development.

The Metropolis

Led by expectation of continuing growth and tempted by cheaper land and the opportunities of an open landscape, developers continued building at the outskirts of the area. The primary restriction — and a very real one — has been and will continue to be water, but other controls on growth reflect the changing form of the Valley's political, economic and social geography during these two decades. While municipalities continued competing with their neighbors, regional identities and even a

metropolitan identity began forming. The process had emerged in the East Valley during the early 1980s, and with fits and starts it appeared in debates within the state legislature and prompted questions of public facilities. The more striking shift occurred in the West Valley, traditionally less populated, divided into more jurisdictions and less sensitive to development. To a great degree John F. Long served as the major catalyst; having worked for decades to promote the West Valley, by 2000 his vision for a public consciousness became a reality.

But the emerging power of the East and West sides of the Valley did not vitiate the larger reality: that every community faced the same major issues. Water provides the basis of growth

and survival in the desert. The system of canals and dams served much of the Valley's population's needs, but groundwater has been a second major source. Starting in the 1920s Arizonans began thinking about accessing water from the Colorado River, and in 1968 Congress provided the initial funding for the Central Arizona Project (CAP), transporting this water over desert and mountains to the central part of the state. In the 1970s, with dwindling national enthusiasm for expensive water projects and growing environmental concerns, the federal government arranged a compromise: it would complete the CAP provided that Arizona correct the falling levels of groundwater.

The resulting Groundwater Management Act (1980) defined water areas and required all Valley municipalities (organized into the Phoenix Active Management Area) to take less groundwater. Between 1985 and 1998 area cities reduced their groundwater usage by one-third. Yet the larger water problem remained. Some cities, particularly in the West Valley, still depended almost entirely on groundwater. Furthermore, overall water usage (i.e. from SRP or CAP) within cities rose, increasing 10 percent in Phoenix after 1995. Some commentators suggest that overall water

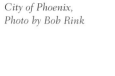

"Tall Stack" construction at the junction of I10 and I17, 1980s
City of Phoenix, Photo by Bob Rink

usage is not a major problem; but others argue that increasing use and competing interests require careful area-wide planning.

Transportation also became a metropolitan issue. Although Phoenix streets remain a major concern of city government, by the early 1980s highways and mass transit dominated the city's discussions of transportation. Moreover, these discussions were now inextricably part of a regional conversation. Construction had finally begun on the Papago Freeway, but traffic conditions throughout the Valley were seriously worsening and the progress on other freeways was glacial. Finally, nudged by the federal government and encouraged by the Valley's prosperity in the mid-1980s, a concerted regional effort won overwhelming voter support in 1985 for a comprehensive, regional plan involving 231 miles of freeways. Financed by a 20-year half-cent county sales tax, the plan also promised some consideration of mass transit.

Following some initial construction and enthusiasm, the process bogged down. Debates increased over exactly where the roads should go and when they should be built. Decisions on those issues affected the cost of the roads and development in the Valley. Building part of the far west loop was cheaper in the

Rafting on the Salt River east of Phoenix
Mesa Convention & Visitors Bureau

long run, but critics complained that this encouraged growth there and did nothing to solve traffic problems elsewhere. Residents being displaced by the crosstown Paradise Freeway objected loudly, and the costs for that section rose far beyond projections. The economic downturn reduced sales tax revenues, which slowed progress still more. Finally, a growing chorus argued that just building freeways would at best postpone the crisis, and that mass transit had to be a more significant part of the solution.

Attempting to resolve these complaints, in 1989 planners went back to county voters asking for an additional half-cent sale tax for ValTrans, an extensive, 103-mile rail system, but voters refused. In 1994, with revenue still lagging and construction falling further behind projections and needs, voters were asked to extend and increase the tax for roads, and again they refused. The planners went back to the drawing boards, abandoned the Paradise Freeway, and considered various notions, including toll roads or selling access to high-occupancy lanes. Economic recovery torpedoed these proposals and sped up construction. In fact, mileage completed by the early 1990s had noticeably reduced traffic congestion, and later work extended the benefits to other areas of the Valley — at least temporarily.

Mass transit remained an issue because population growth continued to undermine gains from freeway construction, but even more because more cars created additional air pollution. Bus ridership in Phoenix did increase by 60 percent from 1986 to 1990, but it stayed at the same level thereafter, despite more buses, extensive advertising campaigns and redesigned routes and schedules. Hopes for a light rail system had never died, despite common criticism that it was inappropriate for areas with such low-population density and the belief that voters would never part with their money to abandon their cars.

Conventional wisdom triumphed in 1997, when Phoenix and Scottsdale voters rejected light rail proposals, and again in 1999 when Chandler also opposed the idea. But the tide had already begun to turn. Earlier, some conservative Republican legislators from the East Valley had commented positively about light rail, and in 1996 Tempe began preliminary investigations. When Phoenix voted on a revised proposal in March 2000, the slim defeat of three years before became a 2-1 margin in support. This victory transformed the debate: Tempe voted to join Phoenix in creating a linked system, and the other major suburbs shifted their planning to a more serious level.

A related problem — air pollution — touched all Valley communities and required both county and state action. Valley residents had complained of air pollution beginning in the early 1960s, and by the 1980s it had become a crisis. Particulates, ozone and especially carbon monoxide levels plagued Valley residents, and according to a 1996 study, cost them $32 million per year in economic and health consequences. The worst problem was carbon monoxide, caused almost entirely by cars. In 1981 Valley air violated the maximum standards of the Environmental Protection Agency on 37 days, and in 1984 the total was 99 days, the worst record in the nation. In 1985 the Center for Law in the Public Interest filed suit to force the state to comply with EPA standards. Ensuing negotiations led to a 1988 state law mandating the use of fuel additives during the winter, higher emission testing standards and efforts to reduce automobile driving. Considering the plan inadequate, the Center appealed to federal court, which ordered the EPA to demand stricter standards. After several postponements, it did, threatening to withhold federal highway funds ($75 million for 1993 and $230 million over four years) to force compliance.

In response, the state legislature raised the standards for gasoline and auto emissions testing, mandated "no-burn" days to prohibit fires on high pollution days, and provided a token $10 million for mass transit. (Valley mayors promised more bus shelters and bike lanes.) Initially these measures brought little improvement, and in 1995 the Valley suffered repeated no-burn days and air quality alerts. The following year the EPA noted that despite some improvement over the decade, the Valley ranked worse than any Western city except Los Angeles. Subsequently, however, the number of air quality violations fell, reflecting the effect of existing standards, beneficial weather and emergency actions like Governor Jane Hull's sending state workers home early on December 30, 1998, to avoid topping the permissible carbon monoxide level. Given the connection between automobiles and pollution, and with the vast majority of Valley residents convinced that air quality is bad and getting

worse, additional action in the future seems likely. Finally, efforts to solve this problem will require coordination among and beyond Valley communities. As Governor Hull noted, "Air quality doesn't seem to stop at the county line."

Education in the Valley

In Arizona local school districts, not city governments, control education. However, the state also exercises considerable influence: defining standards, limiting local school spending and providing state funds. Thus, debates over schools necessarily involve local and state participants. Over the years local control has presented several problems. Racism prompted intervention, for example in 1953 when court orders banned the segregation of African American children, in the 1970 protests over discrimination at Phoenix Union High and in the 1973 U.S. Department of Justice order which mandated the busing of children from Guadalupe.

Wealth disparities between different districts, growing after World War II, generated additional challenges. The problems appeared most clearly outside the Valley where rural counties suffered from economic stagnation, while mining areas experienced boom and mainly bust. By contrast, Valley school districts struggled more with problems of tremendous expansion. In the 1950s John F. Long built a school for Maryvale when it was unable to do so, and later community developers increasingly included school construction in their plans. Rapid growth during the 1980s and 1990s in East Valley suburbs posed similar problems. In the early 1990s, for example, growth so staggered the Gilbert school district that the city attempted to declare a moratorium on all new residential zoning requests. At the same time, however, older Phoenix districts — initially those in the center city but over time in various neighborhoods — found themselves with fewer students and a declining tax base.

Throughout the 1980s and 90s, Phoenix and the surrounding communities had difficulty keeping up with the demand for schools and services.
City of Phoenix,
Photo by Bob Rink

With an enrollment of more than 50,000 students, Arizona State University is one of largest institutions of higher learning in the country. *Arizona State University News Bureau, Photo by Tim Trumble*

By the late 1980s inequities and inadequacies in funding (the state ranked 39th nationally in non-capital spending) were matched by declining quality of education — one national educational group gave the state's schools a "D." A reform coalition organized a major ballot initiative (ACE) for 1990, calling for additional spending over 10 years. Critics complained about a lack of accountability and ineffective programs, but supporters like Alhambra superintendent Carol Grosse responded that "We know many programs that work. What we need is the funding." But facing a weakened state economy and conservatives' suspicion of public schools, and with opposition from major businesses and active hostility from the *Arizona Republic*, the measure lost by a two-to-one margin.

During the next decade conservative legislators continued to starve public schools while reducing taxes, attempting to permit vouchers (an effort which failed), easing the supervision of home schooling, allowing the creation of "charter" schools, i.e. alternative public schools, and creating the AIMS test to measure student achievement. State law restricted increased spending by local districts — a special burden for rapidly growing areas. Districts with dilapidated schools and with students needing extra assistance simply could not afford additional taxes.

The issue changed dramatically in 1994. Ruling on a lawsuit filed by the Arizona Center for Law in the Public Interest, the Arizona Supreme Court required the state legislature to reform the financing of public education and remove the major inequities in school buildings and equipment. After the Court struck down three inadequate plans, the legislature finally passed a satisfactory measure in July 1998, providing $400 million, including $235 million to construct classrooms throughout the state.

Unfortunately, this too proved inadequate: a facilities survey in the spring of 2000 showed needs totaling at least $1 billion more than the legislature had allocated. (In the Murphy School District in southwest Phoenix, for example, every building roof leaked.) Noncapital needs had worsened substantially during the previous decade and presented even greater problems. Education Week's national report showed that real dollar funding had declined six percent, putting Arizona 50th in the nation. Teachers were paying for basic classroom supplies, while their salaries had been dropping in real dollars compared to other states. Not surprisingly, some schools lost a fourth of their teachers every year, and Arizona's "grade" for improving teacher quality was a D minus. Average class sizes had increased, and many districts had been forced to curtail art and music programs. And test scores showed horrific pupil failures: in five south Phoenix districts, the average test scores were in the 24th percentile.

Although the Republican majority refused to act on Governor Jane Hull's proposal to increase funding, a bipartisan coalition, including Phoenix legislators Sue Gerard and Chris Cummiskey, managed to pass the proposal and refer it to the voters. Unlike the 1990 plan, this proposition won endorsements from all of the educational organizations and institutions, and from the major business organizations. The issue had come full circle: key groups and a majority of the population again considered education crucial for the economic health of the valley and the state. Despite competition from other propositions which also raised taxes, the measure passed the state with 53.5 percent and with 56.2 percent in Maricopa County.

To Grow? or How to Grow?

If education forced Phoenicians to work with other communities, the basic question of growth required even more regional awareness. Some residents championed the city's rank as 6th largest city, and saw the Valley's growing and more diverse population as a sign of progress. To them, this growth represented fulfillment of the dream first contemplated in the 1940s. But for others, the dream was becoming a nightmare. Growth was destroying Phoenix's sense of community; sprawl and low-density housing were consuming the surrounding desert; and the resulting air pollution and traffic snarls were polluting the air and endangering health. By the 1970s some natives spoke sadly about the demise of small-city lifestyle and the integrated social networks they had valued so highly — what Jack Pfister termed a "native's remorse." The economic crisis of the late 1980s prompted discussions about unplanned sprawl, real estate speculation and the danger of "becoming another L.A." To some, growth had transformed the Valley that had originally attracted them into the type of place they had fled.

"When we came, the Valley was an Eden," wrote western novelist Glendon Swarthout in 1991. "There was ample room, a

Viewing Phoenix from the Squaw Peak summit
City of Phoenix, Photo by Bob Rink

population which fit, air as clean as a mirror, and a lovely lifestyle. Then for 30 years we let the businessmen and politicians who ran the Valley lead us down the garden path of unplanned growth. Crime, traffic, heat, air pollution, bankruptcies, unemployment, corruption — the quality of our lives is pathetically diminished and what have we been given as compensation? Professional sports."

After the economy rebounded, the pace of growth accelerated and these criticisms were voiced more widely. In 1995 Terry Goddard suggested, "If you are a recreational bulldozer driver or enjoy the tangy smell of exhaust fumes in the morning, times are great in Phoenix," but that most people felt "the qualities that brought us or kept us here are vanishing." Opinion polls taken in the late 1990s proved the accuracy of Goddard's assessment: three-fourths of the Valley residents thought it was growing too fast; half would leave if they had a chance. By the 1990s, then, the Valley became an area of competing visions — of land use, of lifestyles and of the future.

(Both photos) Phoenix's metropolis status has brought events as various as Pope John Paul II's 1987 visit, Grand Prix auto racing (1991), and the 2001 World Series (opposite page) *City of Phoenix, Photos by Bob Rink*

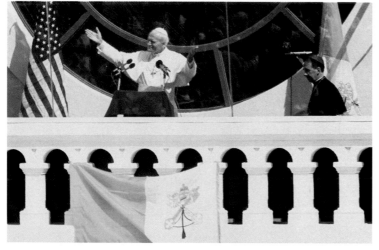

Desires to find solutions grew apace. Following major newspaper discussions, the Morrison Institute at Arizona State University began an annual series evaluating growth and public opinion. In 1995 the Greater Phoenix Economic Council began holding public summits and polling Valley leaders, and in combination with a variety of Valley groups in 1996 it created the Greater Phoenix Quality of Life Stewardship Council. While Valley business leaders and groups were talking, other citizens associated with a wide range of conservation, environmental and public interest groups began designing legislation to control, direct and perhaps even restrict growth. A draft of this Citizens Growth Management Initiative (CGMI) began circulating in 1997 with the aim of placing it on the fall 1998 ballot. Instead, several things happened.

Governor Hull had been working on her own proposal dealing with growth, but she had received little support from Republican legislators and opposition from the GOP's legislative leaders. These Valley conservatives had generally opposed any interference with growth or private property. However, as Rob Melnick of the Morrison Institute wrote, "the fear that the citizens initiative could pass into law — and there is simply no other way to put it — helped many business and political leaders in the state recognize that the debate over growth had changed significantly," and lawmakers enacted a version of the governor's Growing Smarter (GS) plan in May. This measure required local governments to develop 10-year plans dealing with the environment, open space and transportation; mandated public participation to approve or amend the plan; required developers to pay their "fair share" of costs for public services; and encouraged building in vacant inner land, rather than fringe areas. It also sought voter approval to spend $20 million annually for 11 years to purchase state trust lands for conservation purposes. However, it also prohibited any mandatory state plans or growth boundaries, and it promised not to spend money on open space if the CGMI passed.

Ironically, CGMI was not even on the 1998 ballot. That June, organizers realized they had too little time and money to get enough signatures, so they decided to wait for the 2000 election. Thus, the passage of the governor's GS plan and funding for purchasing land were only preliminaries to the main bout. Following the 1998 election, Governor Hull appointed a commission to examine possible growth-management tools, hoping to amend GS in ways that would head off CGMI.

The Arizona Diamondbacks are shown here celebrating their 2001 World Series victory.
Arizona Diamondbacks Photo by Barry Gossage

Efforts at compromise won over some supporters, most notably former Arizona Attorney General Grant Woods, but failed to convince the larger group. A three-day special session of the legislature enacted a lengthy Growing Smarter Plus which changed the original measure by restricting cities' annexation powers; allowing cities to designate growth areas and non-growth areas where they could deny services; allowing counties to charge impact fees; and expanding voters' control of changes to plans. In addition, the legislature placed on the ballot constitutional amendments allowing the sale for preservation of three percent of the state trust land and the exchange of state trust lands for other public lands.

This set the stage for a contentious battle between these measures and the revived CGMI in the fall 2000 election. At stake were two separate but related issues: controlling sprawl and maintaining open space. In contrast to GS, the citizens' initiative wanted local governments to establish firmer growth boundaries and developers to pay the full costs of expansion. The open space issue was complicated less by opposition to preserving some desert and mountain areas, and mainly because much of the land at issue (particularly in northern and western parts of the Valley)

was state trust land — public lands that must be leased or sold to fund public schools. Besides the problem of getting an adequate price for such land, CGMI supporters claimed that three percent was an inadequate amount of land to protect, while GS proponents emphasized that it amounted to roughly 300,000 acres.

Initially, voters strongly favored both the CGMI and the state lands proposals, with CGMI support at about 70 percent in the late summer. However, support began to drop as opponents launched a furious and expensive attack, with glossy mailings and television ads warning that it was unfair and would bring economic disaster. Although significantly outgunned, CGMI supporters defended their proposal and denounced the lands proposal as a fraud, claiming that three percent would actually be the limit of public land for open space. Down to the day of the election, both proposals were hotly contested. The lands measure narrowly lost, but the CGMI failed by a two-to-one margin. Despite this defeat, the struggle had substantially changed public attitudes and led to increased governmental controls over urban growth. Equally clear is that this was only part of a continuing battle over the future shape and character of the Valley.

Gift Bearers I by Philip C. Curtis
Philip C. Curtis Trust

Living in the Valley
Tradition, Arts and Sports

Making sense of culture is a lot like understanding real estate: much of it involves location. Phoenix is situated in the Sonoran Desert, in the Salt River Valley, and its culture always reflects that, to some extent, whether it is the city's Western heritage or more modern comparison to other desert cities around the world. From architecture to landscape to plants, Phoenicians have grappled with their environment, trying to understand it — and on some occasions, trying to ignore it.

chapter four

Defining the Place

Beginning as an agricultural settlement in a desert area, Phoenix grew up as a "Western" town, in a land of horses and cattle, cowboys and Indians, Mexicans and Chinese, outlaws and lawmen. While a 1940s *Arizona Highways* author could joke about visitors learning that Phoenix included more than those traditional images, a 1980 children's book, *Gila Monsters Meet You at the Airport,* reflected the continuing power of those images.

Like all places, then, Phoenix has been marked and defined, to an extent, by its physical environment and its history. But while embracing the city's Western, frontier past and its desert surroundings, Phoenicians have also sought to bring about change. Some have seen the physical environment as at least partly malleable — if not convertible to a tropical paradise, then to an oasis or at least a grassy Midwestern yard. Moreover, the climate outside of the roasting summertime has encouraged an enjoyment of the outdoors — as participant and spectator.

Other residents have tried to foster culture brought from elsewhere — a regional or ethnic culture, or a "higher culture" in music, art and theater. Such efforts are a standard part of the American experience: all immigrants have brought culture with them and the drive to bring high culture, or "civilization," has been a constant theme in America's westward movement.

The combination of physical and historical environments, and the blended impulses to preserve and transform them, provided Phoenicians with the basic elements of self-definition up to the 1940s. But the tremendous influx of people starting with the war years changed that balance. The ongoing migration from other areas brought in people unfamiliar with Phoenix and holding competing notions of its future. Was Phoenix a "Western" town? Or was it a desert city, like Albuquerque or Tucson? Or was it simply an extension of Southern California? How should Phoenicians relate to the rest of the country in style, in dress, in values?

Spring in the desert
Arizona Office of Tourism, Photo by Alan Benoit

Beginning in the late 1940s the city focused on fitting in with the nation, on being "modern." In housing, consumer culture, city amenities, automobiles and shopping malls Phoenix portrayed itself as largely indistinguishable from the rest of the country. This perspective especially reflected the strongly-held views of the Chamber of Commerce and charter government folks, who focused on attracting businesses and immigrants. The promotional view of Phoenix also emphasized the active, outdoor lifestyle which the city's climate and environs encouraged. This included backyard swimming pools, outdoor sports like golf and tennis, and activities further afield like boating, hunting, fishing, camping and skiing.

At the same time, Western and desert aspects of the city's culture did not disappear. Advertising, entertainment and tourism were only several of the venues where the more traditional elements of valley life were visible. Efforts to cultivate fine arts in the desert   music, theater and art — represent an even more deliberate effort to transform the valley's culture. The city elite did not want Phoenix to be considered a "hick town," and they recognized that culture and education were signs of urban status. They also understood these were important attractions for many persons considering a move to the Valley, and that improving them would advance the city's economy. Besides this functional,

Mesa Chamber of Commerce, Photo by Robert Silberblatt

Phoenix urban cowboy, c. 1985
City of Phoenix, Photo by Don Stevenson

Annual Heard Museum
Guild Indian Fair & Market
Heard Museum

booster approach, some of the elite plus others in society labored from a love of the arts, and some were themselves amateur artists.

By the 1970s the impact of population and size began to show. Both the elite and the average citizens sensed a loss of community resulting from rapid population turnover, the construction of large subdivisions and the physical spread of the city. Western culture seemed less connected with sprawling suburbs, and the desert grew more distant and time-consuming to reach. One response to the challenges of cultural loss was to reaffirm the importance of the Sonoran Desert environment. A second involved building community through neighborhood

Phoenix Municipal
Stadium and Legend City
(background), 1964
*Arizona Historical Society-
Central Arizona Division*

associations. Identification with a revived downtown provided yet another alternative, as Phoenicians (like residents of Tempe and Scottsdale, too) perceived that transformation as a sign of community vitality, and increasingly used the various opportunities for relaxation and education.

Sports constitute a final form of community identification and culture, creating strong loyalties but also prompting major protest. Arizona's lifestyle and Valley culture included sport activities, but it was spectator sports that increasingly fostered identification and conflict. Although Arizonans never developed a style quite like "Hoosier Hysteria," high school athletics traditionally attracted public attention and substantial audiences. By the 1960s ASU teams in various sports received national coverage and had many devoted fans. But professional sports held far greater significance for more people. Beginning with minor league teams, Phoenix finally attracted its first major league team in 1968. During the next three decades, interest in acquiring teams in additional sports grew rapidly and for numerous reasons. What makes this manifestly a public issue, rather than only a private cultural matter, is the debates over

providing public facilities, for this not only involves questions of proper public expenditures, it also competed with other possible expenditures — for cultural institutions, for building urban infrastructure, or for schools.

Living in the West

Scottsdale might have claimed to be "The West's Most Western Town," but all Valley towns shared in that general culture — although not the wooden, "cowtown" architecture of Scottsdale's old downtown. A calendar of Valley activities in the 1950s noted, "Some of the outstanding events are the big Arizona State Fair, November; the biweekly Desert Sun Ranchers Rodeos in Wickenburg; weekly travelcades by the Spanish-attired Dons club, topped by the annual search for the Lost Dutchman Gold Mine in the Superstition Mountains; the Wickenburg Gold Rush Days, January;… the Phoenix Jaycees World Championship Rodeo in March," and finally "dances like the Cattle Rustlers Ball and the Valley of the Sun Square Dance Festival and Fiddlers Jamboree." Although they faced increasing competition, events like these continued during the following years.

Western clothing had a more limited life span. Although jeans were already a national style, local clothing manufacturers produced other, Western-style items for a while longer. By the 1990s some stores continued to sell these items, but most restricted their marketing to boots, belts and bolo ties. Finally, as late as the 1960s dining in Phoenix best displayed the city's Western origins. Much like Model T buyers in the 1920s who could choose any color as long as it was black, you could order any meal you wanted in Phoenix as long as it was steak (or chili). Even in the *Pointe West* magazine, the champion of cosmopolitanism in the Valley, steak houses comprised nearly half of the restaurant listings, many others were "American," with just a smattering of other specialties (mainly Italian).

Jackie Cooper rides "Bungalon," Phoenix Rodeo 1942

Arizona Historical Foundation

While a distinctive Western architecture and style were waning through most of the Valley beginning in the 1960s, several projects in this era attempted to build on — and even profit from — Western themes. Because they required substantial space, they were built on the periphery of Phoenix, but it was the city's population they targeted. Legend City, an amusement park with an "Old West" theme, opened for business in 1963. Covering 59 acres south of Papago Park, it offered a range of amusements but went bankrupt in 1966. Bought by the U-Haul company and re-opened in 1969, it struggled until closing again in 1976. Reopened once more in 1977, the park offered such Western fare as a Western Stunt Show, a Mexican Village and a ferry ride on the *Legend City Queen*. Despite being part of the Phoenix Activity Complex, which included the zoo and Pueblo Grande Museum, and developing an identification with Wallace and Ladmo, the popular stars of a local children's television program, *Legend City* submerged for a third and final time in 1982. Some contended that the park's limited hours doomed it, but others said the determining factor was the periodic stench wafting from the nearby Phoenix Stockyards, an authentic Western "attraction."

A second Western enterprise, the Wild West "town" of Rawhide, opened in 1971. Located in a desert area well north of Scottsdale city limits (at the time), it was built to resemble an 1880s western town. Organized around numerous stores, it featured several activities — a High Noon shootout and gold panning — and food. Over the years it expanded the stores,

increased the activities, and added a small museum and a Native American Village. By the end of the 1990s it received over 750,000 visitors annually, and its success over 30 years reflects a blend of living museum, theme park, commerce and concessions. But like much of the old West, Rawhide now is jeopardized by the continuing expansion of Scottsdale's subdivisions.

Roughly 10 miles further north another effort suffered yet another fate of many original Western towns. In the 1950s Herman King, a banker from central Illinois, began vacationing in Arizona and dreaming about the Old West. When King retired to Cave Creek in 1971 he began building a town intended to reflect the 1870s. He laid out 20 buildings and planned to fill them with antiques which he and his wife had collected over many years. King died unexpectedly in February 1972, but his wife and daughter pressed ahead. Frontier Town opened eight months later, with full stores and numerous weekend activities, but Dorothy King's deteriorating health prevented her from managing the town effectively. By 1980 only four stores were open full time, and King's daughter decided to sell. She sold some properties, including the Silver Spur Restaurant (renamed the Satisfied Frog), but ultimately kept the stores, remodeling them into a shopping center. While some of the original theme remained, the overall impact had changed.

A final example of the continuing fascination with Western themes is Pioneer Arizona Living History Museum, for which planning began in 1956. Unlike the three commercial enterprises, Pioneer Arizona is nonprofit, and unlike either Frontier Town or Rawhide, it is composed of authentic buildings moved from various places in the state to a site north of Phoenix along I-17. The complexities of the project kept the museum from opening

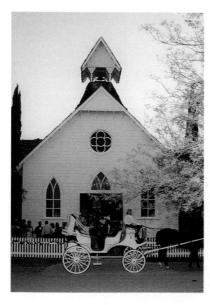

until 1969, but it grew steadily and by 2000 included 28 structures. It resembled the other two "towns" by using a time theme (focusing on the 1858-1912 territorial period), but it differed by including the full range of town structures — public buildings (a jail and a school house), commercial buildings (a bank) and different styles of private residences.

Highlighting Tradition

An appreciation of Valley traditions has blossomed during recent decades. By the 1970s several communities had organized historical societies, and they proliferated rapidly during that decade, including the founding of the Phoenix Historical Society. By the 1990s most cities had museums (typically within a larger public building), with the highlight being the new Phoenix Museum of History (1996). The city also owned the Pueblo Grande park and museum, first acquired in the 1920s and 1930s and expanded after 1968, which reflected the continuing fascination with the Valley's prehistory. The Arizona Historical Society opened its Central Division building in 1989, which included substantial museum space. Numerous other museums also opened which dealt with special historical topics in the Valley's history: the Phoenix police, the Salt River Project, telephones, railroads, military and the Arizona History Room of First National Bank (now Wells Fargo). The initial focus of many of these museums, like the constructed towns, was in the territorial period, yet increasingly they began to address more recent topics.

In Phoenix itself, the emphasis on new and "modern," so prominent as the city first grew after the war, began competing by the 1970s with an interest in older structures. Encouraged by the establishment of Heritage Square, the collection of historic houses relocated to downtown, interest in preserving buildings and neighborhoods also grew because of various renovation and redevelopment projects in the city. The most significant impetus was the demolition of houses in the path of the in-town Papago Freeway. Residents of the affected neighborhood organized the Roosevelt Action Association, which sponsored a survey of

properties and resulted in sections of the area being placed on the National Register of Historic Places. The Encanto Citizens Association and other groups organized soon thereafter. Responding to the growing interest, in 1985 the city created the Historic Preservation office and began an ambitious program. In 1989 voters passed a Historic Preservation Bond Fund, providing $15 million for preservation. In 1990 Arizona voters created the Arizona Heritage Fund, allocating lottery funds to preserve natural and cultural resources, with $1.7 million annual for historic preservation. By 2000 the *Phoenix Register* included nearly 5,000 historic structures, mostly individual homes in 22 districts, but also including refurbished public buildings like the Orpheum Theater.

The Valley has been home to a rich variety of ethnic and racial groups whose history and culture are displayed in numerous institutions and events. The Chinese, for example, first arrived in Phoenix in 1872, and like many immigrants, established restaurants and grocery stores catering to their tastes. The growing popularity of these businesses among non-Chinese, plus the variety of Chinese volunteer and cultural institutions have fostered a visible Chinese presence. Highlighting this are Chinese Week, a week-long celebration in Phoenix of Chinese culture, and construction of the Chinese Cultural Center, a "modern Chinatown," with gardens, pagodas, traditional architecture and commercial businesses. Like Chinese culture, Greek culture has been associated with food and restaurants. It has an additional institutional base in the Greek Orthodox Church, which sustains culture in ways such as holding language classes. An annual Greek festival highlights the food, music and dancing. When Phoenix first began its Hello Phoenix! ethnic festival in 1978, it included representatives from 36 groups.

African American and Hispanic cultures have created institutions to present information on their traditions in the Valley. In 1993 the George Washington Carver Museum and Cultural Center began in the building which formerly housed the segregated high school for African Americans. Headed by

The Pueblo Grande Museum features a prehistoric Hohokam archaeological site that is more than 1,000 years old. *City of Phoenix, Photo by Bob Rink*

Heard Museum, described by *USA Today* as "the nation's most prestigious private Indian arts center." Opened in 1929 on the grounds of the Dwight and Maie Heard estate to house their collection of Native American materials, the original purposes included archaeology plus the collection and preservation of "primitive art." Expanding the structure four times between 1958 and 1999 to accommodate its substantial and growing collection of objects, pictures and archival materials, the Museum changed even more during that time in its purposes and mission. Operating until Maie's death in 1951 as largely a private, personal gallery with limited public access, during the 1950s the Museum established regular hours, created a Guild of volunteers who conducted tours, opened a bookstore and museum shop and began an Indian Fair and Market.

More profound changes in the Museum began in the late 1960s when it started presenting Native cultures as "present and changing," rather than past and "primitive." During the next decades, as the Museum acquired substantial collections including jewelry, ceramics, textiles and basketry from the Fred Harvey Company and from traders, it increasingly addressed itself to the broader Phoenix community and accepted a larger educational role. Most importantly, in 1990 the Heard defined its mission as not only presenting and interpreting objects, but also "to help those cultures sustain themselves." The direction of the Indian Fair and Market passed more to those

former City Councilman Calvin Goode, it holds archival materials and photographs and also houses an art gallery. Chicanos por la Causa established Museo Chicano in the early 1990s as a museum and cultural center presenting diverse Latino cultures. Included in a 1994 Ford Foundation program dealing with arts and community development, it was also included in the city's 2001 bond program. Unlike most of the historical museums, Museo Chicano emphasizes the link between present and past, an important connection in a society where the Mexican historical holiday, Cinco de Mayo has become a common day of festivities.

By far the most prominent organization dealing with the culture and traditions of a minority is the

Hispanic citizens make up a third of the state's population and their culture is an influential part of the Phoenix lifestyle.

Scottsdale Chamber of Commerce, Photo by Paul Markow

creating the material, and exhibits critique historical institutions like the boarding schools.

Explaining Life in the Desert

One of the Heard's interesting programs, begun in 1987, is a partnership in Desert Connections, with the Phoenix Zoo and the Desert Botanical Gardens, which promotes conservation and the protection of desert plants and animals. Both organizations, but especially the latter, have played major roles in educating the public about the plants of the Sonoran region. The Desert Botanical Garden began during the 1930s on land in the state's Papago Park (formerly a national monument but lost the designation to land in Tucson after the Papago saguaro population declined). Reopening after the war, the first annual cactus sale in 1948 drew 18,000 people, and crowds continued to grow over the years. When Phoenix bought the park from the state, it leased 145 acres to the Garden, which built a visitor center. By the mid-1970s, with a membership of nearly 1,400 and a paid staff of 14, the Garden began expanding its activities. Under the direction of Rodney Engard, in 1977 it created a docent program to provide an interpretive program for visitors and in 1978 it began Luminaria Night, which

became a highly popular annual program. Deciding to sell only nursery-propagated plants, in 1978 the Garden built a propagation greenhouse. This position related to the Garden's growing interest in public education: in 1976 it produced pamphlets explaining desert gardening and in 1977 in conjunction with the Salt River Project, it sponsored an annual contest to give public recognition to landscaping which employed drought-resistant plants.

After 1980 the Garden expanded its efforts in ecological and environmental education, offering workshops and field trips for schools; in 1984 the demonstration desert garden opened. The Garden created an interpretive master plan in the 1980s, building looped trails, and the Plants and People of the Sonoran Desert Trail, completed in 1988, became a model ethnobotanical exhibit. In 1993, working in conjunction with five other agencies, the Garden built the Desert House, to study conservation.

As its goals expanded, so too did the Garden's financial needs, which it met from both public and private sources. In 1983 it began receiving money from COMPAS, the cooperative fundraiser for the Art Museum, Zoo Symphony and Heard Museum; and in 1999 it began a major capital campaign. In 1992 it received a National Science Foundation grant for its interpretive services, and in 1988 voters endorsed $1 million for improving the physical facilities. By 2000 it had over 9,000 members, received over 250,000 visitors annually and considerably increased the awareness of Phoenicians about the character, beauty and limitations of the desert environment in which they lived.

Just as the Desert Botanical Garden has become a public champion of the desert environment, so too has the Phoenix Zoo evolved into an institution of "ecosystem exhibition, education, and conservation." At its beginnings in the early 1960s, the Zoo represented an effort to bring outside culture to Phoenix. Some supporters considered zoos a mark of "substantial" cities, while others felt that, like museums, they exposed visitors to interesting things from elsewhere in the world. Robert Maytag, heir to the appliance fortune, helped start the Arizona Zoological Society with his efforts, vision and $100,000. Tragically he died before its opening in 1962. The Zoo began as a completely private operation, although the city provided the land. This created some public sense of connection and responsibility, but it also put the Zoo's existence in doubt for the first several years. Only major contributions by Eugene Pulliam and the Maytags enabled it to survive past 1964.

The Zoo's initial design set pie-shaped areas for each continent. This ambitious and categorical approach to organizing displays was paired with a style that occasionally crossed into other genres of treating animals. The Children's Zoo was the first section completed, "part barnyard and part fantasyland." Chuck the Chimp became a public figure for his art and was brought out to meet people and mug for cameras. Finally, in 1968 the zoo hired an animal trainer to develop shows that might increase attendance. The 1970s marked a transition period for the Zoo. A new design used habitats instead of continents because it was cheaper, but it also had the advantage of focusing on the animals rather than abstract categories of where they lived. The zoo still collected diverse animals from different areas of the world, but the occasional circus-like atmosphere disappeared. Attendance exceeded 600,000 by 1980 and membership rose to over 10,000, but revenue from these sources and from concessions could only pay the operating expenses; any expansion required a private donation.

The Zoo shifted its goals considerably during the 1980s and 1990s, which reflected national trends among zoos and a

Mesa Southwest Museum
Mesa Convention & Visitors Bureau

growing ecological consciousness. The Zoo remained a place for housing various types of animals, but it defined its role as being an "advocate for the natural world." It noted that although "historically zoos have represented animals as creatures separate from plants, landscapes, and human influences," the three were actually mutually dependent. Thus, beginning in the late 1980s the Zoo worked to protect endangered species elsewhere in the world and in Arizona, including the Mexican wolf, the thick-billed parrot and the black-footed ferret. (It had earlier helped preserve the Arabian oryx.) Besides cooperating with the Heard and the Desert Botanical Garden in Desert Connections, it partnered with SRP to sponsor Clean Air Day, and in 1999 it began an Arizona Wildlands project to increase desert awareness. More than any organization in the Valley the Zoo has engaged in education, creating a wide variety of programs, from those that reach the average visitor

(Far left)
Ruby the elephant gained national fame as the Zoo's "artist in residence" in the 1980s. The *Smithsonian* magazine covered her story, and her paintings brought in revenue for the Zoo.
*Phoenix Zoo,
Photo by Dick George*

A painting by Phoenix Zoo elephant artist, Ruby.
Phoenix Zoo

(the interpretive Safari Train rides) to teacher education to numerous children's programs like Zoo Camp and Night Camp. What began as an effort to bring the world to people in ordered cages, changed into an active agency attempting to bring people to their world and to explain how it worked.

"High Culture" and the Arts

Today, the term "culture" can mean many different things, in Phoenix or elsewhere. Places can foster a culture, in the case of Phoenix, a desert culture. "Popular culture" refers to a people's culture — the people of a region (like the Southwest or the South, for example), or people of ethnic or racial groups. Another common term, "mass culture," represents something different — a national (or international), mass-produced and mass-marketed, commercialized set of products and the cultural forms they engender. Phoenix is, of course, plugged in to the proliferation of Best Western Motels and Holiday Inns, to McDonalds and other fast food restaurants, to chain stores like Sears, JCPenny, Osco, Target, Home Depot, Best Buy, and Safeway, and to brand name products from Amana to Zippo. And Phoenix also hears the same country or rock music (albeit with different garage bands getting their "start"), and sees the same television or movies (rented from Blockbuster). Telling this story would be telling the story of America — or vice versa — and is best done elsewhere.

Of course, mass culture had greater effect by the 1980s than in the 1950s, and some local institutions

had more staying power. Radio and television exerted major influence from their beginnings. Two radio stations began in 1922 — KTAR and KOY — connecting the Valley to the outside world. And after broadcasting for 20 years Howard Pyle was elected governor (in 1950) and Jack Williams went first to city council and mayor and then to governor (in 1966). KPHO became the Valley's first television station, but by 1957 three more had started, giving Phoenix one more than many larger cities. Viewer options expanded further in 1961, when ASU began the public television station KAET. Local programming varied in importance for these stations, but one program of great longevity and appeal was "The Wallace & Ladmo Show." Produced by the independent station KPHO, it ran from 1954 to 1989, the longest-running daily television show in U.S. history.

While "culture" means different things in contemporary society, Phoenicians in the 1940s and 1950s (like those before them) had no doubt what the term meant — the "high culture" of theater, art and classical music. This clarity reflected America's cultural origins and westward movement, as migrants had imported pianos, started local groups, and invited performing artists because of their own interests and, sometimes, talents. But boosterism played an equally important role: the city's early leaders recognized that urban status required more than tall buildings or a burgeoning economy. Mayor Sam Mardian noted in the 1970s that "any city, if it amounts to anything, has to develop culturally." Furthermore, boosters understood that fine arts could greatly effect the Valley's economic future, since the economic leaders and workforce they wished to attract were educated, middle- and upper-middle class persons who generally supported the arts. A key part of developing the arts was adequate facilities, but continuing support provided the greatest challenge.

Organized theater has the longest history of the Valley fine arts, beginning in the 1920s with Phoenix Little Theatre (PLT). From 1924 to 1951 this amateur group presented six to eight plays a year in a renovated stable on the Heard property at Central and McDowell. The city's 1949 bonds funded a new 394-seat facility on those grounds as part of a new Phoenix Civic Center, and the troupe prospered during the 1950s, reaching 1,400 subscriptions in 1959. The Arizona Repertory Theatre, a professional group which started around 1960, joined PLT and the Phoenix Children's Theatre in 1965 to form the Phoenix Theatre Center, which required financial help from the city to expand the PLT facility. But the Repertory group soon quit, complaining of financial and scheduling problems, and then folded. Construction disasters on the Children's Theatre facility prompted their departure in 1967, leaving PLT with a crushing debt. To relieve that burden they scheduled mostly comedies, which did help their finances but hurt their reputation. In the 1980s they came upon a successful scheduling formula: opening with a musical, emphasizing comedies and including one or two dramas. In the early 1990s the group changed its name to the Phoenix Theatre, reflecting its shift from community to professional status.

Professional theater in Phoenix advanced considerably after 1980. The Arizona Theatre Company, which started in Tucson during the 1960s, first performed in Phoenix in 1978, and it began offering a full season in both cities in 1983.

The Phoenix Little Theatre, founded in 1924, is the Valley's oldest theater company. This is the cast of *Romeo & Juliet*, 1960. *Arizona Historical Society-Central Arizona Division*

Its opportunities blossomed with the opening of the impressive Herberger Theater Center in 1989, for ATC was the main tenant of the larger theater. In dealing with this shift to a larger stage, the company benefited from a major five-year grant from National Arts Stabilization given in 1992. A second professional company, Actor's Theatre of Phoenix, began in 1986. After several years in a small renovated theater, they became the primary user of the Herberger's second stage in 1989. Unfortunately, this created a serious financial burden; attempting to solve this it by presenting small-cast plays created some dissension within the company. Reorganization in the mid-1990s, aided substantially by a National Arts Stabilization grant, put the company in a much more solid position by 2000. The array of

quality live theater during the 1990s also included performances of the Southwest Shakespeare Company (in Mesa), several alternative theater troupes, two ethnic companies — El Teatro Bravo! and the Black Theatre Troupe — a variety of suburban community theater companies, as well as productions by ASU, in all a vast increase over several decades. The construction of impressive, new facilities — the Herberger and ASU's Galvin Playhouse — plus the remodeling of older facilities like Gammage Auditorium, the PLT theater and the Orpheum aided this proliferation, as well as offering attractive locales for touring companies.

The Herberger Theater Center, opened in 1989, is the Downtown Phoenix home to the Arizona Theater Company, the Actors Theatre of Phoenix, and ChildsPlay as well as host to a wide variety of concerts and events. *City of Phoenix, Photo by Bob Rink*

Art

The early Phoenix leadership generally appreciated and assisted live theater in the Valley, but art and music fired their enthusiasm. They donated more money and raised funds through COMPAS, many served on organization boards, and they arranged greater public support from the city. This reflected the strong personal interests of some, but for others it represented a narrower sense of what would most benefit Phoenix. The Phoenix Art Museum had its origins in the Federal Art Center during the 1930s, which provided employment for local artists, and the Phoenix Fine Arts Association which provided art classes to the public. The museum officially opened in 1949, in a small building near the Civic Center, but it took another decade before it achieved sunstantial form. And as later president

The Phoenix Art Museum's 1999 expansion integrates art and architecture with the southwestern landscape, accommodating larger traveling exhibitions, an expanding collection and a growing arts audience.

City of Phoenix, Photo by Bob Rink

Sam Applewhite noted, "Of course, the man who put the Phoenix Art Museum over was Walter Bimson."

The city's leading banker and involved with much of the economic development in this era, Bimson had a longstanding interest in art. His brother Carl recalled that as a boy in Colorado Walter was "always crazy about art." He took a course in show card lettering, he did air brushing, wood burning and pen drawings. He started college in journalism, wanting to be a cartoonist, and applied for a job at the *Denver Post*. He then switched to architecture, but financial problems forced him to leave school and work for a bank. While doing that he took correspondence courses, which pulled him to Chicago and a career in banking. Throughout his life Bimson collected art and during the 1950s he organized city leaders to support the museum. Rhes Corneilius, of Phoenix Title company, served on the museum board and admitted "I had no interest in art at that time — I just did it as a civic venture, of course, and because somebody asked me to be on the Board." Bimson's efforts succeeded in raising private funds for a building, constructed in 1959, and for an addition six years later. His arguments for the institution's economic importance also appear in the views of Mayor Sam Mardian, who favored city financial aid for expanding the building although he had no particular interest in art, "just the overall interest in knowing that a community needs cultural activities to attract the city the type of people that Phoenix seemed to be attracting — in electronics."

A crucial part of the museum's success was obtaining art donations. Bimson provided some of his own pieces and persuaded others to do the same. The Musuem's director, Forest M. Hinkhouse, successfully collected art works in the Valley and in the East, obtaining an Oriental collection, for example, from Henry and Clare Luce. Perhaps the most notable gifts came from Lewis Ruskin, the founder of a Chicago pharmaceutical chain who moved to the Valley in 1955. In 1958 he gave the Museum seven Renaissance and Baroque paintings

This Old House — By Reg Manning, Arizona Republic Staff Artist

ISN'T THAT PICTURE TOO DISREPUTABLE TO DISPLAY IN OUR PHOENIX ART CENTER?

THAT'S A PICTURE OF OUR PRESENT ART CENTER

worth $320,000; the next year he gave 24 paintings worth $2.5 million. The museum's collection matured over the years, totaling over 15,000 works by the 1990s and prompting an expansion in 1996 which doubled the museum's size. The 2001 bond election provided funding for additional gallery space. Western art was not neglected, and the annual show of cowboy art remained quite popular, but this comprises only one of nine general categories of the museum's holdings, which include a fine collection of Asian works.

Besides promoting the museum, Bimson and others sought to encourage local artists. Bimson provided a $500 prize offered annually at the State Fair to local artists; he bought many of the prize-winning pieces and displayed them at the Valley National Bank. The most substantial and successful effort to help a local artist involved Philip Curtis, who had first come to Phoenix 1936-1939 to direct the New Deal's federal Art Center. Returning after the war, Curtis began developing a national reputation, but as Ruskin discovered in 1961, Curtis was distracted from painting by the need to sell his art. Working with nine other investors (including Bimson and Kax Herberger), Ruskin created the Philip Curtis Trust: a $25,000 fund to support the artist for three years, with repayment from the sale of paintings. The investment was a good one, as the artist's production and reputation increased, and the investors were repaid. In 1982,

Reg Manning, the *Arizona Republic*, April 28, 1957
The Reg Manning Collection, Arizona Collection, Arizona State University Libraries

Lewis Ruskin
(left of fireplace) and members of the "Curtis Trust" donated art and led the crusade to establish an art museum in Phoenix.
Philip C. Curtis Trust

recognizing the extent of Curtis's reputation, the Art Museum created a Curtis study center, including some of his paintings and archival materials.

Private support provided the primary basis for the development of art in the Valley, but public investment — in facilities like the museum and in activities beyond that — also proved crucial. In 1985 the Phoenix City Council established the Phoenix Arts Commission to encourage the arts through grants, education and public advocacy. In 1986 the city committed to devote one percent of all construction project costs to art (following a program begun in Glendale in 1983). Evident in numerous areas, perhaps most visibly along the Squaw Peak Freeway, the program prompted additional projects in other Valley communities, particularly Scottsdale and Tempe. In 2000, after 50 years of advocacy and development, the Valley had become a very different place for art. It was home to numerous artists (the state included an estimated 10,000), encouraged by a substantial number of galleries in Scottsdale, a fine art program and Museum at ASU and an increasing number of museums throughout the Valley.

Music

Classical music experienced a more turbulent history during these decades, although it too reached a quality unanticipated in 1940. The audience for this music developed from many sources and influences — presentations in schools and radio, for example, and individuals participating in musical groups or efforts — but listening to live, professional performances did much to create a love of music. In this regard, the efforts of Jessie Linde bore extraordinary fruit. A tireless booking agent and promoter, Mrs. Linde brought artists to the Valley, educated the audience in etiquette, and helped build support for local performances and new facilities.

The Musicians Club of Phoenix constituted the pioneering organization for musical performance by Phoenicians, and Blanche Korrick was one of the most influential and enthusiastic supporters. A singer trained in Chicago and New York, she had performed on the Chatauqua circuit before marrying department store owner Charles Korrick. Arriving in Phoenix in 1920 she was appalled: "Nothing but cards and drinking. No music, no culture of any kind." But she stayed, joined the Musicians Club, and over the years held many of its recitals in her home; for several years she hosted radio broadcasts of the performances. Building on this interest, in 1947 she and other influential music-lovers organized the Phoenix Symphony Association — she served as president of the fund-raising Symphony Guild — and hired John Barnett, the assistant conductor of the Los Angeles Symphony.

Barnett conducted the first concert in November 1947, bringing fill-in players from Los Angeles. For two years he

continued on page 122

2001-2002 Phoenix Symphony Orchestra
Phoenix Symphony

■The plaque reads "Memorial to Mrs. Archer E. Linde, talented and tireless impresario who… gave this community cultural advantages it otherwise would not have been privileged to enjoy. For at least 15 years before death ended her career in 1965, she never failed, in each public appearance, to make a strong appeal for an adequate civic concert hall." Placed in Symphony Hall as an alternative to the suggestion from many that the hall be named for her, the plaque honors a woman who was a cultural fixture for three decades and whom actor Charles Laughton called "the toughest and sweetest gal in Phoenix."

After searching for medical help from the Mayo Clinic and elsewhere, Jessie Linde came to Phoenix in 1920 with her mother and two-year-old daughter, looking desperately for relief from crippling arthritis. Although never "cured," she found the desert heat provided great improvement. Her husband Archer saw the difference and left Chicago to work as an accountant for A. J. Bayless Markets. Before her marriage Jessie had studied voice at the St. Louis Conservatory of Music — and in Phoenix she joined the Musicians Club. She assisted Cordelia Hulburd (also her piano teacher) with bookkeeping for the Club's Musical Events series, which brought performers to the Valley. The economic collapse of the 1930s put the series $10,000 in debt. Eventually a major booking agency paid the debt and included Phoenix in its national Community Concerts series. At the suggestion of several agents and after some initial hesitation, Mrs. Linde began her own booking agency in 1936 and continued the Mrs. Linde Series and the Linde Box Office for nearly 30 years.

A key part of her success was judging what Phoenix would want to hear — although since the season lasted from November to March, she also considered the tastes of winter visitors. She only paid the artists after they performed, but she guaranteed their fee, so if she guessed wrong her husband paid the difference. (She joked that she had several times lost her husband's shirt.) She corresponded with agents and visited them in New York and Los Angeles. She took a personal interest in the artists, and she brought many of them into her home. Leopold Stokowski married a Russian princess in her living room, and she prepared a honeymoon breakfast for Leonard Bernstein and his bride. When Charles Laughton tried to cancel a performance by complaining that his medicine made him sleepy, she threatened to announce to the audience that "Mr. Laughton is too doped to appear tonight," prompting a miraculous recovery. On another occasion he fascinated her grandchildren at the breakfast table, because "they'd never heard English spoken quite that way." When Marian Anderson, the African American contralto, performed in 1942, Phoenix hotels were segregated, so Jesse invited the singer to stay in her home.

Jesse sold tickets by mail and from a booth that she operated, first in Goldwater's, and then over the years in other downtown stores. She kept track of all season ticket holders as well as many others in a file which reached 5,000 cards, and on each she noted people's musical and seating preferences. She used her contact with patrons to encourage their interests in various artists and, more notably, to desegregate the audience for the performances of African American artists, first of Marian Anderson and later for Paul Robeson and others. She also instructed the audience, noting publicly the need to be on time. In programs she mentioned the need to be quiet and gently reminded patrons: "Hats. You will remove them, won't you? It is so difficult to see through them, under or around them."

The greatest challenge to performances in Phoenix was the absence of an sizable auditorium with decent acoustics and an adequate stage. The only hall with sufficient seating was the Phoenix Union High School Auditorium, but the stage was very small and the acoustics were bad — terrible under the balcony. Jesse made a civic auditorium her personal campaign. Before concerts she would urge the city to build such a structure, and eventually her pleas had an effect. From the discussion or dreaming stage in the 1950s, to the planning stage in the mid-60s, to the completion of Symphony Hall in 1972, her infectious spirit and commitment provided the crucial drive. Her impact on the city, then, included both the building and the music that filled it. ■

(Above) Actor Charles Laughton lovingly called Mrs. Linde "the toughest and sweetest gal in Phoenix." *Pointe West Magazine, November 1962.*

(Below) Phoenix Symphony Hall Terrace at night *City of Phoenix, Photo by Bob Rink*

commuted to Phoenix, until the Board decided to hire a resident conductor. The musicians varied in musical training and ability. Some held jobs unrelated to music, while others were music educators, like violinist Helen Swindall who had graduated from New York's Juilliard School of Music. The Symphony performed in the Phoenix Union High School Auditorium until 1964, when it moved to ASU's new Gammage Auditorium, although some people objected that a Phoenix group should not have its home in Tempe. In 1969 the Symphony entered a five-year period of artistic and financial conflict, including the firing of two conductors. The city helped ease the group's financial troubles by contributing $50,000 in 1973, and a musicians' strike was narrowly averted in 1974. The good news included the hiring of

The Grammy-winning Phoenix Boys Choir
Phoenix Boys Choir

A scene from Arizona Opera's production of *The Barber of Seville*, part of the 2000-2001 season. *Arizona Opera Company, Photo by Tim Fuller*

Eduardo Mata as conductor in 1971 and the opening of the Symphony's new home, Symphony Hall, in 1972.

The Symphony moved up a level in 1981, becoming a full-time, professional orchestra, and in 1986 the board made a deliberate commitment to making Phoenix a major symphony with an expanded season. It hired James Sedares as conductor, who led the orchestra in making three recordings, took them on

a brief tour and championed new music. Herman Michael was hired in 1997 to continue this progress, but in 1998 the long-standing financial problems erupted into crisis. Despite annual fee waivers and other financial contributions from the city, as well as private funding-raising efforts, the Board had been unable to raise the musicians' base salary of $23,490, ranking last of the 40 major orchestras in the country. The musicians threatened to strike, but at the last moment contributions from two civic leaders and promises of additional funds raised the salaries and averted the crisis. A much-expanded concert series, with varied programs and performance times, were intended to help expand community support.

The Symphony has been central to the vitality of classical music in the Valley, but other groups have added to the increasingly rich offerings. This includes those groups with which the Symphony collaborates — the ASU Choral Union, the Phoenix Boys Choir and the Phoenix Bach Choir — as well as various choral groups, the Phoenix Chamber Music Society, chamber ensembles, community orchestra, and the ASU Music School faculty and students. The most important musical organization after the symphony is the Arizona Opera, begun in 1972 in Tucson, and like the Actors Theater Company soon began performing in Phoenix. However, by 1983 the Arizona Opera was nearly bankrupt. Hiring Glynn Ross as the general director saved the organization, and when he retired in 1997, it was solvent, respected and presenting 35 performances a year in the two cities.

Despite periodic crises which the Symphony and other arts experienced, by 2000 the arts seemed to be entering a better and more stable era. Private financial contributions nearly doubled in the late 1990s, a sign of the decade's affluence but even more, a maturing of the community. Instead of identifying with communities from which they had come, increasing numbers of wealthy Phoenicians saw the Valley as home and gave it their money. In addition, Valley attendance at arts performances and institutions increased, jumping nearly a third in the late 1990s, reflecting the increased opportunities as well as the improved quality. Finally, polls showed that the public believed that Valley arts were getting better. The area increasingly provided a more cosmopolitan experience. Perhaps the change is most easily reflected in the current variety of restaurants, which range widely from Ethiopian to Polynesian, from Caribbean to Armenian, or from Middle Eastern to French. The annual Scottsdale Culinary Festival highlights the emergence of haute cuisine in the Valley.

The Early Days of Valley Sports

Sports have always been important in American communities, but their role and importance have changed during the past 50 years in the Valley. The root attraction is recreation, as participants or spectators. The Valley has consistently offered opportunities and social encouragement for various forms of athletic activity from individuals jogging, golfing or swimming to team sports like baseball, soccer or football. From the city's early days, Phoenicians recognized that sports could attract tourists and promote development. Golf has played a unique role in providing activity for residents, attracting tourists and influencing housing developments, as witnessed by the nearly 200 courses in 2000. Nationally, as sporting events grew larger, they acquired greater economic significance for spectators. The increasing scale took sports beyond the realm of simple recreation and made them matters of public policy, for good or ill.

The Phoenix Open Golf Tournament was the Valley's first public sporting event, beginning in 1932. With a purse of $600 it did not attract a large field of competitors, but with the help of the Royal Order of Thunderbirds and the increaing popularity of the sport the numbers grew steadily after the war. Different types of racing gained popularity and facilities after the war: Greyhound Park debuted in 1954 and Phoenix Trotting Park opened for harness racing in 1965. Phoenix International Raceway drew auto-racing fans to the West Valley, while downtown Phoenix hosted a Grand Prix car race for several years starting in 1989.

The growth of ASU and its athletic program provided additional opportunities for sports fans, particularly the competition with the University of Arizona and Tucson. The baseball program began in 1959, and led by Coach Bobby Winkles, quickly achieved status as a national power, winning

The Standard Register PING LPGA tournament in Phoenix is one of the premier golf events in the women's tour.
Banner Health Foundation of Arizona

Phoenix International Raceway
Phoenix International Raceway

Fiesta Bowl 2000
Fiesta Bowl, Photo by Jeff Kida

Chicago Cubs spring training game, 2000
Mesa Convention & Visitors Bureau

The architect's rendering of the city's first "civic auditorium" — Arizona Veterans Memorial Coliseum. Built in 1965, the Coliseum served as the Phoenix Suns' home court for 20 years.
Arizona State Fair

national championships in 1965, 1967 and 1969. Coach Jim Brock continued this record with titles in 1977 and 1981, but even successful college baseball teams like ASU's drew crowds of only modest size. The basketball team attracted more fans, particularly with the good teams coached by Ned Wulk during the early 1980s, but coaching changes and scandal tarnished that program. Football quickly became the major college sport, pulling in tens of thousands of fans, even in the heat of early fall Saturday evenings. The program's heyday came under Frank Kush during the 1970s, when five teams finished the season ranked in the top ten. The best year was 1975 when "The Catch" by John Jefferson helped beat UA, and the team defeated Nebraska to finish second in the nation. Only the 1986 PAC 10 championship and a Rose Bowl victory over the University of Michigan generated as much enthusiasm from local fans. ASU football also contributed to the development the Fiesta Bowl in 1971. By the mid-1980s it had become a Valley-wide festival and one of the nation's premier football bowls.

The first professional team sport in Phoenix (as in most of America) was baseball. After an interruption from World War II, the Arizona-Texas League resumed play in 1947 with the Phoenix Senators still a member of the Class "C" league, along with Mesa, Tucson, Bisbee, Globe-Miami, El Paso and Juarez. Playing in 1954 as the Phoenix Stars, the team drew 114,450 fans, but thereafter air conditioning and television drew more and more fans away from the ballpark. The shift of the major league teams to California added further impetus to a major reshuffling of minor league baseball in the Southwest. Phoenix received a franchise in the AAA level Pacific Coast League in 1959 but low attendance sent it fleeing to Tacoma the following year. A contributing factor was the aging stadium at Central and Mohave, which the city replaced in 1963 with a structure near Papago Park. Minor league baseball returned in 1966 with the Phoenix Giants, who drew a respectable 152,508 fans.

The Valley had a further connection with baseball beginning in 1947 when the New York Giants arrived for spring training and the Cleveland Indians settled in Tucson. The Chicago Cubs came to Mesa in 1952 and several clubs alternated as a fourth team during the 1950s. In the following decade, as baseball added teams, some decided to train in Arizona, forming a small but stable Cactus League alternative to Florida's Grapefruit League. Going beyond baseball, construction of the Arizona Veterans Memorial Coliseum in 1965 provided a venue for an unlikely second minor league sport: hockey. In 1967 the Phoenix Roadrunners began playing in the Western Hockey League.

Phoenix Joins the Big Leagues

The position of professional sports in the Valley entered a new phase in 1968 with the arrival of the Phoenix Suns, an expansion franchise in the National Basketball Association. Essentially an unsolicited team brought by investors rather than fans or the city, news of the franchise received no newspaper coverage for a week after the award. However, the Suns were only an expansion team in what was still a second-tier sport. And the 12-player payroll in the first season was under $200,000. Beginning with the worst record in the league (16-66), the team rapidly improved, making the playoffs in 1970. For 16 years under Coach John MacLeod the team developed a very good record, including a triple-overtime loss to the Boston Celtics in 1976 championship and solid fan loyalty. At the same time, the Valley's growing interest in sports, an awareness of increased consumer spending on recreation and entertainment, and a desire to acquire the signs of urban status created strong pressures to obtain major league franchises in the other three major sports — baseball, football and hockey. What endangered this drive was the national competition for teams, the requirements and cost of facilities and the huge increases in costs associated with professional sports.

The first Phoenix Suns,
1968-1969
*Phoenix Suns
Archive Services*

Phoenix did not worry about competing for teams, since it had been successfully wooing businesses for decades. However, it did need facilities of different sizes and shapes to meet the needs of different sports. Furthermore, the expectations of teams and fans about the accommodations in a facility had been increasing sharply. Because building stadiums and arenas had become so expensive, after 1962 all but one of the major stadiums across the country had been financed at least in part with public funds. Apart from any other factor, the question of using public funds made the recruitment of major league sports into a public and political issue. Beginning in 1988 the Valley has rocked with controversy over aspects of this subject.

Some critics of public funding objected to the placement of stadiums, or the use of state power to tax or to compel the sale of land. Conservatives objected to any tax, while liberal protesters pointed to more important public needs that were being unmet. Proponents responded that teams assisted economic development and fulfilled social purposes, and that they provided useful public facilities. They also argued that these structures were simply too expensive to be built using only private funds. Critics responded that teams were businesses that could or should be able to pay for a place of business, that owners would make vast sums from the facilities, or that their wealth was sufficient to pay for these facilities. Some agreed with Maricopa County Supervisor Tom Rawles, who complained in 1993 that "if they can't pay for a stadium, it's because they're paying inflated and unjustifiable salaries." Owners and their supporters argued that costs had risen greatly over the previous several decades because of the amenities which fans expected, and that profits could not fund such facilities. But however one balanced these factors, owners clearly felt they could not pay. Equally important, they often had alternatives, for many cities pursued "major league" status. Between 1980 and 1992 20 cities sought a major league baseball team, 24 pursued football teams and five teams actually moved.

The actual debates for this issues began in 1988, when the St. Louis Cardinal franchise of the National Football League transferred to Phoenix, following failed efforts to lure the Baltimore

continued on page 128

América West Arena has been home court for the Phoenix Suns since 1992 and for the WBA Phoenix Mercury since their first season in 1997.
*Courtesy of America West Arena,
Photo by Barry Gossage*

Colts and the Philadelphia Eagles. This event aroused great enthusiasm because football was highly popular and the second "major league" sports franchise in the Valley. Many Phoenicians believed this would enhance national awareness of Phoenix as the 9th largest city in the nation. Having a local team also made it possible to host the Super Bowl, which offered further symbolic but also real economic gains. (Phoenix won and then lost the chance to host 1993 Super Bowl, because it lacked a King holiday, but it hosted the 1996 Super Bowl, which reportedly brought in $187 million.) Thus, part of the Phoenix development strategy by the late 1980s was acquiring various professional sports teams. As Phoenix mayor Terry Goddard claimed, in anticipation of acquiring a major league baseball team, "Baseball is big business. It gives us a shot in the arm that we can't get any other way. It brings in the new taxes that we need to pay for other things that this city needs: police, fire, whatever."

According to the initial arrangement, the Cardinals would play temporarily in the ASU stadium, with a public stadium to be constructed in the near future. But what had been anticipated in the rosy glow of the Cardinals' arrival soon receded like a desert mirage, partly because of the Cardinals' actions. Attracted by stories of the Valley's enthusiasm for football, the team's owner, Bill Bidwill, raised ticket prices to the highest in the league — $36 for an average ticket, compared with $29 for the next highest team. The team's poor play (finishing at 5-11 in their second season) fueled the fans' anger and attendance plummeted to the second worst in the league. As one columnist joked, "Bill Bidwill-bashing has become the Valley's favorite pastime," and support for a public stadium diminished to near invisibility.

The rising competition for resources and the changing public mood further complicated the issue.

Phoenix Mercury Center, Jennifer Gillom
*Phoenix Mercury,
Photo by Barry Gossage*

The economic slump beginning in the late 1980s reduced the availability of both private and public money for a major stadium. Since the new owners of the financial institutions were from outside the Valley, they were at least more cautious about investments in sports. Public investment became less likely because falling tax revenues meant that even basic public responsibilities like schools were struggling for money. Finally, a rising conservative movement preferred tax cuts to new expenditures.

Football also faced growing competition from other sports. In 1989 the Suns had been in town for 20 years and generally successful. Their record had fallen in the mid-1980s, but in 1989 they completed a surprising and highly touted return near the top of the league's standings. Jerry Colangelo, general manager and part owner, felt they needed a more attractive arena than the functional coliseum. A deal was finalized in July by which the Suns agreed to provide $44 million toward building a multi-use arena; America West Airlines committed to $26 million over 30 years for having their name on the building; and the city of Phoenix would purchase the land (for up to $12 million) and contribute $35 million for the building, which it would finance by a tax on motels/ hotels and car rentals. Colangelo chose a downtown location for the arena. Phoenix Councilwoman Mary Rose Wilcox strongly endorsed that decision and the basic agreement arguing that sports is "one of the biggest economic development tools a city can use." The building opened in May, 1992, to rave reviews and near constant use. When profits exceeded projects, Colangelo renegotiated the contract with the city to provide faster repayment. Even more importantly, the team nearly reached the top: led by Charles Barkley and Kevin Johnson the Suns lost a heart-breaking championship series to the Chicago Bulls in 1993.

continued on page 128

■Growing up in the working-class Italian neighborhood of "Hungry Hill" in Chicago Heights, Jerry Colangelo dreamed of a life beyond the steel mills. "I used to think," he said "that if I could just make $200 a week, $10,000 a year, I could live on the other side of the tracks." Hard work and his athletic skills created such opportunities for him. After high school he turned down professional sports contract offers to accept an athletic scholarship for basketball and baseball to the University of Kansas. He later switched to the University of Illinois (after Wilt Chamberlain left Kansas to play professional basketball), where he made the All-Big Ten basketball team. Graduating in 1962 without an NBA offer, he worked in a tuxedo rental/dry cleaning business under a verbal partnership agreement with an older friend who was "kind of a father." But after three years the friend closed the business, leaving Colangelo with nothing — nothing except a lesson about the values of loyalty and honesty in business.

Chance led him to a job in merchandising with Dick Klein, and in 1966 when Klein and other investors bought one of the NBA's new franchises, the Chicago Bulls, Colangelo came along as scout and director of merchandising. When the NBA expanded again in 1967, Seattle offered him the number two job, which he turned down; the following year both new franchises — Milwaukee and Phoenix — tried to hire him as general manager. The winter weather, the opportunity and a salary of $22,500 brought him to the desert, a long way from Hungry Hill.

Initially, the Suns were a hard sell: brought by investors rather than fans, they received limited news coverage, basketball did not seem a "natural fit" for Phoenix, and the team drew only slightly more fans than the minor league hockey team, also new. But mid-way through the second season, Jerry took over as coach, guiding the team into the playoffs against the Lakers. During the following years he built fan interest and business support. By the mid-1980s basketball had grown in popularity, and the Suns franchise seemed solid, but declining performance and drug charges against three players produced a crisis. The owners decided to sell the team and, as promised, gave Colangelo first chance to buy. He quickly found investors for $20 million, borrowed $24 million, and bought the team. Through clever trades (for Kevin Johnson) and shrewd negotiations with free agents (Tom Chambers) he soon put together a new and successful team. In 1992 he added Danny Ainge and Charles Barkley, and the team made it to the NBA finals, losing a heartbreaker to the Chicago Bulls. By 1993 the value of the franchise had risen to an estimated $125 million. After repaying the purchase loans, investors made a 600 percent profit and Colangelo's shares had ballooned to an estimated $22 million. By 1997 the Suns were estimated to be worth $220 million.

He displayed similar management skills in creating the Valley's baseball franchise. Responding to the request from Joe Garagiolo Jr., and Jim Bruner, Colangelo put together a group of investors who raised the huge franchise fee, established the team and partially financed a stadium. What makes this seem at all easy is only the considerable success which the franchise and stadium obtained after several years of operation. Some baseball executives criticized his salary offers to certain players as inflationary. But Colangelo viewed some of this as equity: after winning an arbitration dispute with new player Jorge Fabregas, he gave Fabregas what he had originally requested. A 1998 *Sports Illustrated* poll of agents and NBA executives revealed a key factor in his success, reporting the conclusion that "His word is gold. One of the few." The Diamondbacks' epic victory in the 2001 World Series marked the fastest success of any expansion team and vindicated Colangelo's strategy.

Colangelo's most significant accomplishments are the successful completion of the America West Arena and the Bank One Ballpark (BOB). As noted elsewhere in this history, both projects created controversy and complaints about the use of public money for private purposes. The counter-argument is that such facilities serve public purposes — by providing mass entertainment and by fostering activities that private funds could not create. Even more significant for Phoenix was Colangelo's insistence that the facilities be located downtown. Although not a unique preference, the national trend through the 1980s was to locate sports facilities in suburbs. Given the cost and availability of land, a suburban location would have been cheaper and more profitable, especially for the baseball stadium. Colangelo's decision had an enormous impact on downtown. A few years after America West Arena opened, some 40 new businesses had opened in the area; BOB encouraged even more. In conjunction with other public facilities, they have created a critical mass and encouraged more substantial investments in hotels, offices and even residential structures. It was a result that would have made an urban planner proud.■

■(Above left)
At two different times, Colangelo played substitute coach for the Suns.
Phoenix Suns Archive Service

■(Above right)
Just four years after Colangelo established a major league baseball franchise in Phoenix, the team took home the 2001 World Series championship.
Arizona Diamondbacks, Photo by Barry Gossage

jerry colangelo

Baseball Concerns

While negotiations for the America West Arena were being finalized, the city was also planning a multi-use stadium for the Cardinals and a future major league baseball team. But after Bidwill refused to pay what the city suggested, and as questions grew about a multi-use stadium, city officials decided to propose only a baseball stadium financed by a tenth of a percent property tax in order to raise $100 million. On October 3, 1989, Phoenix voters approved a number of bond proposals but firmly rejected the stadium spending by a 3-2 margin. This ended the city council's formal role in promoting a stadium and demonstrated that property taxes were an unattractive way to finance a stadium. As for future prospects, Mayor Goddard was pessimistic: "It would be a very long shot, if not impossible. This was our best shot."

In addition, Arizona's eight-team Cactus League faced a threat in 1989. The state, and especially the Valley, appreciated the national recognition and roughly $150 million tourist dollars, which these teams brought. When Florida cities sought to lure Cactus League teams, Governor Rose Mofford, an all-star softball player in the 1940s, appointed a task force, which recommended providing newer and improved facilities. In 1990

the legislature quickly passed a bill permitting Maricopa and Pima counties to tax motels/hotels and rental cars to finance stadium improvements. The municipalities responded enthusiastically, requesting even more money than was available and building to the satisfaction of all teams except the Cleveland Indians, who had previuosly decided to leave Tucson for Florida. While the price for individual stadiums was not significant, the expenditures quickly totaled a healthy sum.

Thus, in early 1990 there were no plans to build a stadium for football or baseball; despite the public's rising interest in attracting a major league baseball team, there was no clear notion of how to finance a stadium; and other stadium/arena projects seemed to have preemptively claimed any likely tax monies. But during its spring 1990 session, after parliamentary maneuvering and with relatively little discussion, the legislature passed a significant measure: it allowed Maricopa County to create a stadium district with taxing power to fund a ballpark.

This had no effect immediately, but it soon would. In 1990 County Supervisor Jim Bruner and Joe Garagiola Jr. requested an expansion franchise from the Major League Baseball (MLB) owners, but with no stadium and too little money, MLB turned them down.

In April of 1993, with rumors that MLB was planning to expand again, Brunner and Garagiola sought help from the one man in Arizona sports with a record of success, Jerry Colangelo. After investigating, Colangelo decided to participate. He quickly put together funding for the franchise fee, and in November began negotiating with the County Supervisors (acting as Stadium District representatives) to finance a domed stadium. After lengthy discussions, which capped the county's obligation at $238 million, on February 17, 1994, the county supervisors voted 3-1 (with one abstention) to approve plans for a stadium in downtown Phoenix and a quarter-cent county sales tax to pay for it. The three proponents acknowledged that the issue was controversial, but argued that the benefits exceeded the cost, and that the deal would give the county between $1 and $2.5 million annually, plus all non-baseball revenue.

The supervisors' decision produced a fire storm of criticism. The Sun City Taxpayers Association filed a lawsuit, petitions for a referendum repealing the tax garnered tens of thousands of signatures, while radio talk shows and letters to newspapers amply reflected the depth of the hostility to this action. But the protests were ultimately ineffective: the lawsuit was thrown out of court, the petitions were insufficient (after ineligible signatures were removed) to place the repeal on the ballot, and such a repeal rested on legally dubious grounds anyway. Electoral protests had a greater effect: Supervisor Ed King was defeated for re-election, and Jim Bruner lost his bid for a Republican congressional nomination. Before the contest both men had seemed likely winners. The most shocking result was the shooting of the third supporter, Supervisor Mary Rose Wilcox, on August 13, 1997, by a mentally ill man enraged over this issue. (Though seriously wounded, she did recover.) Shortly thereafter, Jerry Colangelo ordered bulletproof glass installed in his ballpark office. In the end, Colangelo's group won the franchise, the tax lasted only two and a half years, the stadium opened in 1998 to public admiration and the Diamondbacks drew impressive crowds. However, the virulent reaction to the subsidy and the method of its passage soured politics in the Valley and limited further action on a football stadium for some years.

A conference on the mound during the Diamondbacks' 2001 season
Arizona Diamondbacks Archives

ASU Stadium is the current home of both the ASU Sun Devils and the Arizona Cardinals.
ASU News Bureau, Photo by Tim Trumble

The Cardinals Get a Stadium — Probably

Meanwhile, Cardinal plans suffered ups and downs. The team regained some public support and attendance by lowering ticket prices in 1990 and by slow team improvement, but they lost ground by hiring Buddy Ryan, an abrasive, pompous and ineffective general manager and coach, who was finally fired in 1995. With Phoenix focused on baseball, the Cardinals began thinking about other Valley communities, changing the team's name from Phoenix to Arizona in 1994. They also responded positively in January of 1996 when the East Valley Partnership suggested they consider a privately financed, multi-use facility — a conference center and a stadium, which would rent to the Cardinals 10 days a year. This initiative gained momentum when the newly relocated hockey team, the Phoenix Coyotes, indicated their willingness to leave America West Arena for another facility.

The first East Valley plan, in September 1997, included a National Sports Center having a stadium facility for three

sports, a sports-related theme park, and a hotel, convention center, restaurant and shops to be financed primarily by a one-quarter cent sales tax in East Valley cities. Tempe and Scottsdale quickly rejected this project, and the Coyotes decided to look elsewhere. But Mesa remained interested. It was struggling terribly to define itself and to create an attractive downtown area — a particularly frustrating effort given the increasing success of Phoenix, Scottsdale and Tempe. This proposal followed a frequent suggestion that sports be used as a basis for identity, planning and growth. In June 1998, the East Valley Partnership unveiled a new and more ambitious plan for a $1.5 billion complex, including a huge integrated stadium and convention center surrounded by large hotels, restaurants and shops, and with residential and recreation areas. The problem, again, was financing — a 20-year sales tax — and, again, Tempe dropped out. The Mesa city council endorsed a revised project, but dissenters criticized the tax and questioned the size of the project. Voters agreed and in May, 1999, soundly defeated the project by a three-to-two margin. By contrast, Scottsdale voters approved a stadium district with a hockey arena at the center of a redeveloped Los Arcos mall, and six months later approved using sales taxes from the area to refinance the project.

Concerned that the Cardinals might move, the following November Governor Hull created a task force of prominent businessmen to design a workable stadium proposal. The issues included getting a greater financial commitment by the Cardinals, and finding an inoffensive method of financing. The new proposal imitated the successful strategies of the past decade. It proposed a taxation method used twice before — a tax on hotels and car rentals — as well as charges on stadium activities and use of sales taxes generated in the area. The aim was to avoid taxing residents who did not attend football games. Finally, the proposal was both broadened and focused: it included a multipurpose stadium, but also more Cactus League facilities, tourism and amateur sports facilities. While the location was not specified, an East Valley site seemed at the top of the list. It was, in short, a balanced and carefully tailored proposal that voters approved in November, 2000.

Soon after the vote was certified, four bids for the stadium site arrived — from Mesa, Tempe, downtown Phoenix and the West Valley. The latter proposal, another in a series of proposals involving land donations by John F. Long, represented a substantial and coordinated West Valley effort and received serious consideration, but the site committee awarded the stadium to Tempe. Problems soon emerged. The Tempe site was judged to interfere with the nearby Phoenix airport, so the site committee retracted its decision. Among various

Luis Gonzales reacts to his game-winning hit in the bottom of the ninth inning, game seven of the 2001 World Series.
Arizona Diamondbacks, Photo by Barry Gossage

alternatives a Mesa site eventually seemed most promising — but certain, fully 18 months after the voters had spoken. Perhaps the only clear conclusion of this process was the new power of the East Valley. But at the same time the West Valley demonstrated its increased importance when Glendale announced that they had landed the Coyotes, luring them from an increasingly controversial relationship with Scottsdale.

The football stadium and the hockey arena represent important changes in the Valley. The earlier decisions to locate the America West Arena and the baseball stadium in downtown Phoenix reflected the city's dominant political power and supported downtown redevelopment. The placement of the other facilities in the two sides of the Valley represents not only a symbolic division but also a real shift of power within the Valley. While the emotional identification with any of these teams will surely cut across municipal boundaries, their economic impact will have specific local consequences.

the Diamondbacks won the game, setting off wild celebrations, topped off by a daytime parade which attracted as many as 400,000 people. Besides the needed infusion of revenue for the team, the World Series victory confirmed Jerry Colangelo's wisdom in spending heavily for free agents. In a mixture of description and prescription the *Arizona Republic* proclaimed the importance of sport in shaping the identity of Phoenix:

"This desert place no longer is an isolated outpost; it no longer is just another adolescent Sun Belt metropolis exhilarated at the sight of its own growth. It is a city of champions."

While this clearly presaged a new theme in city rhetoric, it also reflected a real belief that a national baseball championship somehow reflected the city's new importance. Moreover, the enthusiastic response from citizens reflected a modern urban reality — that in a rapidly growing city with a mobile population some people's community identification can be substantially shaped by professional sports.

The Home of World Champions

Some called it the greatest World Series, others simply said that the 2001 contest was one of the best ever. Phoenix had led its division for much of the season, but the team suffered injuries to key players, and in August the Diamondbacks faltered and briefly fell out of first place. Regaining the lead, the team faced fierce competition from San Francisco, but managed to bring home the second division title in four years. After defeating St. Louis in the playoffs, they faced the aging National League champions, the Atlanta Braves, who had rallied at the end of the season and seemed to be angling for a storybook finish. But the Diamondbacks ended those hopes and entered the World Series against the New York Yankees: the youngest baseball franchise and the quickest to reach the Series faced the legendary Yankees who were seeking their fourth consecutive title.

Behind pitchers Curt Schilling and Randy Johnson in BOB, the team took the first two games, but it lost three close games in New York, two of them in the 9th inning. Returning to Phoenix the team's offense exploded in game six, setting the stage for a dramatic seventh game. Down 2-1 in the 9th inning,

Phoenix Past and Future

Sixty years brought enormous changes to living in Phoenix. From a somewhat remote, medium-sized, agricultural community it became the sixth-largest city in the nation, with all the connections and relationships that implies. One of the significant changes was that Phoenix became more like the rest of the country. This occurred partly because both Phoenix and the nation adopted the same mass culture, partly because the flood of newcomers continued importing customs and identities rooted elsewhere in the nation, but also because Phoenicians wanted to identify with the nation — to escape a "provincial" mentality.

Phoenix's growth attracted great attention because it reflected a conscious, successful plan and because it occurred so continuously, on a large scale, and in such a relatively short period (an adult's lifetime). Aware that their city stood out as a national exemplar of economic and population boom, Phoenicians sought evidence of its ascending status. Population rank and rate of growth were the first and most obvious symbols. Emergence as a center of high tech industry and a tourist mecca provided additional signs. Attracting major league sports franchises offered highly visible symbols of national status, since this involved both valued elements of a national culture and significant businesses. In addition, teams provided some residents with an emotional connection to the area which other elements of Valley life did not engender. Finally, Phoenicians valued evidence of the city's increasingly cosmopolitan status. The founders' original vision had drawn from urban models of the earlier 20th century, and identified live theater, fine art and classical music as crucial elements for achieving national status. Although growth in these areas had been somewhat uneven, most observers would agree that by the end of this era Phoenix resembled the nation's larger cities in its support of "high culture." Other elements of a cosmopolitan culture are harder to measure, but many pointed to the growing range of culinary options, diverse cultural institutions and festivals and the emergence of a downtown social life.

As much as some Phoenicians touted the city's rising status and national reputation, a competing perspective focused on place. As opposed to those who valued Phoenix as a malleable, "plastic" environment which could be molded into a form defined elsewhere, others cherished the area as it existed in nature and history. For every newcomer seeking to recreate the place he or she had left, another immigrant viewed the desert and mountain environs with awe and wished to preserve them. For every long-term resident pleased with growth and change, at least one other felt misgivings about the machine they had set in motion.

A growing awareness of Phoenix as a place also includes its history. Numerous cultural institutions demonstrate an increasingly complex understanding of the city as a Southwestern place. The city's growing diversity highlights the linkage between present and past; the rising Hispanic population is a particularly visible reminder of the area's origins. As a place of residence, Phoenix is also a collection of communities of which individuals and families attempt to make sense and make familiar. Confronting a vast and burgeoning city, containing a highly mobile population, Phoenicians have increasingly sought to create neighborhood institutions and connections to overcome the centrifugal forces of urbanization. In struggling with issues like sprawl, growth, pollution, and traffic Phoenix resembles places across the nation. But its goals, experiences and surroundings tell a key and unique part of the American story.

For every newcomer seeking to re-create the place he or she had left, another immigrant viewed the desert and mountain environs with awe and wished to preserve them. *Mesa Convention & Visitors Bureau*

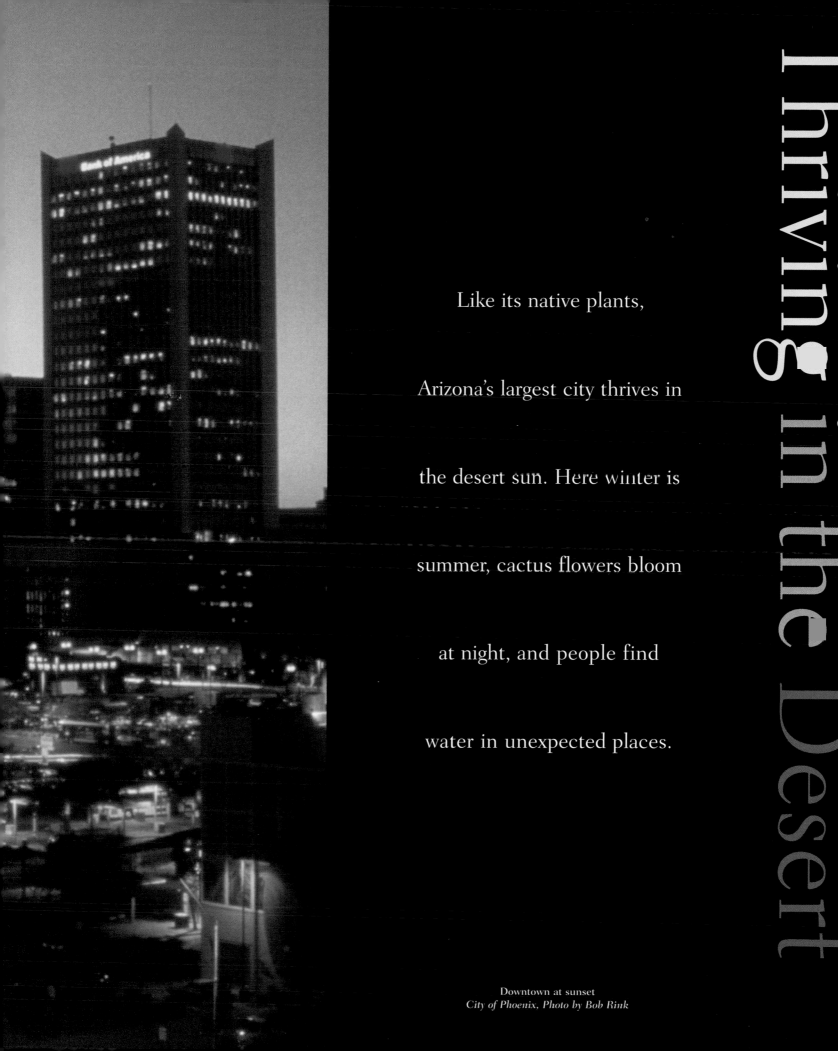

Thriving in the Desert

Like its native plants,

Arizona's largest city thrives in

the desert sun. Here winter is

summer, cactus flowers bloom

at night, and people find

water in unexpected places.

Downtown at sunset
City of Phoenix, Photo by Bob Rink

The beauty of desert plants often surprises

new visitors to the Valley. The surrounding

Sonoran Desert is home to numerous

species, and many of these are commonly used

in urban landscaping.

(Above) Easter Lily Cactus bloom
(Opposite page left to right)
Cacti, creosote and desert marigolds
Blind Prickly Pear Cactus in bloom

All photos *Desert Botanical Garden, Photos by César Mazier*

Penstemon *Desert Botanical Garden, Photo by César Mazier*

Aloe species *Desert Botanical Garden, Photo by César Mazier*

Engelmann Hedgehog Cactus *Desert Botanical Garden, Photo by César Mazier*

Easter Lily Cactus blooms *Desert Botanical Garden, Photos by César Mazier*

Claret Cup Hedgehog Cactus in bloom *Desert Botanical Garden, Photo by César Mazier*

Outdoor living and diverse physical activity remain essential,

defining elements of a Phoenix lifestyle.

The Valley greets every New Year with Fiesta Bowl events, including a parade through downtown. *Fiesta Bowl*

Downtown Phoenix in the winter is a favorite spot for charity walks and bike rides.
City of Phoenix, Photo by Bob Rink

Water sports abound in this desert! Five large lakes surround the Valley of the Sun.
(Top) *Greater Phoenix Convention & Visitors Bureau, Photos by Jessen Associates, Inc.* (Bottom) *Photo by Bob Rink*

The Superstition Mountains east of the city are a horseman's paradise. *Mesa Convention & Visitors Bureau*

The built environment includes a wide range of styles and structures. Some reflect the state's Spanish heritage, the Valley's early Victorian designs or more "fanciful" castles. While modern structures abound, the height limit on buildings has given Phoenix a different feeling than that of other cities near its size. The blending of purpose and style is apparent in the BOB baseball stadium, which combines an external design that matches its warehouse district, a neotraditional internal design of the stands, and a field with modern features such as a moveable roof.

The Heard Museum's colonnade *The Heard Museum*

The Rosson House, Heritage Square *City of Phoenix, Photos by Bob Rink*

Downtown attractions: BOB and the Peacock Fountain at Symphony Hall
Greater Phoenix Convention & Visitors Bureau, Photos by Jessen Associates, Inc.

Tovrea Castle *City of Phoenix, Photo by Bob Rink*

partners in phoenix

Phoenix builders, contractors and development companies, along with city government, plan and shape tomorrow's skyline, providing and improving working and living space for area residents.

Building a Greater Phoenix

ARIZONA CENTER

In the late 1980s, the 18-acre plot of land located at the corner of Van Buren and Third streets in downtown Phoenix was in the middle of a rather dilapidated area. Previously the site of Phoenix Union High School and several other old developments, it was intended for redevelopment by the city. A nonprofit group called the Phoenix Community Alliance (PCA) had been designated by the city to administer the development of this area.

Arizona Center has become a must-see attraction in downtown Phoenix.

At the time, PCA was one of a number of groups in Phoenix that had a vision to spark the revitalization of the old and somewhat seedy downtown area. In looking for a development company to partner with, PCA's executive vice president, Stephen Dragos, turned to The Rouse Company, a highly successful development and management company based in Columbia, Maryland. Dragos had previously worked with The Rouse Company and was aware of the company's continued track record for success with its projects in Baltimore and Boston, both of which were internationally known models for urban mixed-use redevelopment projects. Such was the beginning of Arizona Center.

Given the real estate climate at the time, putting together a major redevelopment project was no easy task. Even with the blessing of the city of Phoenix and PCA's partnership with The Rouse Company, building Arizona Center was a highly complicated undertaking. In addition to bringing together the large number of partners and corporations involved in the project, there were also the tasks of assembling the land, obtaining adequate financing and finding the right mix of tenants to make the project successful.

Groundbreaking for Arizona Center took place in October 1987 with a crowd of 250 gathered under a tent for Mayor Terry Goddard's dedication. New construction began with two primary goals in mind: To spark the revitalization of downtown Phoenix and to bring retail merchants and residents back to the area. In pursuing these goals, the strategy of The Rouse Company was to anchor the project with leading, first-class office development. As an attribute, the retail element also became an impetus for other projects.

Focusing first on office development, the center's original and anchor tenant was the major utility company Arizona Public Service (APS). Because APS was a partner in the project and also very instrumental to the redevelopment plan of the downtown area, Two Arizona Center — also known as the APS Tower — was built first. Designed by the architectural firm of Howard, Needles, Tammen and Bergendoff, the tower opened in March of 1989 with APS occupying the entire 20-story office building.

Despite its address, One Arizona Center was the second tower to be built. Also 20 stories, it was designed by architect Harwood K. Smith and is occupied by many prominent Arizona businesses including Snell & Wilmer, LLP and Pinnacle West Capital Corporation, which is APS's parent company. Other major tenants include the Harlem Globetrotters basketball team and the international accounting firm of KPMG, LLP.

Continuing The Rouse Company's success in Phoenix, the Shops at Arizona Center and the spectacular 3.5-acre Gardens at Arizona Center opened in November 1990. This open-air oasis of food, shopping and beautiful, shaded multi-tiered gardens quickly became a popular destination for locals and tourists alike. With stylish boutiques, fabulous eateries and the ambiance of fountains, misted patios and walkways, Arizona Center became a truly perfect place to visit both day and night.

The next step in its role as a catalyst for the rejuvenation of downtown Phoenix was Arizona Center's partnership with the AMC Theatre Corporation, which was contracted to build the first cinema located downtown in several decades. Opening its doors in March 1998, the 24-screen movie theater features state-of-the-art audio and stadium-style seating in all 24 of its auditoriums.

Today, Arizona Center is one of Phoenix' "Points of Pride" and a very active participant in the myriad of community happenings that take place in downtown Phoenix.

Arizona Center is managed by The Rouse Company's affiliate, Rouse Office Management of Arizona, Inc. The Rouse Company, one of the largest publicly held real estate development companies in the United States, also owns and manages a variety of 200 mixed-use commercial properties, office projects and shopping centers. Its prestigious properties comprise nearly 53 million square feet and include Boston's Faneuil Hall, New Orleans' Riverwalk, New York City's South Street Seaport, Baltimore's Harborplace and Miami's Bayside.

In an area where conventional wisdom wasn't enough, Arizona Center has been an extremely successful project for almost 15 years. Thanks to its part in the rejuvenation of the area, nearby residential growth is now booming with new high-end apartments, lofts and condominiums gracing the landscape. Also making the area a magnet for social activity are the nearby America West Arena, Bank One Ballpark, Herberger Theater, Phoenix Civic Plaza Convention

By day or by night, Arizona Center is an open-air oasis of food, shopping, relaxing gardens and fun.

Center, Symphony Hall, Museum of History and the Arizona Science Center.

So what, exactly, is ahead for The Rouse Company and Arizona Center? Future plans for the center include a 400-room luxury hotel as well as additional office components as the market demands more space. Above all, The Rouse Company will continue its commitment to deliver one of the best high-quality venues that Phoenix has to offer.

(Far left)
The Gardens at Arizona Center offers a spectacular 3.5-acre oasis of palms, fountains, sculptures and beautiful shaded gardens.

For a casual lunch, a quick bite before a movie, or a fabulous dinner, the restaurants at Arizona Center are a must.

CITY OF PHOENIX

The sun is not the only thing shining brightly in Phoenix these days. For America's premier Southwest city, a booming, diverse economy anchored by high-tech industry continues to flourish. Sky Harbor International Airport now ranks fifth in the world for takeoffs and landings. And its once sleepy downtown has emerged as a sports, cultural and entertainment mecca drawing 12 million fans, conventioneers and visitors each year.

The City of Phoenix, with the help of its residents and city leaders, has transformed itself mightily during the last half century, and the catalyst that has spearheaded the change is captured in one word: development.

Consider that in 1950 the city had an area of 17.1 square miles and a population of 106,000. That placed it 99th among U.S. cities. Today Phoenix covers more than 475 square miles and has a population of 1.3 million, ranking it sixth in the country. Recent census figures rate Phoenix as the fastest-growing city among those with populations greater than 1 million, attributed largely to a highly skilled work force, a modern infrastructure, a competitive tax and regulatory environment, and outstanding quality of life.

Supporting this diversified economy and growth is an award-winning city government dedicated to providing high-quality services and a sound, predictable business climate. In January 2000, after a year-long, in-depth study of management efficiency by the Maxwell School of Citizenship and Public Affairs at Syracuse University, Phoenix was the only city among the nation's 35 largest urban centers to earn an overall grade of "A." Put in perspective, the award is the Pulitzer Prize of city management. The director of the study observed that Phoenix is a "veritable innovation machine... never satisfied with the status quo."

In April 2001 the city of Phoenix was ranked No. 1 in a comprehensive national study that measured how well the top 50 U.S. cities deliver government services to local citizens. Conducted over a three-year period by the Reason Public Policy Institute, the study also praised Phoenix for making its public records not only accessible but also understandable to its citizenry.

Accolades such as these have attracted major employers representing a wide spectrum of professions, industries and interests, most notably high-tech. All told, the greater Phoenix area is a roaring $50 billion-plus marketplace driven by technology. World-leading companies such as Intel, Avnet, Motorola Semiconductor, AlliedSignal, Honeywell and the Boeing Company have discovered and taken advantage of the living and working benefits found in the Valley of the Sun.

One of the abundant resources luring these renowned enterprises and others are the superb fiber-optic and integrated switching digital networks that assure fast and reliable data, voice and video communications. Phoenix has more than 300,000 miles of fiber. There is also diversity and redundancy, with 26 telecommunications carriers and new providers entering the market to meet the growing demands of business.

High-tech, however, is not the only game in town that's prospering. Regional headquarters have also discovered Phoenix. USAA, American Express, Charles Schwab & Co. and MFS Management Investment are among the diverse and notable employers with major local operations.

Other thriving industries include manufacturing, tourism, trade and service. Phoenix's location, coupled with its highway and rail networks, plays a principal role in this success. Phoenix is ideal for service not only to the Southwest, but also to Southern California, the West Coast, northern Mexico, Colorado, Texas and international markets.

Another major component in the picture is the expanded Sky Harbor International Airport, nestled in the center of Phoenix. In 2000 it handled more than 36 million travelers, distributed over

The downtown Phoenix skyline shines as brightly as the city's booming and diverse economy.

370,000 tons of air cargo and served 108 cities with nonstop flights. Developing the international service market for Phoenix has been a top priority for the city and airport. Since 1995, British Airways, Air Canada, Air Jamaica and Lufthansa were recruited and have launched direct international flights to and from Sky Harbor.

Phoenix also boasts the Southwest's foremost meeting headquarters: Phoenix Civic Plaza Convention Center. Located in Downtown Copper Square, the 24-acre facility has been hosting national and regional conventions, trade shows, consumer events and theatrical productions since 1972. During its storied history, it has accommodated over 35 million people, playing host to an average of 350 events annually.

Moreover, its 45 conventions represent yearly attendee expenditures of more than $160 million and draw more than 1 million people to downtown Phoenix each year. The convention center has contributed over $1 billion in local economic impact throughout three decades.

Phoenix Civic Plaza is surrounded by more than 90 restaurants, top hotels, unique retail shops, a 24-screen movie theatre complex, history and science museums, America West Arena and Bank One Ballpark — all within walking distance. The crown jewels of the downtown theatre district — Symphony Hall, historic Orpheum Theatre and Herberger Theater Center — are also just a short stroll away.

Such amenities add to the one thing businesses and residents unfailingly associate and credit Phoenix with: quality of life. "Phoenix offers the best of both worlds: it's an entrepreneurial hot spot and a terrific place to live," said Mayor Skip Rimsza. "With the recent success we've enjoyed on desert preservation, transit and a new bond program, the best is only going to get better."

Recent voter approved initiatives include:
• A parks and desert preserve initiative to purchase and preserve 15,000 acres of the Sonoran Desert.
• A 20-year sales tax to vastly improve and alter the transit system in the city of Phoenix. A light rail system will meander through the heart of Phoenix, with stops near Phoenix Sky Harbor International Airport and extended to Tempe and Mesa. The new system will also include more local fixed-bus service, expanded Dial-A-Ride service and new facilities such as bus pullouts and shelters.
• A $750 million bond to increase, improve, purchase and/or preserve items such as police, fire, environmental sites, libraries and affordable housing for seniors.

Blessed with this type of community support and visionary leadership, there is no telling how much more Phoenix, like its legendary namesake, will continue to flourish.

AMPAM RIGGS PLUMBING

V. Keith Riggs founded a small plumbing company with his wife, Mary, in 1948.

Keith II, Robby and Bob make up the second generation of the Riggs family business.

If one word can sum up Keith Riggs Plumbing, it has to be integrity — for integrity is what the family-owned and operated business was founded on. In 1948, when Keith and Mary Riggs first started their small plumbing company on Washington Street in downtown Phoenix, they were looking not only to work for themselves instead of someone else, but also, and perhaps more important, to provide long-term security for their family. And that is exactly what they did.

Taking great pride in the quality of the service provided to its customers, Keith Riggs Plumbing grew steadily, even though its growth often fluctuated with the economy in Phoenix. After a few years, the business expanded and relocated to Mesa, where it continued to provide a wide range of plumbing work for both residential and commercial customers.

One thing was evident from the day he started his plumbing business: Keith Riggs was not the type of boss to sit behind a desk and shuffle paper while overseeing his employees. Instead, he took pride in being out there with his workers, never expecting them to do anything that he wasn't willing to do himself. In short, Keith Riggs was fondly considered "one of the guys" by his employees.

Because Keith Riggs Plumbing was indeed a family business, all of Keith and Mary's children became involved at an early age. Starting as a full-time employee after her graduation from Brigham Young University in 1964, Judy Riggs Palmer eventually became the company's office manager. In 1965, after two years of junior college, eldest son Russell "Rusty" Riggs started working full time and became the youngest journeyman plumber in Arizona at that time by earning his plumber's

license at the age of 18. Following the family footsteps, Gerald "Gerry" Riggs joined the company in 1969 after two years of college. Not to be left out, daughters Alma and Vicki also worked in the office for many years.

It isn't often that a close-knit family can also work well together. The Riggs family, however, was that kind of family. Rusty served as company president from 1980 to 1997 and then as CEO until he retired in April 1999. Gerry began serving as president in 1997, a role that he still fulfills in true Riggs tradition. And keeping the family ties close, Alma's husband, Gary Goodman, joined the company after graduating from Arizona State University in 1974, while Vicki married Sam Sherwood after he joined the company in 1977. Both Goodman and Sherwood eventually became partners in the business. When Keith Riggs passed away in August of 1988, the groundwork had been laid for the family business to be passed on to his children.

Quality work and integrity continued to feed the company's success. In the early 1980s, Keith Riggs Plumbing had begun to focus on single-family residential plumbing. Not only did this allow the company to simplify its purchasing, bidding and warehousing process, but it also sparked the company's growth. By the 1990s, Keith Riggs Plumbing's growth averaged 10 to 15 percent a year, and in 1993 the company's sales exceeded $1 million per month for the first time. Before long, it was a rare day if sales fell below the $2 million a month mark.

Today, capturing approximately 20 percent of the new home market in the valley, the main thrust of Keith Riggs Plumbing is still single-family residential production homes.

While the majority of its business is still within the Phoenix Valley, the company has also expanded to include the Prescott area.

By merging with AMPAM, the largest nonunion plumbing company in the United States and a company that focused on residential and heavy commercial plumbing, Keith Riggs Plumbing has been able to achieve a better capital base for growth funding. This merger also enabled the company to purchase Southey Plumbing, a smaller local competitor with revenues of $5 million a year, in October 1999. Also in 1999, the company added a custom and light commercial division, which focuses on custom homes and small commercial projects.

IF ONE WORD CAN SUM UP KEITH RIGGS PLUMBING, IT HAS TO BE INTEGRITY — FOR INTEGRITY IS WHAT THE FAMILY-OWNED AND OPERATED BUSINESS WAS FOUNDED ON.

The company attracts and retains employees who would much rather work for Keith Riggs Plumbing than one of the larger companies in the state. In fact, most employees have worked for the company an average of 10 to 15 years, while several have been employed for 30 to 35 years. And that, in and of itself, says a lot.

Integrity is still at the heart of the company's core values — it is paramount in everything Keith Riggs Plumbing does. Those values also include visionary leadership that continuously creates an abundant future, valued employees who are the company's most appreciated resource, and satisfied customers as a result of a primary focus on excellence.

Because it believes in giving back to the community that has so wholeheartedly supported its business, Keith Riggs Plumbing contributes its time, materials and financial assistance to worthwhile causes including Habitat for Humanity and the United Way. Additionally, the company works closely with local high schools and trade schools to provide career opportunities for young people who are looking to enter the plumbing profession. The company has an internal training program that teaches plumbing from scratch.

There is no doubt that Keith Riggs' vision of excellence was a primary factor in his company rising above the others located in the Phoenix Valley. Today, his memory lives on as AMPAM Riggs Plumbing continues to lead the way with integrity and excellence.

The Keith Riggs Plumbing fleet, c. 1959

COLTON CONSTRUCTORS, INC.

More than 30 years ago, COLTON Constructors began changing the face of the greater Phoenix area by constructing pre-engineered metal buildings. Today the full-service general contractor constructs buildings of steel and conventional construction materials and has completed more than 1,000 successful building projects.

After 16 years with Fiberglas Supply and Contracting Company, John G. Colton moved his family from Indiana to Phoenix in 1967 to partner with a former customer. After three years and the completion of several hundred buildings throughout the state of Arizona, John decided to go into business for himself. He founded COLTON Building Systems Company on January 23, 1970, to handle pre-engineered metal building projects as a Design/Build service to owners, architects and general contractors. The company established itself as a full-service general contractor in 1975 with the addition of COLTON Construction, Inc.

With thousands of contractors in the construction industry, COLTON Constructors sets itself apart with quality, timely completions. Pre-engineered steel structural systems are erected in the field. Using steel with tilt-up concrete walls saves time and money while simultaneously providing strength and stability. In 1984 COLTON established its steel erection services as a separate business, Eagle Steel Erectors, Inc. This allows other Contractors and Owners to take advantage of Eagle Steel's quality steel erection performance.

John's son, Bob, graduated from Arizona State University's School of Construction in 1979 and joined COLTON Construction. COLTON Building Systems and COLTON Construction merged into COLTON Constructors, Inc. in 1992, combining the company's steel building expertise with general construction. This merger has resulted in successful projects that have included everything from using tilt-up concrete walls with metal roofing systems to multi-level structural steel buildings to conventional construction.

Bob took over as president and CEO in 1995 and has tripled the business since that time. Today COLTON Constructors' projects reach into California, Colorado, Oklahoma and Texas. The company opened a regional office in the Dallas/Fort Worth area in January 2001.

COLTON Constructors builds projects for the automotive, aviation, industrial/manufacturing, office/tenant improvement, warehouse/distribution and specialty industries. The company's growing list of satisfied clients includes General Motors Corp., Intel, Salt River Project, Federal Express, Swift Transportation and Phelps Dodge, as well as national account clients Universal Technical Institute, Sunstate Equipment, Ewing Irrigation and Unifirst.

COLTON Constructors' Mission is "To provide distinctive and personalized service from conception through completion." The company uses an iceberg analogy to convey how much has to happen below the water level before the construction phase actually begins. It is all part of the company's Design/Build approach to construction, an approach it has used since its inception. Design/Build involves managing an entire project from the planning and design stages through construction into occupancy.

The company provides services in project support, contracting, metal buildings and management. Its reputation and

Phoenix Country Day School — AIA Western Regional Award Winner COLTON Constructors is completing its sixth project for the Phoenix Country Day School Board with architect Hugh Knoell and School Architectural Representative Ken Allison.
Photo by Hugh Knoell

A to Z Equipment Rental & Sales — COLTON Contructors has completed nine projects for A to Z Equipment Rental & Sales, working closely with A to Z owner, Fred Matricardi.
Photo by Laine Wahl

respected track record have secured strong relationships with the banking, bonding and insurance industries. COLTON Constructors is committed to total financial responsibility, including 100 percent payment and performance bonds and lien protection.

COLTON Constructors' Design/Build program works with outside, qualified professional architects and engineers, providing functional design with more competitive pricing than conventional projects. By coordinating costs with functional use for each proposed building project, the Owner always retains control over the project before the money is spent. Quality projects are the result of excellent Owner/Constructor relationships before, during and after construction.

A successful construction project starts with the site location and real estate. The company organized COLTON Realty, Ltd. in 1981 as a service to its customers. It became COLTON Commercial in 2000, run by John's other son, Dan, who brought 16 years of commercial and industrial real estate experience to the company. COLTON Commercial services COLTON Constructors' land requirements for Design/Build projects with out-of-state companies, as well as for local company expansions or relocations.

With years of experience and knowledge in code compliance and other regulations affecting the construction industry, the COLTON name is synonymous with quality throughout Arizona and the Southwestern United States COLTON Constructors partners with its clients as part of the construction team. The company embraces complexity and is quick to solve problems. It has zero tolerance for accidents and puts safety before profits.

COLTON Constructors attributes its success to its employees, who are dedicated to hard work. Employees work together as a team in a family atmosphere. They are motivated, enjoy their work and take pleasure in a job well done. The company has rewarded its employees since 1974 with profit sharing for successful team results and a bonus program for individual performance. Employee support, benefits and recognition are high priorities.

In addition, industry and community involvement have always been high priorities for John Colton. Since 1993 he has been actively pursuing a tax change to directly benefit property owners, the construction industry and the Arizona Department of Revenue. He helped found the Arizona Chapter for the Associated Builders and Contractors, which promotes free enterprise and merit shop philosophies. John served as president in 1977 and on a special board by request in 1987. A long-time, active supporter of ASU's School of Construction, he served as

Tempe Mitsubishi — Bud Thurston and Tom Sparrow have worked with COLTON Constructors on Design/Build projects for: Honda Cars of Mesa, Mesa Mitsubishi, Honda Service Center of Gilbert, Tempe Hyundai and Acura of Tempe, which is currently under construction.
Photo by Todd Photographic Services

president of the ASU Construction Industry Advisory Council from 1981 through 1986. In 2001 he started a research fellowship endowment fund at ASU to further improve the construction industry for the direct benefit of Construction Owners.

COLTON Constructors intends to maintain a high-level profile in the construction industry and continue to earn the trust and confidence of its customers. The company has built its business on integrity with repeat and referral customers. It has constructed 10 or more projects for several clients. Quality always comes before profit with COLTON Constructors, whose buildings stand the test of time and continue to change the face of Arizona and the Southwest.

Although no longer part of the company's logo, the eagle holds great significance for COLTON Constructors, as evidenced by the many eagles in its Tempe office. One such eagle displays the caption, "They can who believe they can." John Colton has always believed he can. His company continues to uphold that spirit of determination.

Aviation Facility, Goodyear Airport — a $6.5 million project for Dimension Aviation, a subsidiary of Sabreliner Corporation
Photo by Todd Photographic Services

GREAT WESTERN HOMES

Great Western Homes, a newcomer among homebuilders in Phoenix, is thriving in the competitive new home market. Although the company is only eight years old, thanks to the vast experience of its diverse management team and expert guidance by Scott Smith, company owner and president, the Mesa-based builder is holding its own among the pack.

As an entry-level homebuilder, Great Western Homes currently builds approximately 500 new homes a year, bringing in over $85 million in annual revenues — a real accomplishment considering that the company had $600,000 in revenue in 1994. Smith, however, takes more pride in the fact that while his company's homes come in all sizes, designs and price ranges, each and every one is a quality home and a very good value for its buyer.

Most of the homes the company builds are located in the east and southeast Valley of Greater Phoenix. With houses priced between $80,000 and $400,000, Great Western Homes' target market is primarily first-time and first-time move up buyers. Smith's success is attributed to the quality of his company's homes and neighborhoods, along with the fact that he offers first-time buyers as many incentives as possible, thereby making it easier for them to purchase a new home.

Smith, who is trained as a CPA and attorney, was originally hired by Great Western Homes as a financial consultant. Afterward, he went to work for the company full time. In 1995, during the Valley's longest housing boom, Smith took over as president. His success at the helm of the company eventually led to his buying out the shareholders to become the company's sole owner.

Today, Smith resides in a Great Western Home in a Great Western Neighborhood with his wife and children. And while he has led the company to be named No. 48 on the Arthur Anderson Arizona 100, Smith believes his success has been greatly influenced by his management team. For example, Vice President of Sales and Marketing Robert Stapley has been with the company since its inception and has more than 25 years of industry experience in new home sales and marketing. Smith is quick to admit that managers like Stapley have been a vital part of the growth of Great Western Homes. They also have been an integral part of Smith's business philosophy, which is to hire good people and let them do their jobs.

Smith's commitment to excellence extends out into the communities in which Great Western builds its homes. The company is active in many local activities that benefit both Great Western neighborhoods and its children, such as sponsoring Little League teams, local sports camps and Shakespeare theatre.

So with all this success behind him, what's ahead for Smith and Great Western Homes? According to Smith, the company will continue to look for opportunities that spark his creative interests as well as the interests of his superior management team. But above all, it will continue to build quality Great Western Homes in quality Great Western Neighborhoods.

Scott Smith, president and owner of Great Western Homes

Great Western Homes come in all sizes, designs and price ranges

ROWLAND COMPANIES

When Bill Rowland founded Rowland Companies, a Phoenix-based construction/development manager and general contractor, in 1984, he was committed to building a construction company of excellence. He knew then what all Rowland Companies employees know now: "It is not one thing done 1,000 times better that makes their work a matter of excellence. It is 1,000 things done just a little better that creates a margin of excellence."

That philosophy still holds true for Rowland Companies, whose logo is a pyramid representing owners, architects and contractors all working together in a collaborative team effort to successfully complete a construction project. But the pyramid has another significance for the company as well: It represents the lasting value of great design and quality craftsmanship, reminding the company and its clients of the oldest surviving Egyptian pyramid dating back more than 4,500 years.

Because design and construction are distinctively different arts, Rowland Companies does not attempt to do both, but rather concentrates on the construction aspect. The firm provides construction/development management and general contractor services throughout the western United States. From its inception, the firm has strived to establish long-term relationships with its clients. In fact, many of Rowland's projects come from repeat customers and referrals in health care, religious and other general commercial construction areas.

Rowland builds specialty surgical hospitals, surgery centers, churches, education facilities, senior housing facilities, commercial buildings and multifamily housing. In addition, its custom home affiliate, Rowland Luxury Homes, builds custom homes in affluent communities throughout Phoenix and North Scottsdale starting at $1 million.

Understanding its clients' businesses and needs has set Rowland Companies apart in the industry. The firm focuses on what is important to the end user. Communication is a key component of Rowland's entire process. Keeping communication lines open helps the firm control costs, stay within budget and remain on schedule, all with no surprises.

Rowland Companies has earned numerous prestigious awards as a result of its unwavering commitment to excellence, including *Arizona Business Magazine's* No. 1 General Contractor in Arizona Under 100 Employees in 2000, and No. 1 Custom Home Builder in Phoenix in 2001.

Giving back to the community is vital to Rowland Companies, which encourages all employees to participate in community events. Rowland employees provide direct support to specific organizations, including the American Cancer Society, Central Phoenix YMCA, St. Mary's Food Bank, Christmas in April and Free Arts of Arizona. Rowland also supports the creative arts by contributing to the cost of tickets for employees to attend theatrical productions at the Arizona Theater Company, Ballet Arizona and Phoenix Symphony, as well as various other theatrical productions.

The future is bright for Rowland Companies, which will continue to focus on health care, religious, senior living, general commercial and luxury residential communities. The firm will remain committed to excellence in every aspect of its work, passing on a legacy of integrity and quality craftsmanship. Rowland Companies has played, and will continue to play, a significant role in shaping the character of the greater Phoenix area.

Rowland Companies is one of the premier builders of churches and religious education buildings in Phoenix.

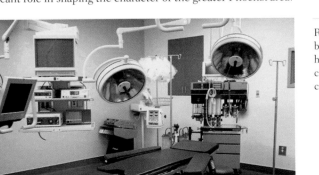

Rowland Companies builds specialty surgical hospitals and surgery centers for the health care industry.

Phoenix financial and insurance companies provide

support for a host of Greater Phoenix organizations.

Business & Finance

SCF OF ARIZONA

In 2002 SCF of Arizona (State Compensation Fund) celebrated its 33rd year of service. However, the earliest workers' compensation systems reach back to the turn of the century as the Industrial Revolution changed the nation's workplace. Because there was no system in place at that time to manage the increased number of on-the-job injuries, many work-related incidents resulted in expensive lawsuits where the employer was only financially responsible for the injury if he was found liable in a court of law.

Needless to say, this early method of compensation was not a good one for either the employer or employee. As a result, several individual states including Wisconsin, New Jersey and Washington started a program modeled after one in Germany whereby individuals were covered and compensated for injuries that occurred in the workplace. Thus, the earliest forms of state funds were formed.

Keeping this history in mind, the constitutional framers of Arizona decided in the early 1920s to create procedures that would allow businesses in the state to purchase insurance for work-related injuries. As a result, a workers' compensation law

Customer service is one reason SCF of Arizona continues to be Arizona's largest workers' compensation carrier of choice.

SCF acquired the ABACUS building in 1986 to meet the needs of servicing a growing economy.

was passed in 1925. This led to the formation of the Industrial Commission of Arizona (ICA). SCF of Arizona was one of ICA's many branches.

The Arizona State Legislature established a state compensation fund as a separate, self-supporting entity on January 1, 1969. Now referred to as SCF of Arizona, it began operating with 470 former ICA employees and 18,807 policyholders. Its immediate mission was to provide a ready market of workers' compensation insurance for Arizona's employers at the lowest possible cost. Keeping this mission as its focus, it immediately set out to improve claims management and enhance policyholder services while providing excellent customer service. By 1979, the number of policyholders had grown to nearly 23,000.

Since its inception, SCF of Arizona has become the leader in the state's workers' compensation insurance industry, providing workers' compensation insurance to literally tens of thousands of Arizona employers and paying benefits to more than 1 million claimants. Yet its contributions to the people of Arizona do not stop there. SCF plays an integral role in bolstering the state's economy, investing millions of dollars in retail and commercial markets. Not only has SCF of Arizona ensured that a ready market for workers' compensation insurance is available to all Arizona's employers, but it sets the standard for service and cost that other carriers try to follow. The result is lower overall costs for workers' compensation insurance for Arizona employers. SCF offices are strategically located throughout Arizona, with nine district offices located in Flagstaff, Lake Havasu City, Mesa, Phoenix, Prescott, Show Low, Tucson and Yuma — with the corporate office also located in Phoenix.

According to Vice President of Insurance Operations Chris Kamper, SCF of Arizona insures 60 percent of the employers in Arizona. What sets it apart from the others is that it handles the workers' compensation insurance for the majority of the smaller companies that private insurers won't cover. SCF insured more than 50,000 policyholders for the first time in 2001.

SCF's formal mission includes fully protecting insured employers against liability for work-related injuries or illnesses incurred by their employees; providing all legally entitled benefits promptly and equitably to injured workers and their dependents; assuring the future stability and solvency of SCF and the workers' compensation system through the prudent investment of reserves and required surplus; and recognizing the value and importance of all SCF customers.

SCF OF ARIZONA PLAYS AN INTEGRAL ROLE IN BOLSTERING THE STATE'S ECONOMY

SCF of Arizona's only business is workers' compensation insurance. It is fully competitive and operates under the same rules, rate structure and regulations as the private insurance companies that provide workers' compensation insurance in Arizona. The governor of Arizona appoints the five-member board of directors.

Providing the highest return on investment dollars to its policyholders is a priority for SCF. As a result, income that is not used to provide benefits to injured workers and/or their dependents, or for operating expenses, is returned to policyholders in the form of dividends. Although dividends cannot be promised or guaranteed, in each year of SCF's existence it has paid policyholder dividends and, in fact, has paid a total of over $888 million since 1970. These accomplishments enhance the total business climate in Arizona and foster growth and opportunity for new businesses and old.

Today's SCF handles approximately 44,000 claims a year, from cut fingers and amputations to fatal accidents that occur on

According to Fred Campbell, third generation president of The Phoenix Brick Yard, which began its longstanding partnership with SCF of Arizona when it purchased a workers' compensation policy in 1927, the 70-year relationship has been built on "trust, service and the willingness of both parties to grow and improve."

the job. It is resolved in its purpose to provide a stable and reliable source of workers' compensation insurance to employers in Arizona at the lowest possible cost. It strives to make sure that all injured workers receive all of the benefits to which they are entitled. Additionally, it endeavors to continually assist those injured workers in an early return to the workplace.

"We consider ourselves to be the frontrunner of the industry," says Kamper. "Others come and go but we stay here. And as we go forward, that stability will remain constant. We will continue to efficiently serve the needs of Arizona businesses."

SCF of Arizona insures a broad range of workers in various occupations in the state of Arizona.

In addition to producing exceptional goods for

individuals and industry, Phoenix manufacturing

and distribution companies provide employment

for area residents.

Manufacturing & Distribution

THE BOEING COMPANY

The Boeing Company — named after founder William Boeing, who began building airplanes in 1915 — is recognized worldwide as a major manufacturer of commercial jetliners. But with the merger of aerospace giant McDonnell Douglas Corporation in 1997, The Boeing Company added a wealth of new defense technologies, including the world-famous, Arizona-built AH-64D Apache Longbow multi-role combat helicopter.

The AH-64D Apache Longbow combat helicopter

Boeing produces the Apache Longbow at its ultra-modern production and research center in Mesa, Arizona, which employs 5,000. The facility, part of the Boeing Military Aircraft and Missile Systems Group, has been the home of the Apache since it went into production in the mid-1980s. The company received two five-year, multi-year contracts for 501 Apache Longbows from the U.S. Army: a $1.9 billion contract to remanufacture 232 AH-64A Apaches into Apache Longbows and a

$2.3 billion contract to deliver 269 more Apache Longbows. Boeing is also producing 67 WAH-64 Apaches for the U.K. and 30 AH-64D Apaches for The Netherlands, and is finalizing contracts with several other international defense forces. Boeing has a goal of delivering "1,000 More" Apaches this decade.

In addition to producing combat helicopters, Mesa's Boeing site develops and produces ordnance systems including a 25mm cannon for ground and sea vehicles, a 30mm automatic cannon for the AH-64 Apache, and 30mm, 35mm and 40mm cannons for a variety of vehicles. Boeing is also working on an advanced 27mm aircraft cannon for use on the proposed Joint Strike Fighter for the U.S. Air Force, U.S. Navy and the U.S. Marine Corps. In all, more than 12,000 Boeing cannon systems are in service in 23 countries. Mesa's site also serves as a strategic manufacturing center for wire harnesses and electrical sub-assembly and produces thousands of components for Boeing military and commercial aircraft.

Boeing emphasizes development of emerging technology companywide, and the Mesa campus hosts an arm of The Boeing Company's research and development organization, known as Phantom Works. The site created the Rotorcraft Pilot's Associate, a futuristic artificial intelligence software system designed to control helicopter mission activities, and the Canard Rotor/Wing aircraft, which lifts off like a helicopter and converts to a high-speed, fixed-wing craft. Phantom Works also developed the NOTAR® anti-torque system, an innovative alternative to the tail rotor on conventional helicopters.

Boeing, which earned the Arizona Association of Industries Manufacturer of the Year in 2000, is a good neighbor worldwide and is committed to its Mesa community through annual donations that total more than $1 million through gifts, grants and its Employees Community Fund. In addition, its employees and retirees volunteer more than 16,000 hours annually to outreach programs ranging from Junior Achievement to fund-raising walks and involvement in local schools. Boeing in Mesa spends $3 million annually on training and an additional $1.1 million on employee tuition at Arizona colleges and universities.

The Boeing Company looks ahead to a future of new opportunities and challenges and remains committed to its communities, to research, and to manufacturing commercial and military aircraft, including the No. 1 combat helicopter in the world.

SPELLMAN HARDWOODS

When James C. Spellman moved his family from Minneapolis to Phoenix in 1962, he came with years of management experience in the lumber industry. Wanting to continue in his trade, he purchased Larry Griffith Wholesale at Grand Avenue and 29th Drive and incorporated Spellman Hardwoods in February 1963, converting the operation to a distribution yard.

Almost seven years later to the day, founder James C. Spellman passed away. Leaving his son, James W., in charge of the family operation. Production and distribution increased through the 1970s despite both major and minor recessions. In 1980 Spellman Hardwoods moved to its location at 43rd Avenue and Highland, which provided more room for inventory and distribution at its 84,000-square-foot facility on four acres of land. The company also built a mill at the new site that runs three molders, two planers and three rip saws, providing the resources necessary to supply millwork to the customers' specifications.

Business has increased with the market over the years. Spellman Hardwoods opened a warehouse operation in Flagstaff in 1983 that duplicates the Phoenix location's inventory and distributes to the northern half of the state with its own trucks. The Flagstaff subsidiary added 18,000 square feet to the company's operations.

The company also expanded locally in 1999, opening a 30,000-square-foot distribution operation on four more acres of land on 44th Avenue. The expansion, about a block and a half away from the main location, provides storage as well as loading and unloading facilities. Anticipating future growth, Spellman Hardwoods has room to expand even further when the need arises.

Since its beginning, the family-owned and operated business has taken a customer-oriented approach to business. As its name implies, the company's specialty is hardwoods — including hardwood plywood, veneers and particle board products — which it provides primarily to furniture manufacturers, cabinet shops, millwork houses and subcontractors. Each customer wants the material in a certain stage or form and Spellman Hardwoods provides the lumber in the form the customer desires. As CEO James W. Spellman said, "To complement our quality products and people, we have built a delivery fleet committed to getting material to our customers when they want it."

The hardwood company plays a vital role in its community, offering its expertise and resources in lumber to various causes. It is a major contributor to the building fund for Brophy College Preparatory and a regular donor to the Westside Food Bank and St. Mary's Food Bank.

Spellman Hardwoods is a member of the National Hardwood Lumber Association, which elected James W. Spellman's son, James N. "Chip," to its board at the 2000 national convention. The company is also a member of the Hardwood Distributor's Association, of which Chip is vice president, and the Pacific Coast Hardwood Lumber Distributors.

With a good management force in place that includes Chip as president and James R. Grant, the elder Spellman's son-in-law, as vice president and a young sales staff, Spellman Hardwoods looks forward to providing its customers with quality material delivered on time at a competitive price for years to come.

Photos by Jay Falter, First Impressions Photography

Phoenix retail establishments and service industries

offer an impressive variety of choices for

residents and visitors.

Marketplace

Partners in Phoenix

EVERGREEN HARDWARE AND ELECTRIC, INC.

Evergreen Hardware and Electric, Inc. was built on the foundation of its motto "Where Money has Value." Today the family-owned and operated business continues to thrive with that motto in mind. And while Bert and Jean Lough have made their business a success story, their beginning was one of simplicity, hard work and family values.

After returning from World War II, Bert Lough went to electrical trade school at night while working a full time job. Although the idea of starting a business was not even a thought yet, his subsequent work as an electrician then foreman and finally an estimator at Banks Electric, prepared him well by giving him the education and work experience that he would need to ensure the future success of his hardware stores.

Two people that Bert and Jean admired very much were Sam and Eveline Lofing. They had taken Bert under wing much as they would a son and taught him sound business practices from their retail business experience. Subsequently, they helped Bert and Jean get started in their first business, Lough's Variety Store on South 40th Street in Phoenix, just south of the airport.

The original Evergreen Hardware store on South 16th Street

Bert and Jean Lough

The variety store opened in 1947. It was built from a U.S. Army barracks building remodeled to have living quarters in the rear and a store in front. In those early days, Jean, who is a natural businesswoman, ran the store herself with help from Bert when he wasn't working at his job as an electrician. As a neighborhood general store, Lough's Variety carried mostly dry goods such as household goods, needles and threads, yarn, batteries, small hardware items, bicycles, candy, toys, pots and pans, paint, glue and, of course, Levi's®, because no one wanted to purchase off-brand jeans at that time.

When the Lofings decided to sell their business on South 16th Street in Phoenix, Bert and Jean bought it. The Lough's kept the name Evergreen, which was derived from the large trees in the area, and added Hardware and Electric to the name. While Evergreen Hardware and Electric began to focus on those items that a hardware store generally carries, it still catered to the neighborhood by offering toys, board games and kitchen goods. Eventually, the store began to carry wooden doors and appliances such as refrigerators, washers and dryers. As their daughter Brenda recalls, Bert and Jean tried carrying a lot of different things to see what would sell. Eventually, electrical and plumbing became their niche.

Bert was adamant about always being open during the posted hours of 8:00 a.m. to 5:00 p.m. Monday through Saturday.

Every morning, he would walk the 100 feet from the family's house to the back door of the store and move display merchandise out onto the front porch — and Evergreen Hardware was open for business. Bert and Jean's three children — Don, Connie and Brenda — grew up working in the family store. Don would make cooler pads and bale excelsior, cut pipe and help load and unload merchandise. Connie and Brenda dusted, cleaned, stocked the shelves and changed window displays. As their business progressed, Bert and Jean hired a few of the local retirees in the neighborhood to help out in the store.

The true growth of the business occurred as customers discovered that Bert had a sincere concern for the many different problems that they encountered on a daily basis. His unique way of solving their problems coupled with the reasonable prices of the merchandise the store carried kept local customers coming back. This reputation became the foundation of Evergreen Hardware and Electric.

The expansion of the business was ultimately triggered when Phoenix' Sky Harbor International Airport acquired the land on which the original Evergreen store was located. For the 18 years following the original notice of intent to purchase the surrounding property for expansion, the airport slowly bought the homes and businesses surrounding Evergreen Hardware. Despite the loss of local customers, the store continued to thrive.

Today Evergreen Hardware owns and operates 10 stores throughout Arizona. The business has evolved from a variety-type hardware store to one that specializes in electrical and plumbing supplies. With 75 employees, Don R. Lough has been in charge of converting Evergreen from a sole proprietorship to a multifaceted corporation. Don, along with Mike Todd and Tony Burns, have been instrumental in the business's expansion, property acquisitions and building projects, while at the same time supplying, maintaining and managing the 10 current retail locations, its warehouses and offices.

Since 1979, Don has served as corporation vice president — a position that is well deserved after leading the business and its growth for over 30 years, with Bert serving as president and Jean as treasurer. Daughter Brenda fills the role of corporate secretary after having managed the office at various times with her sister-in-law, Judy Lough. And in keeping with the tradition of a family business, all of Bert and Jean's grandchildren have worked in the business through the years.

In addition to the success of their business, Bert and Jean, along with their children, have been active with the community, especially in supporting its youth, for over 50 years. Believing that the future lies in the hands of the children, they support such groups as the 4-H, FFA, Juvenile Diabetes Foundation and Special Olympics, as well as the sponsorship of several scholarships through local high schools and the Salvation Army.

There's no doubt about it — Bert and Jean Lough are indeed an example of what hard work, family values and building a successful business are all about.

Jean Lough (left) and Patty White at Lough's Variety in the early days during the holiday season

Sean Todd and Shelly O'Neal stand in front of Evergreen Hardware's office, warehouse, and retail store on South 7th street in Phoenix.

Phoenix media and transportation companies

keep information and people circulating

throughout the region.

Networks

THE TRIBUNE

Once considered a bedroom community, the East Valley has grown leaps and bounds in development, population and technology and now claims more than 1 million residents. As it has grown and evolved, its premier daily newspaper, the *Tribune*, has had to do the same.

Founded in Mesa in 1891 as the *Evening Weekly Free Press*, the newspaper has undergone many names and changes since, but it has continued to serve Mesa and its surrounding communities throughout those changes. Still headquartered in downtown Mesa, it also has offices in Scottsdale, Tempe and Chandler.

Today the city of Chandler is home to Intel, Motorola and Microchip Technology. In fact, 58 percent of all aerospace and high-technology jobs in the state are located in the East Valley. "Tempe has more jobs than it has men, women and children in the entire city," notes Jim Ripley, editor. "It is a net importer of jobs, as is Chandler, as is Scottsdale."

The East Valley also offers its own arts and entertainment opportunities. Residents no longer have to drive into Phoenix to find quality dining and entertainment attractions. Scottsdale and Tempe have some of the finest offerings in that regard. The East Valley has become a region unto itself, evidenced by a market population growth of 34.2 percent between 1990 and 2000.

Freedom Communications, Inc. purchased the *Tribune* in 2000, providing the paper with a strong commitment to liberty, ideas and community. Freedom publishes 25 daily newspapers and 37 weeklies and is dedicated to a community focus on the front page and affecting the lives of the people it serves. That devotion is evident in the *Tribune's* reporters, which include both seasoned veterans and up-and-coming talent who live in the communities they serve and have a personal interest in the stories they cover. Staff reporters are accessible to readers and are interested in their opinions.

The *Tribune* family of products includes the East Valley and Scottsdale editions of the newspaper, *Get Out*, *Value Clipper Magazine*, the *Ahwatukee Foothills News*, the *Daily News-Sun*, *Prospector* and *Surprise Today*.

With a daily circulation of 106,000, local news comes first at the *Tribune*, which offers two editions: one for the East Valley and one for Scottsdale and the Northeast Valley. The editions vary slightly, offering news that is most pertinent to each community's readers. "People are interested in news, first, from the town in which they live, but they care about news from neighboring cities and from around the Valley, too. Our presentation of local news is to make it the first thing readers see when they open the paper, and we devote more space to local news to satisfy the demand for news that is relevant to the lives of people who live here," says Publisher Karen Wittmer.

In addition to local news, the *Tribune* provides national, international, business and sports news, reporting with a local angle whenever possible. It also offers a daily "East Valley Living" section, which provides lifestyle issues and features for readers. Special sections appear in the newspaper throughout the week. "Silicon Desert" addresses the East Valley's high-technology focus by offering pertinent news and information. Tips and trends on living in the Sonoran Desert are provided in "Desert Nesting." In "Perspective" readers can find in-depth commentaries on important local, regional and international issues.

The *Tribune* launched three new weekly newspapers devoted to the communities of South Tempe, Chandler and Gilbert that appear each Wednesday. *South Tempe Voice*, *Chandler Connection* and *Gilbert Guardian* provide readers with an inside look at their local community.

Thursday's paper includes *Get Out*, a weekly entertainment and recreation guide. This guide is also available on racks throughout Phoenix and the East Valley as a free, stand-alone publication. The *Tribune* also publishes *Value Clipper Magazine* — a four-color, glossy coupon booklet mailed to 850,000 homes — the *Ahwatukee Foothills News*, the *Daily News-Sun*, the *Prospector* and *Surprise Today*.

The *Tribune* is an integral part of the communities it serves and is committed to supporting those communities in a variety of ways. One of its unique services is Infolink, an audio-text system that provides information via phone lines 24 hours a day,

coordinating creative or technical writing, photography, layout and design, electronic composition, commercial printing, and packaging and delivery. The service also includes an automated voice response system for local schools and teachers. Infolink enables parents to check messages and find out about homework assignments and field trips, or to leave messages for teachers.

The paper also supports the communities it serves through its "*Tribune* in Education" program, which provides newspapers and educational materials to schools throughout the East Valley and Scottsdale. The newspapers are used to teach reading, vocabulary, math, social studies and literature. The program, designed to complement the work done throughout the year by classroom teachers, is available to teachers at no cost through corporate and individual sponsorships.

The newspaper itself provides corporate sponsorship for community events and organizations, and its employees volunteer their time to local events. The *Tribune* played a key role, along with two other companies, in organizing "Kids Voting." This program allows kids to vote at special booths on election day, introducing them to the voting process and highlighting its importance. Initially offered only in the East Valley, "Kids Voting" has expanded into a nationwide program.

The *Tribune* has garnered numerous awards for its dedication to being the best newspaper in the East Valley. The paper won eight statewide first-place awards from Arizona Newspapers Foundation in 2000, including first place in general excellence and in departmental news coverage. "The honors are great to receive," says Editor Ripley, "but doing the best job for our readers is our primary goal."

As the *Tribune*'s readership continues to evolve, the staff's thinking does the same. Determined to educate its readers on what the East Valley has become, serve the developing region and be its main news provider, the newspaper will continually change and improve so that it reaches those goals. The *Tribune* is committed to being the premier daily newspaper in the East Valley, and as it continues to do its job, people in the East Valley are sure to turn to it as their source for local news.

Local news comes first at the *Tribune*, which features a new weekly newspaper each Wednesday devoted to the local community.

AMERICA WEST AIRLINES

America West Airlines, based in Tempe, Arizona, inaugurated air service on August 1, 1983. With three Boeing 737 aircraft and 280 employees, the airline's original service consisted of 20 daily departures with a total of five cities being served: its hub at Phoenix Sky Harbor International Airport; Colorado Springs, Colorado; Kansas City, Missouri; Los Angeles, California and Wichita, Kansas.

America West Airlines serves more nonstop destinations with more frequency than any other airline in Phoenix.

The United Way, which benefits the Boys & Girls Club, is one of the many charities that America West Airlines supports.

Started in the aftermath of the deregulation of the U.S. airline industry, America West grew at a rapid pace. By the end of 1983, the company had grown to include 10 Boeing 737s and 806 employees with 76 daily departures from 13 cities. Continuing its phenomenal growth, America West achieved major-airline status in 1990 with a fleet of 104 aircraft, 14,000 employees, 672 daily departures serving 62 cities, and annual revenues over $1 billion dollars.

Today, America West Airlines is a low-fare, full-service, major carrier, serving more non-stop destinations from its Phoenix hub across the U.S. with greater frequency than any other carrier — and destinations that include Mexico and Canada. The airline's fleet includes Airbus A320s, Airbus A319s, Boeing 757s and Boeing 737s. Additionally, the airline maintains strategic alliances with Continental Airlines, Mesa Airlines, Big Sky Airlines, Chautauqua, Air China, British Airways, Northwest Airlines and EVA Airways.

Coupled with its excellent service, frequent daily departures and numerous destinations, America West Airlines has a generous community relations program that demonstrates the company's values and good corporate citizenship by supporting many community-based organizations and activities. These activities are strategically designed to enhance the quality of life in America West markets and build goodwill toward the company while generating awareness of the airline and the many quality services it offers.

Among the many community organizations that America West Airlines supports is the Arizona Science Center, a state-of-the-art facility in downtown Phoenix with more than 300 hands-on exhibits, a digital planetarium, and a five-story giant-screen theater. Additionally, the airline sponsors many professional sports teams and college athletic programs including the Arizona Diamondbacks, Arizona Cardinals, Phoenix Coyotes, Phoenix Suns, Arizona State University Sun Devils and University of Arizona Wildcats. The Airline also sponsors select golf tournaments including The Phoenix Open and The Touchstone Energy — Tucson Open.

Believing in giving back to the community, America West Airlines donates $4 million annually through its corporate giving program to help numerous charities and community programs in the areas of education, the arts and sciences, and health and human services. Additionally, the America West Airlines "Do Crew" — the company's corps of dedicated employee volunteers — donates more than 3,000 hours of personal time each year to neighborhood groups, schools and community-based organizations. Last but not least, through programs such as the company's Miles of Hope program, the flying public may donate FlightFund miles to the American Red Cross, the Make-a-Wish Foundation, Angel Flight and the National Runaway Switchboard.

With a proven track record of successful growth and continually supporting the communities that it serves, America West Airlines is indeed committed to value and convenience while making the world a better place in which to live.

City of Phoenix, Photo by Don Stevenson

A broad range of professionals provide essential

services to Phoenix businesses and residents.

Professional Services

e GROUP

landscape architecture/environmental design, inc.

With a name like e group, the Phoenix-based landscape architectural firm stands out in today's technology-savvy society. The funny thing is, however, that the "e" in e group has nothing to do with electronic commerce. The "e" actually refers to the environment as well as the company's original founder, Richard Emik. "Group" signifies the firm's collaborative effort in a highly proprietary industry.

Nestled on Central Avenue in the hub between mid-town and downtown, the company offers landscape architecture, environmental design, land planning and urban design services to land developers, municipalities, government agencies and residential builders. The firm's strength lies in its diverse experience and portfolio, design approach and willingness to go the extra mile.

e group offers Southwest regional hardscape designs with native desert plant materials, at times augmented with non-native materials, to achieve a variety of forms, colors and textures. The company believes that by balancing the project's needs and issues

effectively, it can serve the long-term interests of its clients, the community and the environment. Projects such as the Tovrea Castle Garden Restoration, the Opuntia Exhibit at the Desert Botanical Garden, the Scottsdale Waterfront Development, the Marriott Timeshare at Desert Ridge and the American Express Corporate Campus are good examples. The firm's projects span the entire southwestern United States with a future in Mexico and beyond.

The company's collaborative culture sets it apart in the environmental design industry. e group views its employees as team members, each of which is vital to the entire process. The group also collaborates with other landscape architects and artists on occasion to provide the best team for the project at hand. Modern technology, namely the use of AutoCAD, frees up time, allowing for more collaboration within the office, with clients and in the field.

In addition to being "responsible landscape architects and environmental designers" while satisfying clients' needs, e group is committed to giving back to its community. Several team members donate their time to Arizona State University and other institutions to educate and promote responsible landscape architecture. e group also provides pro bono work for various nonprofit organizations, including the Fresh Start Women's center, ball fields for local YMCAs and master planning for a local community garden.

By taking a diversified approach for the past 25 years, e group has significantly influenced the overall landscape of the greater Phoenix area through various community projects as well as successful public and private developments. As environmental issues and landscape architecture continue to increase in value and confront the world, e group will continue to evolve its services to be of the most benefit to all.

The company is shifting its focus to a broader perspective, embracing new ideas, services and designs. The Internet will play a significant role in transitioning the group from a purely regional service provider to an international presence. Toward that end, e group will continue to expand its services and knowledge as well as pursue new markets in an effort to provide the most benefit to its clients, communities and the environment.

Rendering for the Opuntia Exhibit, by e group

The Richard and Annette Block Cancer Survivors Park in downtown Phoenix integrates the natural desert environment with the existing streetscape.

LEWIS AND ROCA LLP

Few major law firms have such unconventional beginnings as those of Lewis and Roca. In the late 1940s Phoenix was still a very new town. Orme Lewis, however, was old Arizona — his family had lived in the state since the 1870s. A graduate of George Washington University College of Law, Lewis opened his Phoenix law office in 1947. Paul Roca, a practicing Arizona lawyer since 1941, and Harold Scoville, a former county attorney and superior court judge, soon joined him in founding the full-service, Phoenix-based partnership in 1950. More than 50 years later, that partnership flourishes as a premier, progressive Southwest law firm with more than 130 attorneys in its Phoenix, Tucson and Las Vegas offices.

Lewis and Roca is committed to excellence and to making a difference in the community. Its lawyers believe in contributing to the improvement of the law and the legal system. Lewis and Roca has been the most active law office in the state since 1955 in keeping the civil and appellate procedural rules of the Supreme Court current. Public service at Lewis and Roca often means hands-on work. Lawyers serve on civic and professional boards throughout Arizona and Nevada and regularly contribute their time to the local Volunteer Lawyers Program.

Lewis and Roca has always been on the leading legal edge. It was the first major Arizona firm to break the employment barrier and recruit women in 1967. In 1973 Lewis and Roca was the only firm in the Rocky Mountain states with a female partner. Since then, two female partners have moved on to become Arizona's Attorney General and a United States Ninth Circuit Court of Appeals judge.

The firm serves a diverse base of local, regional, national and international clients including some of the world's largest corporations. Lewis and Roca provides a full range of legal services in appeals, arbitration and mediation, banking, commercial finance, bankruptcy, construction, corporate and securities, criminal law, environment, government relations, health care, hospitality, intellectual property, labor and employment, product liability, real estate and land use, telecommunications, trusts and estates, utility regulation, workers' compensation and employers' liability.

Paul Roca and Orme Lewis passed away in 1979 and 1990, respectively, but the firm has continued to thrive because of its commitment to its founding fathers' ideals. Every new lawyer's orientation manual still includes a copy of "Orme's Rules," which state: The client comes first; professionalism is critical; and treat all visitors as you would guests in your home.

As Phoenix continues to expand, the law firm will do the same. Rather than focusing on increasing numbers, however, the firm is more interested in increasing depth in its practice areas. Success means many things. The key element of Lewis and Roca's success is maintaining personally satisfying, highly profitable work for quality clients at the core of its practice. Although names and faces have changed at Lewis and Roca, the firm has not wavered in its commitment to its clients, fellow lawyers, support staff and the community.

Ernest W. Lewis, father of Orme Lewis, practiced law in 1900 with Armstrong & Lewis from offices in the National Bank of Arizona Building located near Lewis and Roca's current Phoenix office.

Orme Lewis and Paul Roca, November 1977

RIESTER~ROBB

On its way to becoming Arizona's leading advertising and public relations firm, Riester~Robb has crashed a UFO on top of Phoenix's tallest building to publicize a museum exhibit and used a peeing dog to help kids in Arizona kick the smoking habit. Creative. Unique. Targeted. These adjectives aren't just industry buzzwords, they are key components of the Riester~Robb credo and philosophy, "Think. Attack."

One of the company's more notable advertising campaigns was created in 1995 when Riester~Robb proposed an innovative campaign heavily based on research with shocking creative messages for the Arizona Department of Health Services' Tobacco Education and Prevention Program. Winning Arizona's Tobacco Education and Prevention account launched Riester~Robb into the national advertising arena. Riester~Robb's tobacco prevention campaign is credited with reducing tobacco use among Arizona adults by more than 21 percent. Within a year, the "Smelly, Puking Habit" anti-tobacco campaign was being featured in the pages of the *Wall Street Journal, New York Times* and *Washington Post*. Elements of Riester~Robb's campaign have since been licensed to 38 states through the Center for Disease Control.

Riester~Robb has continued honing its cause, marketing skills with campaigns for a roster of clients that includes the Valley of the Sun United Way, Arizona Science Center, Hogle Zoo (Utah), City of Tempe Transit, State of Pennsylvania Transit, California Department of Conservation-Recycling Division and the Tohono O'odham Indian Nation. The firm's list of other notable clients includes Intel Startup Develop Online, Deer Valley Ski Resort, Utah Travel Council, Blue Cross Blue Shield of Utah and Idaho, Coca-Cola, and McDonald's in Idaho and Oregon.

While Phoenix provided a firm foundation for a fast-growing company, in 2000 Riester~Robb opened an office in California, and in February 2001 it acquired one of Utah's oldest advertising firms, Salt Lake City-based Harris & Love advertising, and its highly successful interactive division, U235. As a result of this tremendous growth, Riester~Robb now has 90 employees and annual billings of $90 million.

It is no surprise that this company, known for aggressive social marketing, values its employees. Riester~Robb created a child-care center at the Phoenix office and offers flexible schedules to help parents. Riester~Robb provides fun social gatherings and conducts an employee awards program. It encourages employees to rescue stray and abused animals and even allows Riester~Robb staff members to bring their dogs to work at all Riester~Robb offices.

Creatively solving everyday challenges — whether with clients or employees — has well positioned Riester~Robb to continue growing right along with Phoenix.

One of Riester~Robb's most famous print ads

The Riester~Robb building at the corner of 3rd and McKinley Avenues

City of Phoenix, Photo by Bob Rink

Education, health care, religious, cultural, entertainment

and service organizations contribute to the quality

of life enjoyed by Phoenix residents and visitors.

Quality of Life

AMERICA WEST ARENA

Since the doors of America West Arena opened in 1992, nearly 17 million guests have entered through the turnstiles to enjoy sporting events, concerts, ice shows, truck pulls, charity fund-raisers, ethnic festivals, internationally renowned speakers and faith-based conferences. A few people have even been caught sneaking in on the infrequent days when no event is scheduled — just to look around!

Averaging more than 220 events per year, America West Arena has become one of the most successful venues in the United States. It currently serves as home of the NBA Phoenix Suns, NHL Phoenix Coyotes, WNBA Phoenix Mercury and AFL Arizona Rattlers. In its first few years of operation, the arena captured a number of prestigious industry awards, including Best New Concert Venue, Prime Site Award and Manager of the Year. Event promoters love the building's smooth operations, while performers like the intimacy and amenities. Once, on his way out after a concert, Placido Domingo ducked back in and sang a private aria to honor the building's staff.

Despite this high praise, the management team at America West Arena continually seeks ways to improve the facility itself and the service offered by its 1,600 employees. One recent improvement is the complete renovation of a storage area to create the Phoenix Suns Chairman's Club, where VIPs enjoy the luxury of an exclusive bar and lounge on game nights. Improvements that can be enjoyed by everyone include the new seat cushions installed throughout the lower level and the improved flooring in several places throughout the building.

A 15-month renovation is also scheduled to increase the facility's size by approximately 70,000 square feet through the addition of office space, retail, fast food and unique places for people to gather before or after events. Enhancements to the retail Team Shop and Phoenix Suns Athletic Club also are planned.

Any mention of the management team must, of course, start with Jerry Colangelo, the man whose vision gave birth to the arena and whose vigilance has helped keep downtown revitalization at the forefront of business and government discourse. A man with big ideas and a small tolerance for those who say it can't be done, Colangelo has earned the devotion of today's often-demanding professional athletes, many of whom have taken less lucrative contracts in order to play for Colangelo's franchise. Former players often return to take front office or coaching positions, knowing full well the level of commitment Colangelo requires. Alvan Adams, Connie Hawkins, Tom Chambers, John Shumate, Dick Van Arsdale, Cotton Fitzsimmons, Frank Johnson, Eddie Johnson and Neal Walk all returned to the organization following their playing or coaching days.

Colangelo's commitment extends well beyond his basketball family. He exhibits a tireless passion for community giving and economic development. In 1987 Colangelo founded Phoenix Suns Charities, the team's nonprofit foundation that raises funds and awards grants to Arizona nonprofit organizations that assist the needs of children, youth and families. Colangelo's generosity is legendary: each year, the Phoenix Suns and Phoenix Suns Charities give away more than $2 million in grants, sponsorships, tickets and merchandise to provide a valuable assist to those who need it. America West Arena is often a partner in this effort, providing tickets to events and serving as the host site for Phoenix Suns Charities events and other community fund-raisers.

Colangelo's work in the area of economic development is seen on the Phoenix skyline, which would be drastically different if not for the imprint of his commitment to his adopted home. After serving 19 years as the only general manager the Suns had ever known, Colangelo led a group of investors to purchase the franchise in 1987 and has served as CEO ever since. His first priority after taking ownership was to design and build an arena specifically suited to basketball. Downtown Phoenix was

America West Arena provides a world-class entertainment venue to the people of Arizona.

the only location he would consider, believing it to be a vital step to help revive a decaying central city.

The public/private partnership under which the arena was developed became the prototype for a new generation of facilities. The City of Phoenix contributed the land, plus a portion of the construction costs, and in return owns the arena; Phoenix Arena Development Limited Partnership (a division of the Phoenix Suns) covered the majority of the construction costs and holds a long-term managing and operating agreement. Revenues are split between the partners.

With the opening of Bank One Ballpark in 1998 came a reorganization to make the most of the management resources available. A new company, Sports and Entertainment Services (SES), was created to serve the operational needs of both America West Arena and Bank One Ballpark. Paige Peterson serves as general manager, with Alvan Adams as vice president of facilities management. They lead a management team that oversees the major areas of the arena including events, house-keeping, set-up crew, engineering and guest relations.

The guest relations department at America West Arena is a definite source of pride. Its sole purpose is to anticipate and respond to guest needs, thereby ensuring that each visit to the arena is the best it can possibly be. Guest relations representatives assist with unique situations that require special care — wheelchair seating assistance, ticket relocations, personal item check-in and other requests.

Always looking for ways to improve guest service, the guest relations department has a program in place to enlist all arena employees in its mission. Each night, a different employee is selected to serve as Chief Excellence Officer — or CEO — for the event. Rather than working his or her regular position, the CEO monitors the entire event with the perspective of a true CEO looking to see what is going well and what might need to be changed.

Whether CEO or part-time crewmember, every employee at the arena is committed to the highest standards. After all, the next 17 million people who enter through the turnstiles represent new opportunities to introduce guests to everything that makes America West Arena special.

The stars always shine at America West Arena.

ARIZONA STATE UNIVERSITY

Anticipating and responding to the rapidly changing needs of the community is nothing new to Arizona State University (ASU). After World War II, enrollment increased exponentially each year, and in the 1960s, new colleges and schools were added to expand offerings befitting university status. Today, extraordinary growth in Arizona is offering the university its best opportunity ever to be an integral part of the state's long-term, sustained economic viability.

ASU accepts the challenge and responsibility that comes with being a renowned metropolitan research university and has earned its place among the top 100 funded research universities in the nation — without the benefit of having either a school of medicine or a school of agriculture. By matching university talents and expertise with the vision of community leaders, ASU provides indispensable research and support to address the major issues affecting the quality of life in the Valley of the Sun and throughout the nation.

Arizona State University Main Campus in Tempe, Arizona

Palm Walk
Tim Trumble — ASU

Arizona's current and continued competitiveness in the New Economy is directly linked to the government, business and educational partnerships and investments begun more than 40 years ago. ASU's long-term research programs in solid state electronics, computer science, materials, supply chain management, telecommunications, life sciences, environmental sciences and space science have all spurred industrial development.

ASU's commitment to the New Economy includes a plan to recruit the best new minds in emerging research areas in engineering and science; rebuild and refurbish space for high-technology research; and construct new facilities suitable for high-technology research.

The university, with more than 50,000 students, has three anchor campuses and an extended campus in the Greater Phoenix metropolitan area. ASU Main, the original campus founded in 1885 in Tempe, enrolls more than 45,000 students from 50 states and 120 countries. ASU West, located in and primarily serving northwest Phoenix, has approximately 5,000 students; ASU East, in Mesa, is the university's newest campus and serves almost 2,000 students in unique technology and agribusiness programs. ASU Extended Education brings university services into the community at more than 50 locations through flexible programs, technology and schedules.

The quality of education at ASU is reflected by the students who come to the university. The ASU Barrett Honors College, with an enrollment of more than 2,000, is one of the largest and most sought-after honors colleges in the country, and the university is among the top 15 in the country in the number of entering National Merit Scholars. Additionally, ASU is a Truman Scholarship Honor Institution, one of only 17 schools to be selected nationwide.

Minority student enrollment at ASU Main has increased almost 70 percent in the past 10 years, from 5,031 in fall 1989 to 8,536 in fall 1999. ASU has 5,000 Hispanic students, comprising more than 10 percent of the student body, and hosts many outreach programs for minority students in junior high and high schools.

ASU graduate programs consistently rank among the best in the nation in *U.S. News & World Report's* listing of American Best Graduate Schools, including those in the colleges of Business, Education, Engineering, Nursing, Liberal Arts & Sciences, Public Programs, Fine Arts and Law. The magazine also has ranked ASU's undergraduate programs in accountancy, management information systems, general management and production/operations among the top 25 in the nation.

The Student Guide to America's 100 Best Colleges and *Money* magazine rate ASU as one of the 100 best education values in the United States and one of the top public schools for in-state students in the country, respectively.

The university's 25-year-old Disability Resources for Students (DRS) program is recognized nationally for its services and campus accessibility. DRS also has one of the largest scholarship endowment programs for students with disabilities in the nation, offering nearly $100,00 a year in scholarships to its more than 1,300 students.

ASU actively seeks community partnerships that promote economic development, address metropolitan issues, provide linkages with K-12 education, and develop innovative approaches to solving problems of concern to both the university and the community. While many grants support these efforts, ASU funds 48 percent of the programs and partnerships in areas such as teacher training, health, recreation and tourism, early childhood development, urban growth and planning, environment and technology, transportation, and crime.

The university is a $2.3 billion force in the Arizona economy, accounting for nearly 40,000 jobs. For every dollar invested in the university by the state, $7 is returned to the economy,

almost double the average for public colleges and universities.

The ASU Research Park, established in 1984, facilitates technology transfer through university and industry relationships. Park tenants consist primarily of research and development organizations, company regional or national headquarters facilities, and pilot production operations.

The university also provides Greater Phoenix and the state of Arizona with some of the best performing arts and fine arts venues in the world. Gammage Auditorium, on ASU's main campus, is a Frank Lloyd Wright-designed landmark center for the performing arts, seating 3,000 and regularly attracting the nation's finest performers and productions. The Sundome Center for the Performing Arts in Sun City West is America's largest single-level theater with more than 7,000 seats. ASU's Kerr Cultural Center in Scottsdale offers smaller-venue cultural events.

ASU is also involved in local television programming. KAET, Channel 8, an award-winning Public Broadcasting Service (PBS) affiliate, is operated by ASU and broadcasts 24 hours daily.

ASU is a member of the NCAA and the PAC-10 conference. With 18 varsity intercollegiate sports, ASU athletic teams consistently rank among the top 10 in the nation.

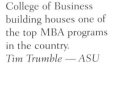

Arizona State University's College of Business building houses one of the top MBA programs in the country.
Tim Trumble — ASU

Hayden Library
Tim Trumble — ASU

Tyler Mall on the Tempe Campus
Tim Trumble — ASU

DELTA DENTAL PLAN OF ARIZONA

Making a Difference — One Smile at a Time

At Delta Dental Plan of Arizona, the commitment to oral health of the people of Arizona is central to its mission. Since its inception in 1972, this commitment has fueled its vision and grounded its decisions. Delta Dental continues to work to improve oral health throughout Arizona by emphasizing preventative care and making affordable dental care coverage available to a wide range of people.

Key to achieving this goal is educating the public on the value of good oral health and its importance to overall health. Delta Dental Plan of Arizona is a leader in meeting this educational responsibility. Through its Foundation, resources support and promote dental health and education for children through Teeth on the Go, an educational program targeting elementary school aged children. Children receive their own toothbrush and floss as well as home instructions on proper dental hygiene. And, educational initiatives don't stop there. The Foundation supports professional educational programs for dentists and hygienists offered through the Arizona Dental Association.

Caring for those in need is nothing new to the dentists of Delta Dental Plan of Arizona. Individuals donate their time with gifts of uncompensated dental service and direct monetary donations. Through its Foundation, Delta Dental reaches out to hospitals and nonprofit organizations connecting care with underserved and uninsured individuals.

Foundation donations have been given annually to support three dental clinics — John C. Lincoln and St. Joseph's Dental Clinic in Phoenix and St. Elizabeth of Hungary Clinic in Tucson. In addition, this year Delta Dental provided funds to Hope 4 Kids International for the purchase of a mobile dental

---

THE CAPACITY TO CARE IS THE THING WHICH GIVES LIFE ITS DEEPEST MEANING AND SIGNIFICANCE. ~PABLO CASALS

---

van — a dental office on wheels — taking oral healthcare to individuals who don't have any way to get to a dental office or clinic. In addition, funds to provide access to oral healthcare for at risk children were donated to Catholic Social Services. Last year's donations underwrote expenses associated with more than 10,000 dental encounters including exams and x-rays, restorations, orthodontics, extractions and oral surgery, endodontics, prophys, and crowns.

Delta Dental proactively addresses industry pressures associated with manpower. Making a significant impact on dental services, it founded the Rio Salado School of Dental Hygiene with a $500,000 donation.

As Delta Dental celebrates 30 years in the state of Arizona, it continues to move forward with even more determination to make a positive difference in people's lives, regardless of their ability to pay — one smile at a time. It's a gift like no other.

(Left to right, back row) Clinic volunteers Michael Radcliff, DMD and Michael Thompson, DDS; Delta Dental board member Oksana Komarnyckyj; Clinic supervisor Kathy Fitzgerald and (seated) Bernard Glossy, FACHE, President and CEO of DDPAZ at John C. Lincoln Dental Clinic

Judge Us By the Company We Keep

Delta Dental Plan is pleased to be the dental service plan of choice for these businesses from 5 to 28 years!

- STATE OF ARIZONA
- COCHISE COUNTY
- COCOPAH INDIAN TRIBE
- CHW, ARIZONA
- YAVAPAI REGIONAL MEDICAL CENTER
- ARIZONA SHEET METAL TRADES TRUST
- CITY OF APACHE JUNCTION
- CITY OF CHANDLER
- CITY OF FLAGSTAFF
- CITY OF SIERRA VISTA
- CITY OF PEORIA
- TOWN OF GILBERT
- CENTRAL ARIZONA COLLEGE
- COCONINO COUNTY COMMUNITY COLLEGE
- MARICOPA COUNTY COMMUNITY COLLEGE DISTRICT
- WOOD PATEL & ASSOCIATES, INC.
- KYRENE EMPLOYEE'S BENEFIT TRUST
- COMPUTER GUIDANCE CORPORATION
- PINAL GILA COMMUNITY CHILD SERVICES
- R&R PRODUCTS
- SUN HEALTH CORPORATION
- SHAMROCK FOODS COMPANY
- COCONINO COUNTY ADMINISTRATION CENTER
- DESERT SCHOOL FEDERAL CREDIT UNION
- CASE GRANDE ELEMENTARY SCHOOL
- WILSON SCHOOL DISTRICT
- CLARKDALE-JEROME SCHOOL DISTRICT
- GLENDALE UNION HIGH SCHOOL DISTRICT

- SACATON PUBLIC SCHOOL DISTRICT
- PHOENIX ELEMENTARY SCHOOL DISTRICT
- FLAGSTAFF UNIFIED SCHOOL DISTRICT
- WINSLOW UNIFIED SCHOOL DISTRICT
- TANQUE VERDE UNIFIED SCHOOL DISTRICT
- PAYSON UNIFIED SCHOOL DISTRICT
- PINE-STRAWBERRY SCHOOL DISTRICT
- ROOSEVELT SCHOOL DISTRICT
- LITTLETON ELEMENTARY SCHOOL DISTRICT
- ADOBEAIR, INC.
- DMB ASSOCIATES, INC.
- VIRGO PUBLISHING
- GILA RIVER INDIAN COMMUNITY
- TOHONO O'ODHAM GAMING AUTHORITY
- INTERFACE DATA SYSTEMS, INC.
- UNITED BEVERAGE COMPANY
- POLYMICRO TECHNOLOGIES, LLC
- PHOENIX SYMPHONY ASSOCIATION, INC.
- META SERVICES
- GILA RIVER GAMING ENTERPRISES, INC.
- ROMAN CATHOLIC DIOCESE OF PHOENIX
- VITAL PROCESSING SERVICES, LLC
- WORLDATWORK
- WALTERS AND WOLF CONSTRUCTION
- FRESH PRODUCE ASSOCIATION
- WEISER LOCK
- NORTH ARIZONA REG BEHAVIORAL HEALTH AUTHORITY
- CANYON RANCH
- SUNSTATE EQUIPMENT COMPANY LLC

UNIVERSITY OF PHOENIX

University of Phoenix is the culmination of the dream of John Sperling, a remarkable man who was born into a life of poverty in the Missouri Ozark hamlet of Freedom School House and fought his way to the top. With his bet-the-farm attitude and self-developed entrepreneurial spirit leading the way, Sperling created the largest private university in the United States and the "for-profit revolution" in higher education.

In the 1970s Sperling, who was a college professor, conceived of the idea that working adults should have the opportunity to earn a college degree within the same timeframe as full-time college students. His research convinced him that working adults required a different educational model than that found in traditional higher education. The nation's colleges disagreed. Many of his peers believed that Sperling's ideas degraded higher education and the academic community ostracized him.

Despite all the opposition, Sperling believed completely in this new concept and wanted it to succeed. He knew, however, that in order for this revolutionary academic structure to survive, he would have to abandon his own academic career and start a private educational institution. Sperling did exactly that. It wasn't easy, especially since the defenders of traditional education sought to destroy his efforts through the regulation process.

Against all odds, Sperling prevailed and founded University of Phoenix in 1976. Shortly thereafter, the University became accredited by the Higher Learning Commission and a member of the North Central Association.

Today University of Phoenix has over 100 campuses and learning centers throughout the United States and Puerto Rico. The University also has two international locations — one in British Columbia and another in The Netherlands. Additionally, it offers educational opportunities to students worldwide through University of Phoenix Online.

By understanding the needs of its students and the communities in which they live and work, University of Phoenix has been able to develop exceptional programs uniquely tailored for adult learners. University of Phoenix offers bachelor's, master's, and doctoral degree programs, as well as professional certificate and customized training programs, all led by academically qualified practitioner faculty. By offering year-round evening and weekend classes and curriculum that is continually updated to meet the needs of students, University of Phoenix has set the standard for adult education.

The University's mission is to provide the highest quality of education available to working adult professionals in a manner that meets their specific needs. "We accomplish this goal through a dedication to excellent customer service and an unwavering focus on our mission," says Laura Palmer Noone, president of the University. "In short, we are committed to providing education that meets the needs of adult learners, any place and any time."

University of Phoenix is dedicated to providing education that has real-world relevance. As such, the University responds to societal and technological advancements by continually updating curriculum and developing programs that fit the changing needs of busy professionals. Curriculum at University of Phoenix is developed and administered through the University's two Schools:

For more than 25 years, University of Phoenix has helped working adult students meet their educational goals.

The John Sperling School of Business and the Artemis School of Education, Health and Human Services.

Comprised of the Colleges of Undergraduate Business, Graduate Business, and Information Systems and Technology, the John Sperling School of Business has developed some of the most comprehensive and unique degree programs available. The School offers bachelor's, master's, and doctoral degree programs, which include Bachelor of Science in Business, Bachelor of Science in Information Technology, Master of Arts in Organizational Management, Master of Business Administration, and Doctor of Management in Organizational Leadership. Many of the programs offer students a choice in specializations such as marketing, e-business, accounting and global management.

John Sperling, founder of University of Phoenix

The University of Phoenix Artemis School develops diverse programs that enhance critical thinking and inspire active learning in the fields of education, healthcare and human services and includes four separate Colleges — Counseling and Human Services, Education, General and Professional Studies, and Health Sciences and Nursing. Degrees offered through the Artemis School include Bachelor of Science in Criminal Justice Administration, Bachelor of Science in Nursing, Master of Counseling, Master of Arts in Education, and Master of Science in Nursing. Also offered are certificates in areas including mediation, nursing informatics and school nursing.

In addition to being accredited by the Higher Learning Commission and a member of the North Central Association of Colleges and Schools, the University's Bachelor and Master of Science in Nursing programs are accredited by the National League for Nursing Accrediting Commission. The Master of Counseling program is accredited by the American Counseling Association Council for Accreditation of Counseling and Related Educational Programs.

University of Phoenix's focus on quality education has earned it recognition from the American Productivity and Quality Center as Best Practices Partner: Technology Mediated Learning in February 2000 and the Best Practices Partner Assessing Learning Outcomes in June 1998. In May 1998, the University was recognized by the Council on Higher Education as Exemplar: Ensuring Quality in Distance Education.

Locally, the Phoenix Campus was awarded the prestigious Arizona Pioneer Award for Quality in 1998. This Arizona State Quality Award recognizes organizations that have established and deployed fundamental quality systems within their operations and have demonstrated positive results.

All in all, University of Phoenix's educational philosophy and operational structure embody participative, collaborative, and applied problem-solving strategies that are facilitated by faculty whose advanced academic preparation and professional experience help integrate academic theory with current practical application.

And a man who fought opposition to fulfill an incredible dream for higher education started it all.

In its 25th year, University of Phoenix reached an enrollment milstone: over 100,000 students.

MAYO CLINIC SCOTTSDALE

Following in their father's footsteps, Doctors Will and Charlie Mayo established a group medical practice in Rochester, Minnesota, in the late 1800s that became famous for its model of care. That model involved physicians working together as a team to provide the best treatment to patients. The concept was built on the idea that two heads are better than one and encouraged a continual search for better ways of diagnosis and treatment. Throughout years of growth and change, Mayo has remained committed to its heritage: thorough diagnosis, accurate answers and effective treatment through the application of collective wisdom to the problems of each patient.

(Far right)
Mayo Clinic Hospital,
northeast Phoenix

Mayo Clinic Scottsdale

In the mid-1980s leaders at the Mayo Foundation, the parent organization that oversees all of Mayo's activities, decided to offer its famous model of care in other regions. The foundation leaders looked at areas of growth, need and opportunity, and chose Scottsdale, Arizona, and Jacksonville, Florida, as the two new sites for a group medical practice.

Mayo Clinic Scottsdale opened in 1987. The outpatient clinic at 134th Street and Shea Boulevard near the McDowell Mountains started with 42 physicians and 220 support personnel, 120 examination rooms, an on-site laboratory, diagnostic imaging, two outpatient operating rooms and advanced satellite telecommunications capabilities. The clinic also included a pharmacy, patient education library and a 188-seat auditorium. Only a year later, a radiation oncology center was added.

Since its opening, Mayo Clinic Scottsdale has grown rapidly, doubling every five years. As a result, the clinic outgrew its facilities sooner than projected. In 1990, nearly three years

ahead of schedule, it began constructing an addition that doubled the size of its original building. The addition included an outpatient surgery center and pain clinic to better meet patient needs.

Because research and education are integral to the Mayo mission, patient care is continually being improved through research, and knowledge is passed on to the next generation through education. To that end, plans to build a research facility at Mayo Clinic Scottsdale were soon under way, and in 1993 the Samuel C. Johnson Research Building opened on the Scottsdale campus. The facility currently houses seven research laboratories and can be expanded to a dozen independent research programs. The lab focuses on biomedical research of molecular and cellular biology as well as molecular genetics. Investigators conduct research projects in such areas as asthma, breast cancer and cystic fibrosis. Ongoing clinical research trials are also under way to ensure that Mayo Clinic Scottsdale patients have access to the newest and most effective medical treatments.

In addition to improving patient care through research, Mayo Clinic is committed to educating the next generation of medical professionals. Today the educational program includes medical student clerkships, Mayo Clinic Scottsdale-based residency and fellowship programs, continuing education courses as well as allied health training opportunities. In 1999 alone, more than 160 residents, fellows and medical student clerks completed educational assignments at the Scottsdale campus.

As the clinic grew, it became apparent that a hospital needed to be built to integrate the inpatient and outpatient practices. In 1998 Mayo Clinic Hospital opened as the first hospital planned, designed and built from the ground up by Mayo Clinic. Located in northeast Phoenix, the 440,000-square-foot facility houses 178 licensed beds, including 112 medical/surgical beds, 20 critical-care beds, six beds in a short-stay unit, 24 skilled-nursing beds and 16 rehabilitation beds.

State-of-the-art digital technology at Mayo Clinic Hospital provides quick access to critical data about patients. The filmless, computerized radiology system used throughout the hospital lets physicians access X-ray images on a computer screen almost immediately after they are taken. Bedside computer monitors in each medical/surgical patient room enable nursing staff to enter important information about each patient without leaving the patient's side. This system gives physicians and nurses keystroke access to a patient's medical history as well as up-to-the-minute information on test results, treatment plans and patient progress.

Mayo's strong reputation and high quality of care draw patients to Mayo Clinic Scottsdale from all 50 states and more than 80 countries. The clinic offers thorough evaluations and a team approach to medicine with specialists, technologists, testing and treatments available in one location. Like the hospital, the clinic is equipped with computerized systems in its exam rooms that help speed the flow of decision-making information to physicians. Laboratory testing and analysis are done on site, as are X-rays, including advanced medical imaging such as CT and MRI.

By the beginning of the new millennium, Mayo Clinic Scottsdale had provided medical care for more than 446,000 patients in 66 medical and surgical specialties. The staff had grown to more than 250 physicians, 1,900 support staff, 50 residents and fellows, and seven research investigators. Combined with that of the hospital, Mayo's total Arizona staff had grown to more than 3,500 employees.

Mayo has a long-standing tradition of giving back to the community, and Mayo Clinic Scottsdale is no exception. The Scottsdale campus feels a strong sense of belonging to its surrounding community. The clinic sponsors a wide variety of school medical clinics, food and clothing drives, blood drives and a communitywide fitness event to benefit a local charity

MAYO CLINIC SCOTTSDALE'S VISION IS "TO BE THE PREMIER ACADEMIC MEDICAL INSTITUTION OF THE SOUTHWEST REGION,..."

every year. It is also a corporate contributor to charities and civic organizations throughout the Valley. In addition, its staff members donate time to more than 100 professional, community, civic and cultural organizations.

Mayo Clinic Scottsdale's vision is "to be the premier academic medical institution of the Southwest region," says Dr. Michael B. O'Sullivan, chair of the Board of Governors. Today Mayo Clinic Scottsdale is an integrated, multicampus system that includes the outpatient clinic, Mayo Clinic Hospital, primary care centers and the Mayo Center for Women's Health. As the clinic continues to grow, its roots and heritage remain unchanged. The words of its founder, Dr. William W. Mayo, continue to be paramount to the Mayo Clinic mission: "The needs of the patient are the only needs to be considered."

(Far left)
The team approach to medicine at Mayo Clinic Scottsdale enables physicians to collaborate and discuss the best treatment for patients.

An electronic medical records system speeds the flow of decision-making information to physicians at Mayo Clinic Hospital.

DeVry University

To find career success in today's knowledge economy, employees need to be technology and business savvy, ready to hit the ground running. For students looking for an education that develops the knowledge and skills needed to flourish in this new economy, DeVry University is where they turn to pursue their education.

Serving the Phoenix area since 1967, DeVry University offers high-quality, career-oriented degree programs in technology, business and management that have evolved over the years to meet the needs of industry and today's knowledge economy. Part of DeVry Inc., an international higher education system, DeVry University has nearly 70 locations in North America that serve over 56,000 students.

Since 1984, DeVry has offered undergraduate programs at its campus on West Dunlap Road in Phoenix, which includes a Keller Graduate School of Management education center,

opened in 1988. A second KGSM center opened in Scottsdale in 1999, and a Mesa center, opened in 1992, became DeVry University Center in 2001 in order to serve both undergraduate and graduate-level adult learners.

At the undergraduate level, approximately 3,500 students are enrolled in DeVry's seven bachelor's degree programs in business administration, computer engineering technology, computer information systems, electronics engineering technology, information technology, technical management and telecommunications management. DeVry also offers an associate degree program in electronics and computer technology.

In designing its curricula, DeVry solicits input from leading businesses in technology fields. The school relies on local advisory boards comprised of representatives from other institutions and businesses that have hired DeVry graduates. These advisory boards help evaluate DeVry programs to keep the curricula on track with technological changes.

Dennis J. Keller (left), chairman and chief executive officer, and Ronald L. Taylor (right), president and chief operating officer, of DeVry University's parent company, DeVry Inc.

Upon graduation, DeVry takes an active role in assisting its students in finding jobs in their fields. It takes pride in its national graduate employment rate where 93 percent of its students who sought employment secured a position — or were already employed — in their chosen field within six months of earning their degree. The school assists students with employment searches through a national employer database, proactive career services staff, ongoing seminars, a career development course and career fairs.

DeVry is also committed to helping its communities and their residents make the most of high-tech opportunities. The school has formed partnerships with Phoenix-area secondary schools and education associations to bring technology into the classroom. Its students and staff help schools design technology-based curricula. It has agreements with many community colleges to allow students to apply earned credits toward a DeVry degree. Staff and faculty are involved with area chambers of commerce and professional organizations, and the school sponsors technology-based educational events and programs to help high school students develop an interest in science and technology.

Every summer DeVry/Phoenix offers high school students an opportunity to take one of its courses free of charge in order to give them a taste of college life. To be eligible for this program, a student must have at least a 3.0 grade point average and a recommendation from a high school faculty member. More than 300 students took advantage of this opportunity in 2000. The students spend four to six hours a day in a classroom setting and receive college credit. The same opportunity is available to high school faculty from the Phoenix metropolitan area as well.

At the graduate level, Keller Graduate School of Management is also focused on education that is relevant to today's business. Having started with 30 students in 1988, today the graduate school of DeVry University serves more than 400 students in the Phoenix area and 9,000 annually nationwide. KGSM offers master's degree programs in business administration, accounting and financial management, human resource management, information systems management, project management and telecommunications management.

Both DeVry's undergraduate and graduate faculty are unique because of their focus on teaching and their practitioner orientation. Because many DeVry students demand practical education and appreciate instructors who have real-world experience, most undergraduate faculty members have experience in a business or corporate environment and bring a first-hand understanding of business to the classroom. All Keller Graduate School faculty members are working professionals in addition to their roles as instructors.

As technology evolves, DeVry continues to seek better ways to utilize it to enhance learning opportunities both in and out of the classroom. One example of developments in this area is the university's online class offerings. It offers an online bachelor of science in business administration degree program with concentrations in e-commerce, accounting and project management as well as all six of its master's degree programs online. These interactive offerings use computer-mediated e-mail and

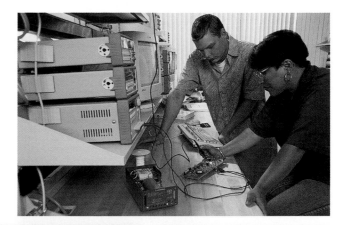

threaded conversations. In addition, they provide for various group and team activities with fellow online students.

In addition to DeVry University, DeVry Inc. also owns and operates Becker Conviser Professional Review, which offers courses to prepare students for the state-administered certified public accountant, certified management accountant and chartered financial analyst exams. Like DeVry University, Becker Conviser also focuses on student success, with its students passing the CPA exam at twice the rate of non-Becker alumni.

The mission of DeVry University is to provide high-quality career-oriented undergraduate and graduate programs in technology, business and management to a diverse student population. It has been fulfilling that mission in Phoenix for 35 years. It continues to fulfill that mission through offering career-oriented degree programs, continually improving its offerings and providing career-development strategies and employment assistance.

As technology becomes more and more essential in the world of business, a growing number of students will take advantage of DeVry's offerings. DeVry University will continue to produce the technology and business leaders of tomorrow for Phoenix, America and the world.

DeVry's hands-on undergraduate education builds the technology skills that are in demand by today's employers.

(Far left) DeVry University's Phoenix campus is one of 23 undergraduate sites in North America. One of its three Phoenix-area Keller Graduate School of Management educational centers is also located at the campus. There are 47 graduate centers in the U.S.

Keller Graduate School of Management's practitioner-oriented faculty members bring their real-world experience to the classroom.

GRAND CANYON UNIVERSITY

Grand Canyon University has been drawing people to Arizona since it began in 1949. Originally named Grand Canyon College, it started with 95 students and 15 full-time faculty in Prescott. The college has grown into a university with 250 full-time faculty and staff and 3,600 students from around the world.

The college held its first classes in the armory building on Prescott's Gurley Street, fulfilling the dream many Southern Baptists had of opening a Christian college in Arizona. Although the college anticipated staying in Prescott permanently, college officials began looking for a new location in the Phoenix area to bring the school closer to the homes of most students as well as improve students' chances at landing part-time jobs. Officials settled on an 80-acre parcel of land that was two miles outside the Phoenix city limits at the time. The college erected nine buildings and opened its doors in September 1951. It has remained at that location, 33rd Avenue and Camelback Road, ever since.

North Rim Apartments — student housing

On stage in Ethington Theatre

More buildings, including residence halls and student apartments, have been erected over time and enrollment has steadily increased. Enrollment grew by 55 percent between 1981 and 1989. When the college became a university in 1989, it comprised five separate colleges offering more than 50 majors and two master degree programs.

Of the university's current 3,600 students, nearly 1,600 are traditional, on-campus, undergraduate students. The other 2,000 are graduate, adult education or distance learning students. Canyon, as it is commonly referred to by alumni and friends, anticipates capping enrollment for traditional students at 2,000.

Technology has enabled the university to reach students it otherwise would not have. It allowed Canyon to launch online degree programs, offer a Master of Arts in Teaching degree through a video-based program and develop other Web-based programs. The university offers the Master of Science in Executive Fire Service Leadership online, with plans to bring the Master of Business Administration and a Master of Science in Nursing online as well.

The college began with a mission "to train young men and women in an environment that makes for high scholarship and Christian character." It has stayed true to that mission over the years. The university's undergraduate curriculum is built on a strong core of liberal arts and sciences. Its graduate, professional and continuing studies programs are equally challenging. In addition, the university values the integration of faith and learning.

Reaching its surrounding community is a high priority at Canyon and helps strengthen students' character. Students are heavily involved in community and missions work through Salvation Army, Habitat for Humanity, aiding in soup kitchens and helping serve Thanksgiving and Christmas dinners to needy families.

Students also reach out to their college community through service learning, part of Canyon's curriculum. Service learning combines volunteer service with academics. It is an integral part of English and Sociology, as well as other courses. Students have been involved in after-school tutoring for inner-city children, volunteering at retirement homes and various other independent service learning projects.

When the 1999 Fort Worth, Texas, Baptist church shooting took the life of Canyon alumna Sydney Browning, the university took 64 local neighborhood children under its wings in the name of Browning, who spent her adult life working with at-risk youth. The university is mentoring these children, commonly referred to as Sydney's Kids. When they are ready to attend college, each will have a full scholarship to Canyon, provided they meet admissions requirements.

Over the years, Canyon has gained a reputation for its strong academic programs. Graduates from both the Samaritan College of Nursing and the College of Education are in great demand. College of Science graduates have been accepted to graduate programs in medicine, physical therapy and occupational therapy at nationally recognized schools. Canyon graduates are practicing in classrooms, hospitals and courtrooms across the country. They are in law enforcement, business, government, media and the ministry.

Canyon is also well known for its athletics programs. Its teams regularly advance to post-season play and have won eight national championships. The university offers a host of intramural sports, as well as intercollegiate baseball, basketball, tennis, soccer, volleyball and golf.

The Canyon baseball program, which is often compared to the programs at Arizona State University and other large universities, has produced 10 major league baseball players. The university's baseball clubhouse bears the name of Canyon alum Tim Salmon, who was Major League Baseball's National League Rookie of the Year in 1993. The university also served as a springboard for two NBA basketball players and several professional soccer players.

Canyon's fine arts programs shine as well. The university is known in the community for its award-winning Ethington Theatre Series showcased in Ethington Theatre, which was built in 1973. Students are involved in plays, operas and intercollegiate forensics, as well as various vocal and instrumental ensembles. Canyon was home to Miss Arizona 1989 and 1997. The university also houses the A.P. Tell Art Gallery, displaying the work of Canyon students and professional artists.

Arizona's only private, Christian, liberal arts university, Canyon is a member of the Council of Independent Colleges and the Council of Christian Colleges and Universities. It has been honored in the Student Guide to America's Best College Buys, on the John Templeton Foundation's Honor Roll of Character-Building Colleges, and by *U.S. News & World Report* as a top Western liberal arts college.

The pursuit of excellence in the classroom

Students from all over the world choose Canyon because of its small classes, family atmosphere and the personal attention they receive. Arizona's climate and the fact that Canyon classes are taught by professors rather than teaching assistants add to the institution's appeal.

Today Grand Canyon University is an independent Christian university that intends to continue training young men and women in an environment that makes for high scholarship and Christian character. The university has had a significant impact on the greater Phoenix area, particularly the area immediately surrounding its campus. It will continue to reach out to its community and develop the leaders of tomorrow in the process.

Taking a swing in Brazell Stadium

ALL SAINTS'
EPISCOPAL DAY SCHOOL

Just as Phoenix has changed over the years, so has All Saints' Episcopal Day School, which opened in 1963 with a student population of 60 in kindergarten through third grade. The school added a grade each consecutive year for the next five years until arriving at classes for kindergarten through eighth grade. The school capped its enrollment at 485 and continues to enhance its 11-acre campus to better meet the needs of its students.

Situated west of All Saints' Episcopal Church near Central Avenue and Bethany Home Road, All Saints' Episcopal Day School began as an outreach ministry of the church. It still has very close ties to the church, where students participate in two weekly chapel services. The school welcomes students from all religious backgrounds and places a strong emphasis on morals, values, relationships, decision-making skills and respect for others.

All Saints' takes a collaborative approach to education, encouraging partnerships among students, teachers and parents.

The school's ambitious academic curriculum teaches students to read with comprehension, listen attentively, think critically, solve problems analytically and communicate effectively. Students leave their traditional classrooms for art, music, physical education, Spanish, computer, religion and library, giving them a well-rounded education.

The school provides opportunities for students to develop new skills through student newsletters, the school newspaper, the literary magazine, the school yearbook, fine arts, and competitions in Spanish, math and language arts. Students have opportunities to be involved in Student Council, National Junior Honor Society and Peer Mediation.

Extracurricular activities also abound at All Saints', which is a member of the Catholic Youth Athletic Association. As such, the school fields sixth, seventh and eighth grade teams for boys in flag football, basketball and baseball; and for girls in volleyball, softball and basketball. Fourth and fifth grade students are eligible to participate in intramural sports.

As All Saints' student population has grown over the years, so have the buildings that comprise its campus. The school opened the David John Watson Academic Building, which features eight classrooms and two state-of-the-art computer laboratories, in 1999. A year later the school dedicated the 13,000-square-foot Father Carl G. Carlozzi Gymnasium which includes a performing arts stage. The gymnasium provides a locale for sporting events, performances and social functions.

In 2002, the school opened the new Manning Hall, which replaced the building used for services while All Saints' Church was being built. As the social hall of both the church and school, Manning Hall features a cafeteria, a versatile kitchen that can serve two large groups simultaneously, and a multipurpose area that can be divided into three separate meeting rooms. The second floor of Manning Hall houses two art classrooms.

Family-oriented All Saints' Episcopal Day School has been nurturing the hearts and minds of its students since 1963. The private, not-for-profit school continues to do so in a safe, caring environment. All Saints' is preparing the students of today to be the leaders of tomorrow.

Students of All Saints' Episcopal Day School learn to read with comprehension, listen attentively, think critically, solve problems analytically and communicate effectively.

All Saints' takes a collaborative approach to education, encouraging partnerships among students, teachers and parents.

SCOTTSDALE UNIFIED SCHOOL DISTRICT

No Dream Too Big . . . No Challenge Too Great

The seeds for the Scottsdale Unified School District took root in an era when education was a premium commodity in the Arizona Territory, and one-room schoolhouses were built in a day.

The district opened its first elementary school in 1896 with eight students and a dream to be a district of high-achievers. Over the years, this culturally diverse school district has seen that dream come true. It grew to 475 students in 1922 when it opened its first high school. By 1996, when the district celebrated a century of serving the community, enrollment exceeded 25,000.

Today, the 115-square-mile district is the seventh largest in Arizona with more than 27,000 students in 20 elementary schools, seven middle schools, five high schools, and one alternative school. Nestled amidst desert and mountains, the district's boundaries include most, but not all of the city of Scottsdale, almost all of the town of Paradise Valley, a section of the city of Phoenix, and a small section of the city of Tempe.

The district is governed by a five-member elected board. More than 3,000 employees work for the district, including approximately 1,800 teachers.

Known for its A+ and National Blue Ribbon schools and test scores that rank among the highest in the state, the Scottsdale Unified School District offers a core curriculum to include fine arts, career education, language arts and business classes. A high school international baccalaureate program is offered, as well as programs for the gifted and for special education. Computer labs and media centers augment classroom instruction. Summer school, evening school, all-day kindergarten, and after-school programs round out the school year.

Scottsdale is known for its active and involved parent community. Each school has a site council, as well as an independent parent group. Specific parent and citizen committees have provided input on issues ranging from boundaries to the development of a long-range facility master plan. At a community summit, participants established the following districtwide goals:

- To increase individual student academic achievement and personal growth.
- To provide a positive, respectful and safe learning environment.
- To offer its staff comprehensive professional growth programs that provide skills, strategies and resources for meeting the needs of all students.
- To provide equity in opportunities, facilities, programs and resources for all.
- To ensure that all students and staff are proficient in the use of technology to acquire and manage information, communication, time and task.

The district partners with community colleges, business, civic, and volunteer groups as a way to ensure that students have the skills they need to achieve their dreams. Two such groups, the Scottsdale Arts in Education Council and the Scottsdale Education Foundation, support a variety of special programs and opportunities for students throughout the district.

The Scottsdale Unified School District is committed to increasing individual student academic achievement and personal growth.

SUNRISE PRESCHOOLS

Sunrise Preschools opened its first preschool at Baseline Road and Pennington in Mesa in 1982 with a commitment to long-term staff development through the continuing education of its teachers and caregivers. That commitment has paid off for Sunrise, which currently operates 16 facilities statewide. Sunrise's management staff has more than 175 years of experience among them, and the majority of that staff has served the school an average of five to eight years, a rarity in today's high-turnover child-care industry.

Sunrise Preschools operates 16 facilities statewide.

Headquartered in Ahwatukee, the school continues to research the most helpful and supportive ideas in early childhood education and is committed to setting the standards for excellence in these areas by providing knowledgeable, skillful, nurturing educators; healthy, safe, child-centered environments; partnerships with each family; and meaningful contributions to its communities.

Sunrise Preschools offer child care, preschool and after-school programs — including transportation to and from nearby schools — for children ages 6 weeks to 12 years, with lesson plans devoted to each age group. Using carefully tested programs and materials in each of its locations, the school provides learning centers that include creative arts, library and language, sensory wet and dry, block building, music and movement, science and discovery, manipulatives and math, and dramatic play. Sunrise is dedicated to providing children with a whole body experience through plenty of hands-on interaction.

Daily and weekly lesson plans focus on children's natural interests and curiosity. A typical week might include picture books about butterflies, discussing what caterpillars eat, spotting patterns in a butterfly's wing, watching a cocoon open, and dancing like butterflies with colorful scarves for wings.

Sunrise, one of only a few child-care centers that accept children with disabilities, provides additional staff for what it calls its "inclusion program." Through a contract with the State of Arizona Division of Developmental Disabilities, Sunrise has been approved to mainstream children with disabilities into the regular preschool program.

Sunrise Preschools encourage parent involvement, welcoming them to visit at lunchtime, naptime, storytime or any other time. The school offers monthly newsletters to keep parents informed, as well as conferences, family events and open house festivals. Parents take comfort in closed-circuit TV monitors, which allow them to watch their children interact with others. The school offers extended hours to meet the needs of working parents. Additionally, each Sunrise Preschool houses its own kitchen, which provides snacks and warm meals to the children daily.

The local, home-grown school plays an active role in its surrounding communities. It is recognized as the preschool of choice for many local events, including the Phoenix Open,

which was the first golf tournament to provide on-site child care for spectators. Additionally, Sunrise has served as a child-care provider for Channel 3's annual Women's Expo. The school always has an overwhelming number of employees volunteer for these local events.

Sunrise Preschools take one day at a time. The school's 400 to 450 employees know that tomorrow they will get up, go to their respective Sunrise Preschools and serve children they have grown to love.

Children enjoy hands-on activities devoted to their specific age group at Sunrise Preschools.

Arizona State University News Bureau, Photo by Tim Trumble

As a center for spectator sports and recreation,

Phoenix attracts international visitors and

provides year-round leisure activities.

Sports & Recreation

PHOENIX INTERNATIONAL RACEWAY

There is nothing quite like going out to Phoenix International Raceway early on a November morning. The air is cool and filled with an aura of excitement and anticipation. The men and machinery of the NASCAR Winston Cup Series have gathered for their yearly event in the desert. Yes, this is Arizona auto racing at its best. But it wasn't always that way.

Phoenix has seen auto racing since the mid-1920s, but modern, professional racing's first venue was a one-mile track at the Arizona State Fairgrounds. The 50s-era course was extremely tough for drivers, as hard racing combined with the desert heat resulted in blinding dust and a track surface that was always breaking apart. This deadly combination resulted in numerous accidents. In 1962 Elmer George's car went off the track and into the grandstands, killing the driver and injuring 23 spectators. The fairground's track was deemed unsafe and soon closed.

Soon after this catastrophe, Richard Hogue — who was building a new road-racing course at the base of the beautiful Estrella Mountains, just west of Phoenix — got a call from oval racers. They asked if he could possibly incorporate a circle track into his new raceway and he agreed. The new track, a paved one-mile oval with a kink or dogleg in the backstretch, was opened as an integral part of the all-new Phoenix International Raceway (PIR). The oval's first major event — a 100-mile Indy car race — was held on March 22, 1964, and won by racecar legend A.J. Foyt. Thus began the illustrious history of Arizona's famous raceway, known affectionately as "the Desert Jewel."

Phoenix International Raceway continued to hold road races, but the track soon became known strictly for its oval racing. The Indycars started running two races per year at PIR, and

then NASCAR started coming to Phoenix with its Winston West Series. The fast and friendly Phoenix mile was building a stellar reputation for good times and great racing, a status that began to attract NASCAR Winston Cup stars like Richard Petty, David Pearson, Cale Yarborough and others.

From the mid-70s through 1985, PIR changed ownership three times. Hogue sold the track to Malcolm Bricklin of Bricklin Cars fame, and then Bricklin sold it to a private group of investors. Then in the late 70s, a local sportswriter named Dennis Wood bought the track. Wood realized that for PIR to truly become a world-class facility, it would need a date on the NASCAR Winston Cup schedule. The only problem was that the track would need a lot of improvements before it could get a date.

In 1985 Dennis Wood sold PIR to Emmett "Buddy" Jobe, a successful local farmer who also happened to be a great race fan. He assumed Wood's goal of getting NASCAR to come to Phoenix. In three short years Jobe transformed the 10,000-seat track into a 60,000-seat racing showcase. The only part of the track Jobe didn't completely tear down and rebuild was the unique, general admission hillside viewing area, a mountainside that overlooked turn four where families could watch the same way they had since 1964.

On a sunny Sunday afternoon in November of 1988, Alan Kulwicki won his very first NASCAR Winston Cup Series race at PIR's very first NASCAR Winston Cup Series Race. In the years that followed, the list of winners that included Indycar legends Andretti, Foyt and Unser would be joined by NASCAR greats like Earnhardt, Allison and Elliott.

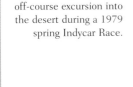

Roger McCluskey, in a new rear-engined Ford Indy racecar, dives under a very young Mario Andretti in an old Offy Roadster in 1964.

Gordon Johncock returns to the pits after an off-course excursion into the desert during a 1979 spring Indycar Race.

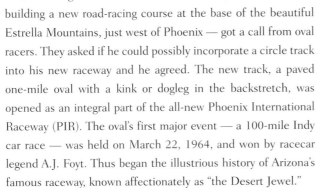

After 12 years of incredible expansion and success, Jobe sold PIR to International Speedway Corporation (ISC) in 1997. ISC bought the raceway with a specific goal in mind: in order to become the leader in motorsports entertainment, it had to acquire the best facilities in the country. And Jobe had, indeed, made Phoenix International Raceway one of the best. Now owning and operating 12 racing facilities across the United States including the renowned Daytona International Speedway, home of the Daytona 500, ISC is definitely one of the leading motorsports entertainment companies in the world.

Today, the picturesque, 650-acre Sonoran Desert facility boasts one of the most diverse racing schedules in motorsports. Major events each year include the NASCAR Winston Cup Series race, the NASCAR Busch Series Outback Steakhouse 200, NASCAR Winter Heat (NASCAR Winston West and Featherlite Southwest Series), the Pennzoil Copper World Indy 200, the Sun Automotive 200 presented by azcentral.com and cars.com Grand-Am road races, and the NASCAR Craftsman Truck Series Silverado 150. With these popular events on its schedule, PIR has become one of the largest revenue producers in the Valley of the Sun with a yearly economic impact of $316 million — substantially more than the Super Bowl brought to Phoenix in 1996. And PIR does it each and every year!

If an exceptional track and a great facility aren't enough of a draw for PIR, the weather in Phoenix definitely is. With very little rain and mild winters in the valley, the raceway has become a favorite for fans everywhere. Additionally, because of its proximity to the sixth-largest city in the United States, the raceway has become a "destination location." Fans who travel to PIR can take advantage of a host of other leisure activities.

Having established its niche in Phoenix, it comes as no surprise that PIR also demonstrates a strong track record of community service. Held each year at the Wigwam, the PIR-sponsored Diamond Ball benefits the West Valley Fine Arts Council. PIR also reaches out to the youth of Phoenix through its Show Car Program, which visits local schools to teach children about the sport of auto racing.

So what's in the future for PIR? Because International Speedway Corporation is committed to maintaining it as a world-class facility, it is willing to spend the capital to make sure people enjoy the raceway, and to continually upgrade it to the standard of other great tracks in the country. With this goal in mind, the future of Phoenix International Raceway is definitely paved with success.

Another record crowd gathers at Phoenix International Raceway to watch NASCAR Winston Cup Series action.

PHOENIX COYOTES/ ALLTEL ICE DEN

On October 10, 1996, the former Winnipeg Jets played their first home game in the National Hockey League as the Phoenix Coyotes. Played against the San Jose Sharks at America West Arena, the game marked a list of many firsts for the team.

Team celebration after winning a playoff game
Barry Gossage Photography

That inaugural season was capped off by another first when the Coyotes went up against the Anaheim Mighty Ducks in the playoffs. Since that debut season, the Phoenix Coyotes have made it to the playoffs every year. This feat, combined with its 1995/1996 participation in the playoffs as the Jets, marks the

AS THE COYOTES' POPULARITY GROWS, SO DOES THE TEAM'S PROSPECT FOR A GLOWING FUTURE.

Jeremy Roenick in game one of the 2000 playoffs against Colorado
Barry Gossage Photography

franchise as one of only six teams in the NHL that has clinched a spot in the Stanley Cup Playoffs for five consecutive years.

While the Coyotes' success in the league continues, so does its success in Phoenix. A strong belief in giving back to the fans that have welcomed them so graciously has helped to make the team one of the most popular in the Valley of the Sun. Phoenix Coyotes charities foundation donates funds to many nonprofit children's charities in Arizona including local schools, hospitals, community centers, shelters and food banks. In the five years since its inception, the foundation has donated over $2 million to local children's organizations throughout Arizona.

Another popular community event is the Cool Coyotes Field Trip, which invites more than 16,000 Valley fourth, fifth and sixth-graders to a regularly scheduled game. It then ties the excitement of professional hockey with the students' curriculum by way of an educational worksheet based on the on-ice action. Outside of the rink, the Coyotes' annual Power Play Tour has become an event that fans of all ages look forward to. The tour brings Coyotes hockey to communities outside of the Phoenix Valley in the form of a free carnival. Fans can meet and mingle with team players, participate in interactive games and win team merchandise. In addition to bringing hockey to existing fans, the tour also welcomes newcomers to the sport, thereby increasing the team's fan base.

As the Coyotes' popularity grows, so does the team's prospect for a glowing future. With the formation of a new ownership group that includes Steve Ellman and hockey great Wayne Gretzky, there are also plans to build a new multipurpose arena in Glendale that will serve as home for the team as well as a venue for concerts and other major events.

"With the new ownership and a new arena," said Joe Levy, Coyotes' vice president of business development, "the team is positioning itself to become even more successful both on and off the ice." There is little doubt that the Phoenix Coyotes will do exactly that, given the team's one underlying goal: To bring Arizona its first major league sports championship.

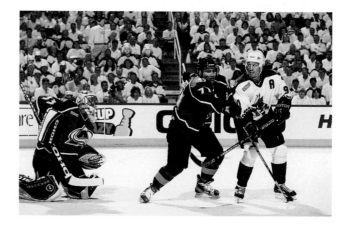

Appendix

					Total		Voter
City Elections 1949-1959							
Year	Office	CGC Candidate	Votes & % of Vote	Main Opponent	Votes	Votes	Turnout
1949				*Civil Action*			
	Mayor	Nicholas Udall	13,270 (60%)	Thomas Imler	3,935	22,157	41%
	Council	(Average candidate)	14,103 (67%)	(Average candidate)	43,342	1,212	
1951	Mayor	Nicholas Udall	17,381 (80%)	E.H. Braatelien	4,381	21,762	39%
	Council	(Average candidate)	14,103 (79%)	(Average candidate)	4,399	21,371	
1953				*Economy Ticket*			
	Mayor	Frank Murphy	12,086 (67%)	Jack Choisser	5,940	18,026	29%
	Council	(Average candidate)	11,665 (67%)	(Average candidate)	5,250	17,380	
1955				*Payers Ticket*			
	Mayor	Jack Williams	12,858 (83%)	Sam Levitin	2,544	15,402	27%
	Council	(Average candidate)	12,918 (68%)	(Average candidate)	3,246	18,992	
1957				*Dem Charter Gov Ticket*			
	Mayor	Jack Williams	17,128 (82%)	Rogers Lee	3,845	20,973	23%
	Council	(Average candidate)	15,911 (79%)	(Average candidate)	4,305	20,216	
1959				*Phoenix Ticket*			
	Mayor	Sam Mardian	28,929 (71%)	Russell Kapp	11,860	40,789	32%
	Council	(Average candidate)	27,731 (72%)	(Average candidate)	11,014	38,745	

Other candidates: In 1949 two for mayor, 11 for council; in 1953 two for council; in 1955 four for council.

■**1A** from chapter 1 page 31

New Manufacturers in the Phoenix Area
1948-1960

Type	# of Firms	# of Employees	% of all Companies	Notable Companies	Products/Sizes
Aerospace	13	7,484	31.7%	AiResearch, Goodyear, Sperry Phoenix, Rocket Power	Three firms w/more 1,000 employees, three w/fewer than 20
Electronics	23	6,990	29.6%	GE, Motorola, US Semiconductor	Three firms w/more than 1,000 employees, 11 w/ fewer than 20
Manufacturing Support	73	2,363	10.0%	Acme Steel, Garland Steel Western Rolling Mills, National Malleable & Steel Castings Co.	Structural steel, steel rolling mill products, plastic. Median # of employees − 17.
Housing and Building	70	2,040	8.7%	Union Gypsum, Jokco Mfg. Palmer Excelsior Materials	Windows, doors, furniture draperies, lights, air conditioning
Clothing	18	1,874	8.0%	E.L. Gruber, Albert of Arizona Grundwald-Marx, Raco Apparel Penn-Mor Mfg.	All clothes, especially underwear. Six firms w/more than 100 employees, eight w/fewer than 50
Food	23	1,187	5.0%	Carnation & Shamrock dairies Rosita Food Products	Five dairies & bakeries w/ more than 100 employees; other were small
Other	70	1,645	7.0%		Average 11 employees
Totals	**290**	**23,583**	**100.0%**		

■1B from chapter 1 page 34

Appendix

	Population Rank		Land Area	
Place	1980	Change since 1960	1980	Change since 1960
Growth Rates for Western Cities, 1960 and 1980				
Los Angeles	3	0	464.7 sq. mi.	9.9 sq. mi
Houston	5	2	556.4 sq. mi.	228.3 sq. mi
Dallas	7	7	333.0 sq. mi.	53.1 sq. mi
San Diego	8	10	320.0 sq. mi.	127.6 sq. mi
Phoenix	9	20	324.0 sq. mi.	136.6 sq. mi
San Antonio	11	6	262.7 sq. mi.	102.2 sq. mi
San Francisco	13	-1	46.4 sq. mi.	-1.2 sq. mi
San Jose	17	40	158.0 sq. mi.	103.5 sq. mi
Seattle	23	-4	83.6 sq. mi.	-4.9 sq. mi
Denver	24	-1	110.6 sq. mi.	39.6 sq. mi
El Paso	28	18	239.2 sq. mi	124.6 sq. mi
Oklahoma City	31	6	603.6 sq. mi.	282.1 sq. mi
Ft. Worth	33	1	240.2 sq. mi.	99.7 sq. mi
Portland	35	-6	103.3 sq. mi.	36.1 sq. mi
Long Beach	37	-2	49.8 sq. mi.	3.9 sq. mi
Tulsa	38	12	185.6 sq. mi.	137.8 sq. mi
Oakland	43	-10	53.9 sq. mi.	.9 sq. mi
Albuquerque	44	16	95.3 sq. mi.	39.1 sq. mi
Tucson	45	9	98.8 sq. mi.	27.9 sq. mi
Spokane	82	-14	51.7 sq. mi.	8.7 sq. mi
Salt Lake City	91	-26	75.2 sq. mi.	19.1 sq. mi
Tacoma	98	-14	47.7 sq. mi.	.2 sq. mi

■**2A** from chapter 2 page 44

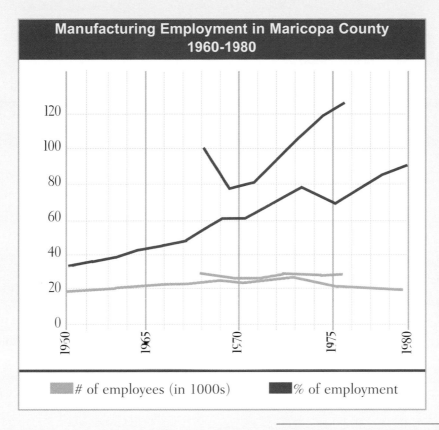

Manufacturing Employment in Maricopa County 1960-1980

120

100

80

60

40

20

0

1960   1965   1970   1975   1980

# of employees (in 1000s)   % of employment

■2B (Left)
from chapter 2 page 71

■3A (Below)
from chapter 3 page 88

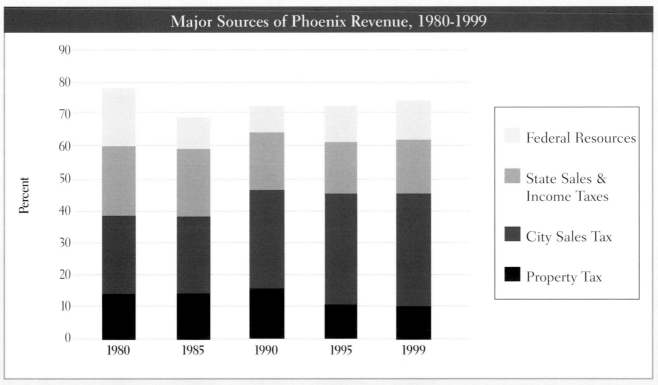

Major Sources of Phoenix Revenue, 1980-1999

90

80

70

60

Percent 50

40

30

20

10

0

1980   1985   1990   1995   1999

Federal Resources

State Sales & Income Taxes

City Sales Tax

Property Tax

Bibliography

Historical Studies – Books

Abbott, Carl. *The Metropolitan Frontier: Cities in the Modern American West*. Tucson: University of Arizona Press, 1993.

Abbott, Carl. *The New Urban America: Growth and Politics in Sunbelt Cities*. Rev. ed. Chapel Hill: University of North Carolina Press, 1987.

Bataille, Gretchen M.; and Albert L. McHenry, eds. *Living the Dream in Arizona: The Legacy of Martin Luther King, Jr.* [Tempe, Ariz.]: Arizona State University, 1992.

Berman, David R. *Arizona Politics and Government: The Quest for Autonomy, Democracy, and Development*. Lincoln: University of Nebraska Press, 1998.

Bimson, Carl A. *Transformation in the Desert: Story of Arizona's Valley-National-Bank*. New York, Newcomen Society in North American, 1962.

Blanc, Tara A. *Oasis in the City: The History of the Desert Botanical Garden*. Phoenix: Heritage Publishers, Inc., 2000.

Bridges, Amy. *Morning Glories: Municipal Reform in the Southwest*. Princeton: Princeton University Press, 1997.

Buchanan, James E., comp. *Phoenix : A Chronological and Documentary History, 1865-1976*. American Cities Chronology Series. Dobbs Ferry, N.Y.: Oceana Publications, 1978.

Doti, Lynne Pierson and Larry Schweikart. *Banking in the American West from the Gold Rush to Deregulation*. Norman: University of Oklahoma Press, 1991.

Fernlund, Kevin J., ed. *The Cold War American West, 1945-1989*. Albuquerque: University of New Mexico Press, 1998.

Findlay, John M.. *Magic Lands: Western Cityscapes and American Culture after 1940*. Berkeley: University of California Press, 1992.

Gammage, Jr., Grady. *Phoenix in Perspective: Reflections on Developing the Desert*. Tempe, AZ : Herberger Center for Design Excellence, College of Architecture and Environmental Design, Arizona State University, 1999.

Garreau, Joel. *Edge City: Life on the New Frontier*. New York: Doubleday, 1991.

George, Dick. *One of a Kind: An Informal History of the Phoenix Zoo, 1961-1982*. Phoenix: Arizona Zoological Society, 1982.

A Guide to the Architecture of Metro Phoenix. [Phoenix]: Central Arizona Chapter, American Institute of Architects, 1983.

Haitt, Pam. *The Arizona Bank: Arizona's Story*. Phoenix: The Arizona Bank, 1987.

Hardt, Athia L., ed. *Arizona Waterline*. [Phoenix, Az:] Salt River Project, 1989.

A History of the Phoenix Police Department. [Phoenix : Police Dept., 1978?]

Iverson, Peter. *Barry Goldwater, Native Arizonan*. Norman: University of Oklahoma Press, 1997.

Johnson, G. Wesley. *Phoenix, Valley of the Sun* Tulsa, Okla.: Continental Heritage Press, 1982.

Johnson, G. Wesley, ed. *Phoenix in the Twentieth Century: Essays in Community History*. Norman: University of Oklahoma Press, 1993.

Jones, Michael D. *Desert Wings: A History of Phoenix Sky Harbor International Airport*. Tempe, Az.: Jetblast Publications, 1997.

Luckingham, Brad. *Discovering Greater Phoenix: An Illustrated History*. Carlsbad, CA: Heritage Media Corp, 1998.

Luckingham, Brad. *Minorities in Phoenix : A Profile of Mexican American, Chinese American, and African American Communities, 1860-1992*. Tucson: University of Arizona Press, 1994.

Luckingham, Brad. *Phoenix: The History of a Southwestern Metropolis*. Tucson: University of Arizona Press, 1989.

Mohl, Raymond A., ed. *Searching for the Sunbelt: Historical Perspectives on a Region*. Knoxville: University of Tennessee Press, 1990.

Morrison Institute for Public Policy. *Growth in Arizona: The Machine in the Garden*. Tempe, Az.: Morrison Institute for Public Policy, 1998.

Morrison Institute for Public Policy. *Hits and Misses: Fast Growth in Metropolitan Phoenix*. Tempe, Az.: Morrison Institute for Public Policy, 2000.

Morrison Institute for Public Policy. *What Matters in Greater Phoenix: Indicators of Our Quality of Life*. Tempe, Az.: Morrison Institute for Public Policy, 1998.

Pollock, Paul W. *American Biographical Encyclopedia. Profiles of Prominent Personalities. Arizona Edition*. 6 vols. Phoenix, Ariz.: P. W. Pollock, 1967-90.

Pulliam, Russell. *Publisher: Gene Pulliam, Last of the Newspaper Titans*. Ottawa, IL: Jameson Books, 1984.

Rice, Trudy Thompson. *St. Joseph's: The First 100 Years.* Flagstaff, Az.: Heritage Publishers, 1991.

Schweikart, Larry. *A History of Banking in Arizona.* Tucson: University of Arizona Press, 1982.

Shadegg, Stephen C. Shadegg. *Arizona Politics: The Struggle to End One-Party Rule.* Tempe: Arizona State University, 1986.

Shappell, Lee. *Phoenix Suns: Rising to the Top with the "Team of Oddities."* Champaign, Ill.: Sagamore Publishing, 1993.

Sheridan, Thomas E. *Arizona: A History.* Tucson: University of Arizona Press, 1995.

Sherman, Len. *Big League, Big Time : The Birth of the Arizona Diamondbacks, the Billion-Dollar Business of Sports, and the Power of the Media in America.* New York: Pocket Books, 1998.

Wenum, John Dale. *Annexation as a Technique for Metropolitan Growth: The Case of Phoenix Arizona.* Tempe: Institute of Public Administration, Arizona State University, 1970.

Wiley, Peter and Robert Gottlieb. *Empires in the Sun.* New York: Putnam, 1982.

Zarbin, Earl. *All the Time a Newspaper: The First 100 Years of the Arizona Republic.* Phoenix:: Arizona Republic, 1990.

Historical Studies – Articles and Essays

Altheide, David L. and John S. Hall. "Phoenix: Crime and Politics in a New Federal City." In Anne Heinz, Herbert Jacob, and Robert L. Lineberry ed. *Crime in City Politics.* New York: Longman, 1983.

Bergsman, Steve. "Del Webb." *Phoenix* (August 1991), pp. 81-89.

Cunningham, Bob. "The Box That Broke the Barrier: The Swamp Cooler Comes to Southern Arizona," *Journal of Arizona History*, 26 (Summer 1985): 145-62.

Doti, Lynne Pierson and Schweikart, Larry. "Financing the Postwar Housing Boom in Phoenix and Los Angeles, 1945-1960." *Pacific Historical Review*, 58 (May, 1989): 173-94.

Gable, William R. "Arizona." In JeDon A. Emenhiser, ed, *Rocky Mountain Urban Politics.* Monograph Series, vol. 19. Logan: Utah State University, 1971. pp. 24-35.

Goodall, Leonard E. "Phoenix: Reformers at Work," in Goodall, ed., *Urban Politics in the Southwest* (Tempe: ASU, 1967), 110-27.

Howard, George W. "The Desert Training Center California-Arizona Maneuver Area." *Journal of Arizona History*, 26 (Autumn, 1985): 273-94.

Melcher, Mary. "Blacks and Whites Together: Interracial Leadership in the Phoenix Civil Rights Movement." *Journal of Arizona History*, 32 (Summer 1991): 195-216.

Stocker, Joseph. "Mrs. Archer Linde, Beloved Impresario," *Phoenix*, 20 (January 1985), 94-96.

Theses and Dissertations

Abbitt, Jerry W. "History of Public Transportation in Phoenix, Arizona, 1887-1989." M.A. Thesis, Arizona State University, 1989.

Brisco, Jerry. "The Department Store Industry in Phoenix, 1895-1940." M.A. Thesis, Arizona State University, 2000.

Brown, Brent Whiting. "An Analysis of the Phoenix Charter Government Committee as a Political Entity". M.A. Thesis, Arizona State University, 1968.

Crudup, Keith Jerome. "African Americans in Arizona: A Twentieth-century History." Ph.D. Dissertation, Arizona State University, 1998.

Dean, David R. "Rising from the Ashes: Phoenix and the Cold War, 1946-1963." M.A. Thesis, Arizona State University, 2001.

Konig, Michael. "Toward Metropolis Status: Charter Government and the Rise of Phoenix, Arizona, 1945-1960." Ph.D. Dissertation, Arizona State University, 1983.

McCoy, Matt. "The Desert Metropolis: Image Building and the Growth of Phoenix, 1940-1965." Ph.D. Dissertation, Arizona State University, 2000.

Jacobson, Judith Anne. "The Phoenix Chamber of Commerce: A Case Study of Economic Development in Central Arizona." M.A. Thesis, Arizona State University, 1992.

Rosebrook, Jeb Stuart. "Diamonds in the Desert: Professional Baseball in Arizona and the Desert Southwest, 1915-1958." Ph.D. Thesis, Arizona State University, 1999.

Russell, Peter Lee. "Downtowns Downturn: A Historical Geography of the Phoenix, Arizona, Central Business District, 1890-1986." M.A. thesis, Arizona State University, 1986.

continued on following page

Bibliography continued

Contemporary Materials - Memoirs

Tom Chauncey; as told to and edited by Gordon A. Sabine. *Tom Chauncey: A Memoir.* Tempe, Ariz.: Arizona State University Libraries, 1989.

Barry M. Goldwater. *With No Apologies: The Personal and Political Memoirs of United States Senator Barry M. Goldwater.* New York: William Morrow and Company, Inc., 1979.

Barry M. Goldwater, with Jack Casserly. *Goldwater.* New York: Doubleday, 1988.

George H. N. Luhrs, Jr. *The Geo. H. N. Luhrs Family in Phoenix and Arizona 1847-1984.* Phoenix: Jean Stroud Crane, 1988.

Edna McEwen Ellis. *Sunny Slope: A History of the North Desert Area of Phoenix.* Phoenix, Ariz.: Art Press, 1990.

Contemporary Materials - Articles

Laing, Jonathan. "Phoenix Descending: Boomtown Gone Bust." *Barron's National Business and Financial Weekly* (December 19, 1988), pp. 8-9, 30, 32, 34, 56.

Martin, Harold H. "The New Millionaires of Phoenix." *Saturday Evening Post,* 234 (30 September 1961): 25-33.

Meunch, Joyce Rockwood. "Sun City Arizona, U.S.A." *Arizona Highways,* 43 (November 1967): 4-

Monroe, Keith. "Bank Knight in Arizona." *The American Magazine,* 140 (November 1945), 24-.

Noble, Daniel E. "Motorola Expands in Phoenix." *Arizona Business and Economic Review,* 3 (June 1954): 1-2

Peplow, Edward H., Jr. "You'll Like Living in Phoenix." *Arizona Highways* 33 (April 1957): 14-35.

Sederberg, Arelo and John F. Lawrence, "Del Webb The Bashful Barnum," *Los Angeles Times WEST Magazine,* (September 14, 1969), 16-20.

Stocker, Joseph. "Phoenix: City Growing in the Sun." *Arizona Highways.* 33 (April 1957): 36-39.

Ullman, Edward L. "Amenities as a Factor in Regional Growth." *Arizona Business and Economic Review,* 3 (April, 1954): 1-6.

"Where Taxes Are Low, Climate Mild, Living Easy." *U.S. News and World Report* 43 (October 11, 1957): 92-97.

Winsted, Manya. "Pioneer Builder John F. Long Celebrates an Anniversary". *Phoenix,* 10 (February 1977), 47-49.

Zellmer, Al M. "Welcome Stranger!" *Arizona Highways* 19 (August 1943): 20-5, 59.

Contemporary Materials - Reports, Yearbooks

Arizona Statistical Review. Phoenix: Valley National Bank, 1949-1994.

Arizona Town Hall. Phoenix: Arizona Academy, 1962-1999.

City of Phoenix. *Annual Financial Report. 1960-2000.* Phoenix: City of Phoenix, 1961-2001.

Historic Homes of Phoenix: An Architectural & Preservation Guide. Prepared by Cooper/Roberts Architects. Phoenix: City of Phoenix, 1992.

The Municipal Year Book, 1951-1998.

National Civic Review, 1949-1990.

Phoenix Forward Task Force. *Phoenix Forward: Citizen Participation in Planning: A Citizen Report on Objectives and Goals for Metropolitan Phoenix.* Phoenix: The Task Force, 1970.

Sargent, Jr., Charles S. *Planned Communities in Greater Phoenix: Origins, Functions and Control.* Papers in Public Administration No. 25. Tempe: Institute of Public Administration, Arizona State University, 1973.

Sargent, Jr., Charles S., ed. *The Conflict Between Frontier Values and Land-use Control in Greater Phoenix: Report on a Conference Held at Arizona State University, November 22, 1975.* Phoenix: Arizona Council on the Humanities and Public Policy, 1976.

Index continued

Index continued

Index of Partners & Web Sites